The
DEVOTION
to the
SACRED HEART
of
OUR LORD
JESUS CHRIST

by *Jean Croiset, S.J.*

Translated from the French
of the final edition published at Lyons, 1694
by Rev. Patrick O'Connell

International Institute of the Heart of Jesus

This book, the seventh in a series on the Heart of Jesus is published by the International Institute of the Heart of Jesus, Inc., Milwaukee (U.S.A.) and Rome.

This is IIHJ Publication No. 7E

Library of Congress Number 76-25383
ISBN 0-917502-01-9

NIHIL OBSTAT
FRANCISCUS LARKIN *SS.CC.*
censor deputatus
Milwauchiae, Wisconsin
die 9a iulii 1976

IMPRIMATUR
GULIELMUS E. COUSINS
Archiepiscopus Milwauchiensis
die 9a iulii 1976

Table of Contents

SECOND PART

The Means of Acquiring This Devotion

THIRD PART

The Practice of This Devotion

Foreword

Sincere efforts for renewal have characterized and still characterize the Roman Catholic Church in the present period of its history which began with the opening of the Second Vatican Council in October 1962. However one important area of the Church's life which has yet to benefit fully from the new insights gained during the conciliar and post-conciliar years is the area which can be called the devotional life of Catholics.

The restoration of the sacred liturgy as the Church's most perfect prayer and as the primary source of religious inspiration and strength has enabled Catholics to esteem and participate in community worship in new and effective ways. But liturgical renewal was meant not to suppress devotional practices but to place them in proper perspective.

Devotion to the Sacred Heart of Jesus, one of the greatest treasures of Christian spirituality, has received the most explicit encouragement from the Church's Magisterium. It can indeed be called the devotion of devotions. When properly practiced, it is "the highest act of religion."

The renewal of this devotion, ardently desired by many sensitive pastors and by countless Catholics who have experienced its benefits, can best be promoted by the twofold approach which has brought about renewal in other aspects of the Church's life: (1) the application of new theological and pastoral insights; (2) a return to the privileged sources of the devotion in Scripture and Tradition.

The reprinting of the present volume is an excellent contribution to the study of the sources of devotion to the Sacred Heart of Jesus as practiced during almost three centuries of the Church's recent history. St. Margaret Mary Alacoque, to whom this devotion in modern times owes so very much, died in 1690. The following year, Father Jean Croiset, S.J., her spiritual director (as was also Blessed Claude de la Colombiere, S.J.), published the first edition of a work on the devotion which he had begun during Margaret Mary's lifetime. Her death enabled him to include a summary of her life, especially of the years after her entrance into the Convent of the Visitation, Paray-le-Monial, France. In 1694, at Lyons, Father Croiset published in French a final edition of his work, entitled, *La devotion au Sacre Coeur de Notre-Seigneur Jesus-Christ*. This text was translated into English from that final edition by Rev. Patrick O'Connell and published in Ireland in 1948. The present volume is a reprint of this English edition.

The aspects of Margaret Mary's life presented to us by Fr. Croiset, the numerous quotations from her writings, and the texts of her prayers reveal to the thoughtful reader an exceptionally holy woman who found the source and goal of her sanctity in the Heart of Jesus. Three centuries separate us from the religious and cultural milieu of 17th century France, but the witness of authentic sanctity, while necessarily expressed in time-conditioned ways, transcends all limitations. That is why Margaret Mary can be held up to all generations as an outstanding example of love for Our Lord Jesus Christ.

The Heart of Jesus was for her — and should be for all Christians — the origin of all the virtuous dispositions she received, and the end towards which she dedicated her entire life. Margaret Mary lived both consecration and reparation to the Heart of Jesus in the Blessed Sacrament with such intensity that everyone who is exposed to her example cannot but be moved to imitate her according to the measure of God's grace.

Father Croiset's presentation of the motives of the devotion (Part I), of the means of acquiring the devotion (Part II)), and of the manner of practicing it (Part III) is no less impressive. His reflections can be considered to be a treatise on the spiritual life. Once again we must remember that almost three hundred years separate the contemporary reader from the original author. We who have had the benefit of the encyclical *Haurietis aquas* of Pius XII and theological studies on symbolism such as those by Karl Rahner, could add still other reflections on the devotion. Yet Father Croiset's work remains a classic. His explanations of and exhortations to devotion to Jesus present in the Blessed Sacrament and reparation for the irreverences and neglect to which this sacrament is subject, retain their value for our own day.

Another merit of his work is the frequent reference to saints and spiritual writers who preceded Margaret Mary and who were known for their devotion to the Heart of Jesus, e.g. Catherine of Siena, Gertrude, Mechtilde, Blosius, Lanspergius.

The meditations proposed all stress devotion and reparation to Jesus in the Blessed Sacrament and are based upon passages selected from the gospels. A wider choice of texts and of orientation could be offered with advantage, but Father Croiset has the merit of calling our attention to that aspect of devotion to the Heart of Jesus which is reparation for sins and failings in regard to the Blessed Sacrament.

On the occasion of the 41st International Eucharistic Congress in Philadelphia, U.S.A. celebrated during this bicentennial year of the United States, the International Institute of the Heart of Jesus has generously made possible the reprinting of this classic work of Father Croiset. In the past this book has inspired thousands of readers throughout the world. Let us hope that in our own day, and in the future, countless others will be helped by this volume better to understand and more generously to practice devotion to the Heart of Jesus and to "the Eucharist, most outstanding gift of the Heart of Jesus" (Pope Paul VI).

EDWARD MALATESTA, S.J.
Pontifical Gregorian University, Rome
JULY 6, 1976

Preface

By

FATHER JEAN CROISET, S.J.

The extraordinary ardor and eagerness shown towards the devotion to the Sacred Heart of Our Lord Jesus Christ, the great fruit that has been derived from it and the great esteem which persons of universally recognized merit have for it, compel us to bring out a new edition of this book to satisfy the demand of the faithful.

There had been, it appears, in the beginning some reason to fear that the very title, *Devotion to the Sacred Heart of Jesus,* while attracting several people to read this book, might turn away many others and prevent them from forming a just idea of this devotion. It is in order to anticipate this difficulty that we have judged it proper to explain in the beginning of this book what is meant by the Devotion to the Sacred Heart of Jesus. Experience has taught us that all those who have formed a clear idea of what this devotion consists in, become convinced that it is reasonable, solid and very useful both for attaining salvation and arriving at perfection.

We have followed practically the same order in this book as in the previous one. Having explained in the First Part the motives which should urge us to practice this devotion, we give the means for acquiring it in the Second Part, while in the Third Part we explain the practice of the devotion and give a number of special exercises of it.

And in as much as the essence of this devotion consists in the perfect love of Jesus Christ, particularly in the adorable Sacrament of the Eucharist, this perfect love of Jesus Christ forms the subject matter of this book. We dwell at greater length on visiting the Blessed Sacrament, on the august Sacrifice of the Mass and on receiving Holy Communion because, of all spiritual exercises, it is these which bring us closest to Jesus Christ, and are most suited to honor His Sacred Heart and to inflame our hearts with ardent love for Him.

1

We trust that reflection on these subjects will help to persuade many to adopt the practice of the devotion and at the same time teach them how to practice it with fruit.

Those who know of the singular merit and sublime virtue of Blessed Claude de la Colombiere, and are aware that God had chosen him in a special manner to propagate this devotion, will be very pleased to find in many places of this book the thoughts and sentiments of this great servant of Jesus Christ about this devotion.

Although it is in no way necessary to quote authorities or revelations or examples to urge Christians to practice this devotion, since it is sufficient to know that its only object is to make people love Jesus Christ perfectly, yet we have judged it advisable to devote two or three chapters of this book to the revelations made to St. Gertrude and St. Mechtilde about devotion to the Sacred Heart; at the same time we are convinced that it would be manifest prevarication on our part, if, through fear of being reputed too credulous, we refrained from giving an account of the admirable means of which God has made use in recent times, to renew devotion to the Sacred Heart of Jesus (through the revelations made to St. Margaret Mary Alacoque).

To deny that there have been pure and chosen souls in every age who have received confidential communications from God would be to condemn what the whole Church believes; and although these divine caresses and familiarities are exceedingly rare, nevertheless no century has passed which has not furnished examples of such in the case of some saint. "Those who have never received favors of a similar kind," says St. Teresa, "sometimes find difficulty in believing in these extraordinary gifts. But such people should consider that if it is a sign of simplicity to believe in all alleged favors, it is a sign of temerity to refuse to believe in any." Now we think it opportune to remark here that the revelations made to St. Gertrude and St. Mechtilde which have been quoted three times in the course of this book, have been examined in our time by the most learned men in Flanders, France, Italy and Germany, as well as in the most famous universities; and that all were agreed that these revelations were full of the Spirit of God, Who alone is the author of them; that learned Prelates and great Saints have esteemed them and approved of them; that the greatest doctors have quoted them with approval, one of them (Blosius) asserting that after the examination to which these revelations have been subjected he did not think that any really prudent and solidly virtuous person would refuse to have respect for them.

The Spiritual Retreat of Blessed Claude de la Colombiere has already made known several years ago the admirable means of which God made use to propagate this devotion. But as the person of whom this great servant of God speaks in this book (St. Margaret Mary) as having received confidential communications from Our Lord, has always taken extreme care to lead an obscure and hidden life — although God has honored her with these extraordinary graces which are the privilege of the greatest Saints — we deem it proper to give an account of her life in this book, since Providence, by taking her out of this life, has given us complete liberty to tell the world about the rare and sublime virtues of this holy soul whom God has chosen to propagate this devotion to the Sacred Heart of Jesus. At the same time, it will be seen in the person of this saintly religious that the arm of the Lord has not been shortened, and if the present is not a time for great miracles, there is no century of the Church's history that is not suitable for great Saints.

"The revelations made to those chosen women are known to the whole world, and have been approved of by pious and learned men; and holy fathers everywhere quote them in their writings and their books. The revelations of St. Gertrude were most diligently examined by very learned men, both before and after her death, one of whom gave his opinion as follows: "Having prayed for divine light, I feel that no one who is enlightened by the Spirit of God could speak evil of or attack what is written in this book (of St. Gertrude), for it is Catholic and holy" (Blosius, Chap. IV, De Auctoritate Revelationum).

LIFE OF
ST. MARGARET MARY ALACOQUE

St. Margaret Mary Alacoque was a religious in the Convent of the Visitation at Paray le Monial in the province of Burgundy.

God had specially chosen her to make known the devotion to the Sacred Heart of Jesus Christ. For this end he lavished on her from the very cradle His choicest blessings with such profusion, and in ways so extraordinary, and she corresponded so faithfully, that the sublime virtues which she practiced from her tenderest youth appear truly miraculous. Her extreme love for contempt, for an obscure and hidden life, and the inviolable silence which her profound humility made her always keep about everything that could bring her honor, would have robbed us of the knowledge of the most of these graces, had not the distrust which she always had for her own lights, her fear of illusion, and the perfect submission which she always had for the orders of her confessor and the commands of her superiors, sometimes obliged her to consult persons in whom she had confidence and to make a record of the most remarkable favors which she received from God. The repugnance which she felt in doing this was so strange that, not being able to conquer it otherwise, she was obliged to make a vow to obey blindly. The following account of her life is drawn from these records written by herself, of graces received, and from information given by her superiors.

As God had destined this virtuous soul to make known a devotion whose object is to make Jesus Christ ardently loved, He had inflamed her almost from the cradle with such ardent love for this divine Savior, that almost from the time that her life began, she allowed herself no enjoyment except what she thought was pleasing to her divine Spouse. From the age of two or three, she had such a horror of even the shadow of sin that her parents, who were aware of it, found it sufficient to say that a thing was an offense against God to make her desist from doing it. Divine grace, anticipating the use of reason and supplying for the weakness of youth, inspired her with such noble and generous sentiments that we have good reason for believing that the like of her had not appeared on the earth for several centuries.

4

From her earliest childhood, a time little suited for the practice of exalted virtue, the heroic actions which she performed give the idea of a person already arrived at the pinnacle of perfection. The Holy Spirit Himself taught her the chief requisite for the interior life by giving her the spirit of prayer, for she had a great gift of prayer. Although she had never learned how to make a meditation and had no practice in it, she found herself suddenly elevated to a high degree of contemplation. From that time all her pleasure was to spend whole hours in prayer; and if she was not found in some corner of the house on her knees, she was sure to be found in the church, motionless before the Blessed Sacrament.

At that tender age, she made a vow of perpetual virginity, which she was accustomed to renew at every Mass after the Consecration. All her life she had a great devotion to the Blessed Virgin, and she was tenderly loved by her. When she had suffered for four years from a kind of paralysis, all remedies were found useless until she was consecrated to the service of the Blessed Virgin for the rest of her life, whereupon she was miraculously cured.

From her earliest youth, the spirit of mortification was joined to that of prayer; she conceived such a hatred against herself and such a great love of the Cross that her only desire was to suffer. She passed entire days without eating, and always abstained from what was pleasing to the taste. She was accustomed to macerate her body with instruments of mortification that would have frightened the most austere penitents; she tied herself so tightly around the arms with little iron chains that the flesh grew over the chains, and they could only be removed by tearing with them pieces of her flesh. From the age of ten or twelve she usually slept on the ground, passing a part of the night in prayer even in the depth of winter.

This ardent love for Jesus Christ, which was the motive of all her austerities, inspired her with an extreme love and compassion for the poor. She had such veneration for them that she often prostrated herself before them. Her charity drew to her a crowd of poor, in whose favor she used frequently to deprive herself of food, and she never sent them away without teaching the principal truths of our religion to those who were ignorant of them.

Thus did this saintly girl occupy the time that she was obliged to spend in the world, where the greatest sin that she remem-bered to have committed, and which she expiated with so many tears and such austerities, was to have taken too much care to dress herself neatly — and even this was to please her mother, who ordered her to do so.

Such extraordinary and sublime virtue soon showed that this soul so cherished by God, was not for the world. She had long sighed after solitude, as she found no enjoyment except in God, and as worldly amusements were a torture to her, reli-gious life alone had any attraction for her. But her parents could not bring themselves to part with her, until after many prayers and eager solicitations she finally obtained what she had so passionately desired. God had endowed her with a great intellect, a solid, fine, penetrating judgment, a noble soul and a great heart. Her perfect modesty, her unalterable meekness, her attraction for prayer, her extraordinary devotion to the Blessed Sacrament and to the Blessed Virgin, her mortification, and especially her profound humility, which caused her to per-ceive none of these virtues in herself, were the effects of this ardent love for Jesus Christ which may be said to have, prop-erly speaking, constituted her distinctive character.

With these fine qualities and these admirable virtues, she entered the Order of the Visitation of the Blessed Virgin Mary, where she failed not to cultivate with great care such a rich endowment, and where she soon reaped all the fruits which might be expected from such virtue.

As she brought to the religious life a heart purified from all passions, a thing which costs so many combats to others, her whole occupation consisted in perfecting those virtues which she brought from the world. This was done under the direction of obedience, which served rather as a break to moderate her austerities than as a stimulus to fervor. Persuaded that the observance of her rule was the surest way to arrive at the high perfection to which God had called her, she made it an unviol-able law for herself to keep her rule all her life with great exact-ness; and she kept it so well, even to the letter, that it would have appeared excessive, if it was not clear that this extraordi-nary punctuality proceeded from her great fidelity, which caused her to neglect no occasion to increase in grace with God and to render herself pleasing in His sight. Besides, she sustained this excessive regularity with such an air of sanctity, and with such a number of virtues, that all that she did was capable of attracting veneration. She had, especially, such a high idea of obedience and she was so perfect in this respect, that it may be said that it was the virtue in which she excelled. She had not even those natural inclinations which ordinary people never completely master and which urge them instintively to do or to desire differently from what they are ordered. Although honored by Heaven with such extraordinary graces, she had never any other rule of conduct but the will of her superiors, being persuaded that whoever withdraws from obedience necessarily recedes from the Spirit of God.

It is difficult to conceive to what lengths she went to detach herself from everything which was not God. She would never agree to accept a pension which her parents wished to give her, and all the remedies which she was obliged to take during her continual illnesses were only tolerable to her insofar as they were compatible with the greatest poverty; during her life, she carried this virtue of poverty to refinement. Whatever was her occupation she was always in prayer. She was so closely united to God, particularly during the first ten years of her profession, that even sleep rarely interrupted this consciousness of His presence, or rather this thought of His presence interrupted her sleep. Her meekness and evenness of temper were all the more admirable because they did not proceed from her natural disposition; she had acquired this admirable tranquility of soul by constant vigilance over herself, by constant interior mortification, and especially by continuous union with God; and grace elevated her to such a high degree of peace and evenness of spirit that she was proof against all the vicissitudes and occupations of life. She was the enemy of all singularity and regarded all thoughts of devotions that seemed incompatible with the least duties of her state as temptations.

Far from being preoccupied with the care of her weak health, she incessantly importuned her Directors and Superiors to obtain permission to macerate her body with new austerities. It would have been difficult for her to add any austerities in religion to what she had practiced in the world, and obedience served only as a break to prevent excess in this matter. However, although she had been all her life weighted down with illness and was of extremely delicate constitution and was, nevertheless, always practicing extraordinary mortifications, in her

humility, she regarded all this as nothing. The severe mortifications practiced by this Sister, who was a life-long invalid,
afford material to confound the cowardice of many people who
pass for pious.

Her extreme care all through life to seek occasions of mortifying herself and her great fidelity in profiting by these occasions,
were a great source of these great graces which Heaven lavished
on her. She had such a great natural repugnance to a certain
kind of food that her parents thought themselves obliged to
make it a condition of their permission to her to enter that she
would never be asked to take it. Towards the end of her
novitiate one of the Sisters offered her, by mistake, this food;
she thought it would be a good opportunity to make a little
sacrifice which would be as pleasing to God as she found it
difficult. Pressed by her desire to deny no sacrifice to God,
she overcame her repugnance. Jesus Christ liberally rewarded
the generosity of His servant. On that evening at prayer, she
felt her heart so inflamed with ardent love for Jesus Christ that
she could not contain its vehemence. The Son of God showed
her how many graces and signal favors this act of generosity
was to gain for her. From that moment interior lights were
more vivid, inspirations stronger, graces more abundant, and
favors of Heaven more frequent. From that moment, she no
longer found any obstacle capable of stopping her on the road
of piety.

Her silence, her conversation, and her whole outward de-
meanor inspired veneration for her person and love for virtue.
Those who knew her had no doubt that she preserved intact
her baptismal innocence. Her Directors spoke of the extreme
purity of her soul, and say that it was an example of the height
of innocence, delicacy and sublime virtue which a soul gov-
erned by God and honored from the cradle by His greatest
graces can reach.

It was by means of this great innocence and by the exercise
of many virtues that she arrived at the height of contemplation
to which she was elevated. If the lives of St. Teresa, of St.
Catherine and of several other saints had not made us aware of
the marvels which God sometimes works in the souls of those
whom He honors with His visits, and to whom He deigns to
communicate Himself in prayer, the life of this saintly Religious
would be sufficient to do so. In fact, the extraordinary graces

and great favors conferred on her by God, and the familiar communications which she received frequently from Jesus Christ, were such that we have reason to doubt whether anything more admirable was ever seen in the Church since the days when Jesus Christ conversed familiarly with His apostles. As she was endowed with a clear intellect and very good judgment, and was extremely humble, on the one hand she could have hardly any doubt that these communications were the work of the Holy Spirit, and on the other hand her humility found it difficult to believe that God would deign to confer such favors on her. In this perplexity, she was obliged to break the silence which her humility had made her keep so long about the extraordinary favors which she had received. She consulted her Directors on the matter, but in order to try the virtue and increase the merit of His servant, God permitted that some of her Directors should not understand her. They even condemned her great attraction for prayer, treated her as a visionary, and forbade her to follow the inspirations of the Spirit that guided her. One can understand the torture which this treatment caused a person who had too keen a judgment not to see that her Directors were deceived, and too great humility not to obey. She spent several years under this hard trial, which she assures us was the hardest she could suffer in this life. But Our Blessed Savior, to Whom she confessed her fear that she might be living under an illusion, told her that He would send her one of His great servants to reassure her.

This great servant was (Blessed) Claude de la Colombiere, who was sent as Superior of the Jesuits at Paray le Monial. This wise Director, so enlightened in the ways of perfection in which he himself had made such great progress, soon recognized that there was something extraordinary in this soul. He examined with great care all that had reference to her interior dispositions. He discovered such treasures of graces in her that he said that he did not think that there was then in the world a soul more cherished by God, or one that Jesus Christ favored with such intimate communications. He reassured her, and ordered her to allow the Spirit of God, which she had hitherto resisted through fear of illusion, to act freely in her. From that time Blessed Claude held her in great esteem; he even consulted her in many important enterprises, and assures us that he received great help through her prayers. When

Blessed Claude was about to leave Paray le Monial, St. Margaret Mary sent him a note telling him that Our Savior wished the sacrifice of his life at Paray. Though he had at the time no appearance of death, yet he died soon afterwards, as she had foretold.

Under the guidance of this saintly Director, St. Margaret Mary made extraordinary progress on the way to perfection. Among all her virtues, that which constituted her special character was a most ardent and altogether extraordinary love for Jesus Christ. The divine fire with which her heart had been inflamed from her youth, went on ever increasing, and, if the love of Jesus Christ is capable of causing death, she (according to the testimony of the Sisters) died of an excess of this ardent love. As soon as she appeared before the Blessed Sacrament; she made prodigious efforts to contain the transports of her love. When she began her prayer, God took possession of her in such a wonderful manner, and poured into her soul such an abundance of lights and consolations, that when she had finished her prayer her whole person was affected by it. These divine ardors became so perceptible during the last years of her life and made such changes in her body, that she suffered from them in an extraordinary way; especially after the Son of God, by a grace similar to that which He had conferred on St. Catherine of Sienna and St. Gertrude, had purified her heart in a sensible manner. She experienced the sweet effects of this extraordinary favor until her death.

From the same source, *i.e.*, from her ardent love for Jesus Christ, proceeded this extraordinary love which she had for humiliations, contempt, self-denial, and all kind of suffering which she called her delicious bread. And although God complied with her wishes so liberally on this point, she was all her life so hungry for these humiliations and sufferings, that she often said that she suffered in a strange manner by the very fear which she had of being a single moment without suffering.

The violence which she did herself continually to conquer her extreme delicacy, the victories which she gained in this matter, are so heroic that we would find it hard to believe that there was ever a person of such strength of will and courage, if we did not know what grace can accomplish in a soul that is specially cherished by God. She was subjected to such rude trials that visible miracles were necessary to sustain her in them. The devil, not being able to overcome her, omitted nothing to make her suffer; but this was not the way to terrify her, because she found only repose and pleasure in suffering.

If obedience had not moderated her fervor, her extreme desire to suffer for Jesus Christ would have carried her to excess. Having one day heard that the last complaint which the Son of God made upon the Cross was of the thirst which He suffered, always ingenious as she was to find new means of imitating her divine Master by sharing in His sufferings, she resolved to pass from Thursday evening to the following Saturday each week without drinking. Although this abstinence was very difficult, she practiced it for a long time until her superior, having learned about it, forbade her to continue it; and to try her obedience still further, she ordered her to drink two or three times outside of meal times on those days. She obeyed, but she soon found new ways of mortifying herself, while obeying. She considered that it would not violate obedience to drink the dirtiest water she could find on these occasions, although this caused her the greatest repugnance. The very thought of it made her shudder, but the only effect this repugnance had on her was to make her reproach herself for her too great delicacy, and resolve to punish her cowardice by drinking it. She did so for several months, causing herself terrible suffering. When her Superior learned of her ingenuity in mortifying herself, she concealed her admiration for such extraordinary fervor and generosity. She called her and reproved her so severely that this saintly Sister for the rest of her life regarded this action, which is indeed worthy of the greatest admiration, as one of her greatest faults.

One of the surest marks by which we can infallibly recognize whether people are led by the spirit of Jesus Christ, is the esteem, and love which they have for obedience, always distrusting their own lights and always deferring to the opinion of their Superiors. It is by this mark that the Spirit of Jesus Christ has been recognized in the conduct of this virtuous Religious.

She writes: "Although my divine Savior has made Himself my Master and Director, nevertheless He wishes me to do nothing of what He orders me without the consent of my Superiors, whom He wishes me to obey, in a manner, more exactly than Himself. He teaches me in particular to be on my guard against myself as my most cruel and most powerful enemy; but He assures me that if I put all my confidence in Him and have perfect obedience, depending in all things on the will of my Superiors, He will protect me. He tells me not to be troubled by anything that may happen, but to regard all the events of life as ordered by His holy Providence and Will, which can, when He pleases, turn all things to His glory. On one Easter Sunday, I happened to be engaged in an employment which frequently prevented me from joining in the prayers of the Community, and I experienced a sentiment of grief. My divine Master reproved me for it immediately, saying: 'Know that the prayer of submission and sacrifice is more agreeable to Me than contemplation or the holiest meditation.' That impressed itself on my memory, and since that time I have no longer experienced any pain at anything which my Superiors ordered me to do."

And in another place she writes: "From this time on, My divine Master has never ceased to reprove me for my faults and to show me how hideous they are. What displeases Him most and what He reproves me for most severely, is want of respect and attention before the Blessed Sacrament, especially at the time of Office and prayer. Alas! of how many graces have I not deprived myself by distractions, by looking around from curiosity, by a more comfortable but less respectful posture? The sorrow which I feel as soon as I perceive that I have offended Him in anything obliges me to go immediately and ask for some penance, for my divine Savior assured me on many occasions that the least penance performed under obedience was more pleasing to Him than the greatest austerities of my own choice. This I can say with certainty, for my divine Savior assured me a hundred times that there is nothing more injurious to a Religious than want of obedience to Superiors or to the Rule, however little it might appear, and that the least objection on this point, the least sign of repugnance, is an intolerable fault in the eyes of God. 'You are deceiving yourself,' my Savior said to me, 'by thinking that you can please Me by these kinds of actions or mortifications of your own choice; know that I reject all these things as fruits corrupted by your own will, and that I have a horror of them especially in a Religious; it would please Me more that a Religious accept under obedience all her little comforts than to afflict herself with austerities and fasts of her own choice.'

"I have found by experience that if I happen to do any of these kinds of mortification without the express permission of my Superior, my divine Savior does not permit me to offer it to Him, but punishes me for it instantly. One day when I wished to continue a penance imposed on me under obedience, I heard the voice of my amiable Savior saying to me: 'What you have done so far is for Me, but what you are going to do is for the demon.' I desisted immediately and resolved to die rather than deviate in the smallest from the orders of my Superior; to accomplish this I am resolved to sacrifice everything, inspirations, desires, visions, and extraordinary graces."

God showed by miracles how pleasing this perfect obedience is to Him. The following, which bears out this, was written by one of her Superiors after her death:

"When, on one occasion, I went to visit her in the infirmary, where she had been for more than a year ill suffering from a strange malady, she asked me for permission to rise the following morning to assist at holy Mass, and anticipated any objections by assuring me that if I consented God would give her sufficient strength. Although there was no prospect that she would be able to do so, I permitted her on condition that she should not get up early and that she should not be fasting. She desired to receive Holy Communion, and, wishing to be dispensed from this condition, she asked the Sister in charge of the infirmary to obtain the complete favor for her, which was the permission to receive Holy Communion. This Sister promised to do so, and on the following morning assisted her to rise, not doubting but that I would grant the permission. God so permitted that I should enter the infirmary just when the infirmarian had gone out to look for me. Astonished at seeing the patient up contrary to my orders, I reprimanded her severely, exaggerating the pretended defects in her conduct, especially her disobedience and her attachment to her own will. 'You will go to Mass,' I added in a tone of displeasure, 'you will receive Holy Communion; but since your own will can give you sufficient strength when you wish, I also wish to command in my turn. You had sufficient strength to get up when you wished and sufficient strength to go to Mass. You will then be able to follow the exercises of the Community for the future; return to your ordinary room, I forbid you the use of all medicines; leave the infirmary now and do not return to it for six months, except to visit sick Sisters when there are any there.' This holy Sister received my correction on her knees with her hands joined, with extraordinary meekness and humility. She humbly asked pardon for her fault and a suitable penance. She then got up as if she had not been ill, and carried out to the letter all that I commanded her. You know, my dear Sisters, that during the six years that I was Superior in your house, this holy Sister had never been in health except during these six months. We all looked on this as a visible miracle, since at the very hour when the six months were up, she fell sick suddenly just as she had been before."

However great the pain she might suffer, she never asked for any relief. When sometimes there was a short interval between her long periods of illness, it was always remarkable for some excess of fervor. Though she was weak during these intervals, yet she always remained on her knees before the Blessed Sacrament. "On one Holy Thursday," writes her Superior, "just as she was recovering from a heavy fit of illness, she asked me so earnestly for permission to spend the night in the church that I could not refuse her. She knelt down in the choir in the evening and remained there motionless until eight o'clock the following morning, when she went and took her place with the other Sisters to recite the Office. She told me afterwards that during that night Our Lord made her share in the extreme sorrows of His agony, and that she had never passed any time of her life in a state more conformable to her inclination because she had never before suffered so much."

This great desire which she had for suffering is brought out in her letters to a Jesuit Father (Father Croiset) in whom she had great confidence and to whom she revealed her most secret thoughts, for she always feared lest she might be suffering from delusions.

She writes: "Nothing in this world is capable of pleasing me except the Cross of my divine Master, a Cross like His Own, heavy and ignominious without sweetness or consolation or relief. Let other people be so fortunate as to accompany my divine Savior in His ascent to Thabor; for my part I wish to know of no other road but that to Calvary, for nothing but the Cross has any attraction for me. My lot will be, then, to be on Calvary until my last sigh, amidst the scourges, the thorns, the nails, and the Cross, without consolation or pleasure but that of having none. And what happiness to be able to suffer always in silence and finally to die on the Cross, crushed under the weight of all kinds of misery, of body and mind, forgotten and despised, for the one cannot please me without the other! Then, Reverend Father, bless and thank my sovereign Master for me, that He honors me so lovingly and so liberally with His precious Cross, not leaving me a moment without suffering. Ah, without the Cross what would I do in this valley of tears, where I lead such a criminal life that I regard myself as a most miserable wretch? That thought makes me fear lest I render myself unworthy of the happiness of bearing the Cross and of making myself resemble my Jesus in His sufferings. I beg of you, if you have any charity for me, to ask this amiable Savior not to reject me on account of the bad use that I have hitherto made of this precious treasure of the Cross and not to deprive me of the happiness of suffering; for that is all the alleviation that I find for the length of my exile. Let us never weary of suffering in silence. The Cross is good at all times and in every place to unite us to Jesus Christ suffering and dying. We cannot really love Him without suffering for Him; and I can say that I do not love Him at all, since it seems to me that I suffer so little, that my greatest suffering is that I do not suffer enough. I make it my pleasure to know that others are filled with the sweetness of the love of enjoyment; for myself I wish for no other pleasure than to see myself sunk in the abyss of the sorrows of pure, suffering love. But I perceive that I am yielding to my own satisfaction in speaking about suffering, but I cannot do otherwise, for my ardent thirst for suffering is a torment which I cannot describe to you; nevertheless I know well that I neither know how to love nor suffer, which shows me that all that I say about it is the effect of the self-love and secret pride which lives in me. Ah! how I fear that all these ideas about suffering are only artifices of the devil to amuse me with vain and sterile sentiments! Let me know simply what you think of all this."

In another letter she writes: "My Reverend Father, I seem never to be at rest except when I see myself in the abyss of humiliations and sufferings, unknown to everyone, and buried in eternal oblivion; or if anyone thinks of me, that it will be only to despise me the more and to give me some new occasion to suffer something for God. This is what I am incessantly demanding from my divine Savior; I do not know whether there is any illusion in this, but I can assure you that with the exception of His love, I cannot ask for anything else; or rather I only know how to ask for one thing for myself — namely, an ardent love for Jesus Christ crucified, and consequently, a suffering love."

In another place she writes: "I do not know whether I am deceived, but it seems to me that my greatest desire would be to love my amiable Savior with a love more ardent than that of the Seraphim; I would not object, it seems to me, that it should be in hell I would love Him. The thought that there will be a place where during all eternity an infinite number of souls redeemed by the precious Blood of Jesus Christ will never love this amiable Savior afflicts me to excess. I would wish, O my divine Savior, if it were Thy Will, to suffer all the torments of hell, provided that I might love Thee as much as all those wretched souls who will suffer forever and never love Thee, could love Thee in heaven. Is it reasonable that there should be a place where for all eternity Jesus Christ will not be loved? Truly, if it were known how ardently I desire to suffer and to be despised, I feel sure that Charity would urge everyone to satisfy me in this respect."

But the virtue of patience does not consist in the mere desire to suffer; we have reason to be on our guard against this kind of desire so long as Heaven does not put our virtue to the test, and it is properly only in the exercise of humiliations and sufferings that we can judge whether we really love the Cross. We have already seen that the life of humiliations and sufferings of this virtuous Sister was in perfect harmony with these sentiments.

Her Superior, who was a Religious of great virtue and merit, seeing the great treasures of graces that God poured out on this saintly Sister, did all in her power to help her attain the high degree of virtue to which God had called her; she believed that the surest and most efficacious means of doing this was to exercise her virtue by humiliating her on every occasion that offered. She succeeded in doing so, for profiting by the unfavorable dispositions of the most of the Sisters of the Community towards this saintly Sister, she paid no heed to her virtue externally, she disapproved of her conduct, she showed that she distrusted the extraordinary ways by which God was conducting her. This severe treatment which she received would have persuaded any other that she might at least try to justify herself with her Superior without doing anything against perfection. But she did not give heed to this sentiment. Everything which she did was interpreted in an unfavorable sense; whether she gave an account of her conduct under obedience in order to appease the Sisters, or accused herself in the excess of her humility, she was always blamed. When accused of suffering from imaginary sicknesses, when called a hypocrite in her devotions, a visionary in her prayers, humiliated within, condemned from without, always persecuted, she never allowed the smallest word of complaint to escape from her, never could the smallest sign of sadness or vexation be observed in her actions or on her countenance.

A person must sometimes do violence to himself not to show forth the sentiments of his heart, but how difficult it is to keep silence when a single word would suffice to avoid confusion that is not merited! A person must have reached a very high degree of perfection not to be even moved by such kinds of humiliation. This was how this holy Sister always acted in these circumstances, to the admiration of those who knew her. As an example of this we give the following: One day when the parlor was occupied, her Superior permitted her to give an account of the state of her conscience in the confessional to Blessed Claude de la Colombiere. Some of the Sisters who were not aware that she had permission to use the confessional, complained to the Superior. She was severely reprimanded in presence of the Community and punished by the Superior herself, who had given the permission. The edification of her neighbor and a hundred other reasons should have, one would think, obliged her to justify her conduct; but the joy which she experienced at seeing herself despised and humiliated made her embrace these little crosses and thank God fervently for them. She received this great humiliation with amazing submission, and no one ever heard her make any complaint about it.

The pleasure which she experienced in being humiliated inspired her with special affection for all those who procured humiliations for her. One of her Superiors at Paray le Monial wrote: "It is true that this illustrious Sister who has died, had great affection for me, but it gives me great pleasure to tell you the source of this affection. Being fully persuaded of the sincere desire which she had to suffer and to be humiliated, I was accustomed to use no moderation in her regard and allowed no occasion to pass to exercise her virtue. When the Superior who succeeded me treated her more gently this saintly Sister wrote to me as follows:

"How can it be that with so many faults and miseries my soul is always hungry after suffering? But when I think that you were accustomed to do me the favor of sustaining it sometimes with this delicious bread so repugnant to human nature, and that now I am deprived of this happiness because, no doubt, of the bad use which I made of it, I am overcome with grief. I assure you that nothing has attached me to you so much as your conduct towards me, which I cannot think of without sentiments of the tenderest gratitude; for you could not have given me more certain or more agreeable proofs of perfect friendship than by humiliating and mortifying one so imperfect as I have been. Although you have not done so sufficiently, considering the reasons I have given you, however, the little consoles me and sweetens the bitterness of life, which is insupportable to me without suffering when I see my divine Master on the Cross. However, I have never learned well how to suffer; there is nothing which I do so badly, although there is nothing which I desire so ardently. The reason is that I do not love God enough, because I love myself too much. O my dear Mother, how bitter it is to live without loving God, and how can anyone love a God crucified without loving the Cross? Without living and dying on the Cross? It seems to me that I lived in security under your control because you had the charity to contradict my inclinations sometimes; alas! I have made myself unworthy of these favors. However, my love for humiliations increases, and I do not know whether it is because I suffer hardly anything at present that the desire to die presses me more than ever. I could never resign myself to ask of God the years which you have advised me to demand, except on condition that they would be employed in honoring the Sacred Heart of my Jesus in silence and in penance, without ever more offending Him, remaining night and day before the adorable Sacrament of the Altar, where this divine Heart is all my consolation here below.

"It might be said that the extreme desire which she had to suffer constantly was efficacious; and when the universal esteem and remarkable veneration which people had for her exalted virtue prevented her from finding new occasions of suffering, God Himself exercised her patience by interior crosses which sometimes reduced her to extremity."

Writing to one of the Jesuit Fathers she said: "My Sovereign Master has granted me much consolation from reading the letter which you were so good as to write me, but this was only after He had for quite a long time, forbade me to read it because of my too great eagerness to seek consolation from it in this painful, suffering state in which He has placed me during this time of the Carnival when so many sinners offend Him and abandon Him. For this seems to me to be a time of such great sorrow and bitterness for me, that I am incapable of seeing or tasting anything but my Jesus in His sufferings, compassionating Him in His sorrows, with which this divine Savior penetrates me so vividly that I no longer recognize myself. Everything serves His divine justice as an instrument to torment this criminal victim in such a way that I cannot do otherwise than sacrifice myself as a victim of immolation to His justice; and I seem to suffer in such a strange manner that I confess that, if His Infinite Mercy did not sustain me while His Justice makes me feel the weight of its rigor, it would be impossible for me to endure it for a moment. Nevertheless, all this takes place in unalterable peace. I content myself with acquiescing in His good pleasure; it suffices for me that my divine Savior is satisfied. I did not think that I could write to you, for I would not wish to say anything in the state in which I am except these words of my amiable Savior: 'My soul is sorrowful even unto death' or these others: 'My God, why hast Thou abandoned Me?'

"However, I can assure you that the more I suffer, the more I feel increase the ardent thirst which I have for suffering; I even fear that I take too much satisfaction in suffering. Finally, the attitude which I am resolved to adopt in all this is to abandon myself and submit myself perfectly to the infinite goodness of my sovereign Master, even moderating this ardent desire which I have for sufferings, leaving to Him the care to do everything. And since I desire nothing in the world except to do His holy will perfectly, it matters little whether it be in consolation or affliction. You could hardly believe how much I suffer in writing all this; for although I am persuaded that I have done nothing at all to merit the graces of my Sovereign Master, the lack of correspondence with them will perhaps be the cause of my greatest condemnation; nevertheless I suffer a kind of martyrdom when He obliges me to speak to you of them."

Urged by the same motive, she desired most eagerly to lead a hidden life and to be forgotten. The first thing which she did on entering religious life was to forbid herself the remembrance of everything which she had left in the world. She regarded the parlor as a place of punishment, and although she concealed her extreme repugnance when sometimes her Superiors obliged her to go there, it is incredible how much this act of obedience cost her.

One of the former Superiors of Paray le Monial wrote to one of the Sisters there: "When, as you may remember, Sister X fell down with a fit of apoplexy, fearing that she should die without the Sacraments I ordered Sister Margaret Mary to go immediately before the Blessed Sacrament and ask our Lord to restore to this Sister the use of her reason. She obeyed, and soon afterwards she told me that Our Lord made known to her that He would hear her prayer on condition that she made a vow at that moment to sacrifice to God what cost her most; this was to go to the parlor whenever she was called there, without showing repugnance. As I knew the great pain it caused her to conquer herself in this respect I exhorted her to make this vow. No sooner had she obeyed than the Sister who was ill recovered the use of her reason and received all the Sacraments. I thought that this vow would have lessened her extreme repugnance; but God willed that she was obliged to do violence to herself up to the time of her death to fulfill her vow; on every occasion that she was obliged to go to the parlor; it seemed to her that she was going to violate her vow, so great was her difficulty in concealing her repugnance."

She had made it an inviolable law never to write to anyone except when absolutely necessary; and then an express command to do so was required.

This great desire which she had to remain hidden and unknown can be seen in her letters and in the extreme care which she took to hide the great favors which she had received. She requested those to whom she wrote under obedience to burn all her letters and to keep her secret inviolable. Her secrets were kept during her life, but the glory of Him Who conferred such great graces on her, and the edification of the faithful, demanded that those treasures of graces be made public after her death. She retained this desire to be humiliated and to remain unknown until her last breath. A few hours before her death, she begged her Superiors never to speak of anything she had told them in confidence that might be advantageous to her, and she asked one of the Sisters to write to a certain priest, asking him to burn all her letters.

Such heroic and solid virtue soon raised her to the sublime degree of perfection for which God had destined her. Although she had long lived a life of such perfection, she thought she had done nothing unless she bound herself by an express vow to do always what she believed to be most perfect. Few people, however holy, would be capable of executing such a project; it would require a St. Teresa to exercise such heroic virtue. A matter of such importance demanded long and serious consideration; it was only after observing faultlessly for years what she proposed to bind herself by vow to do, that she asked permission to make it. Her Director and Superior, who had perfect knowledge of the state of her soul, granted her the permission. She made this vow on the vigil of the Feast of All Saints, and wrote down all the details with her own hand. A glance at the contents of this vow is sufficient to show that when she made it she had already arrived at the pinnacle of sanctity.

"The following is the subject matter of the vow which I have long felt myself urged to make to God and by which, however, I have not wished to bind myself without the advice of my Director and the permission of my Superior. They, having examined it, have permitted me to make it on this condition that if it should cause me trouble or scruples, my Superior can dispense me from it and make my obligation cease in whatever articles of it might cause me trouble. The sole object of this vow is to unite me more closely to the Sacred Heart of Jesus Christ Our Lord, and to bind me inviolably to what He shows me that He desires of me. But, alas! I feel myself so inconstant and weak that I would not dare to make any promise except relying on the goodness and charity and mercy of this adorable Heart of Jesus, for the love of Whom I make this vow, not intending by it to make myself more troubled and constrained, but rather more faithful to my sovereign Master.

"The divine Master has given me grounds to hope that He Himself will give me all the assistance necessary for the practice and the perfect accomplishment of this vow. I seek only by it to give proof to God of more pure and ardent love by crucifying my flesh and my senses for love of Him. May this God of goodness grant me this grace! Amen. May God be praised!"

Vow made on the eve of All Saints to consecrate myself, immolate myself and bind myself more closely and more perfectly to the Sacred Heart of our Savior Jesus Christ:

"In the first place, O my only Love, I will endeavor to subject to Thee and to keep in submission to Thee all that is in me, always doing what I believe to be most perfect and most pleasing to Thy Sacred Heart. I promise Thee that I will spare nothing that is in my power, and that I will not refuse to do or suffer anything whatsoever that presents itself, which conduces to make Thee known, loved, honored and glorified.

2. "I will not neglect or omit any of my exercises or the observance of any of my rules except for motives of charity or real necessity, or of obedience, to which I submit all my promises.

3. "I will endeavor to make it my pleasure to see others elevated, loved and respected, thinking that this is due to them but not to me, who ought to be annihilated in the Sacred Heart of Jesus Christ. I will place all my glory in bearing my cross, in living poor, unknown and despised, desiring never to appear except to be humiliated and opposed, whatever repugnance my proud nature may find therein.

4. "I wish to suffer in silence without complaining, no matter how I may be treated.

5. "I will not avoid any occasion of suffering whether it be bodily pain or humiliations, contempt or opposition.

6. "I will not seek or procure for myself any satisfaction, pleasure or contentment except that of having none in this life; and when Providence will present me with any which I cannot avoid, then I will accept them, renouncing interiorly every sentiment of pleasure, and not thinking whether I am satisfied or not, but rather applying myself only to love my Sovereign, and seeking in all things and on all occasions only to do what

is pleasing to Him.

7. "I will not procure any relief for myself but what necessity obliges me to seek, and I will ask for that simply according to my rule. That will deliver me from the constant pain caused by the fear I have of flattering this body and granting too much to this cruel enemy.

8. "I will leave my Superior entire liberty to dispose of me as seems best to her, accepting with humility and indifference the occupations which obedience will give me, showing most joy for the things for which I feel most repugnance.

9. "Without henceforth troubling about myself, I will abandon myself totally to the Sacred Heart of Jesus Christ that He may console me or afflict me according to His good pleasure; contenting myself with adhering to all His holy operations and dispositions, regarding myself as a victim which ought always to be in the continual exercise of immolation and sacrifice according to His good pleasure, and being attached to nothing except to loving Him and pleasing Him, by acting and suffering in silence.

10. "I will never inquire about the faults of others, and when I may be obliged to speak of them, I will do so in the charity of the Sacred Heart of Jesus Christ, thinking in myself that I would be very pleased to be treated in that way. And when I see anyone commit a fault, I will offer to the Eternal Father a virtue of the Sacred Heart of Jesus opposite to that fault to repair it in some way.

11. "I will regard as my best friends all those who will afflict me or speak evil of me, and I will endeavor to render them all the services, and do them all the good I can.

12. "I will endeavor not to speak of myself, or to speak of myself very little; and never, if possible, to praise myself or to justify myself.

13. "I will not seek the friendship of any creature, except the Sacred Heart of Jesus inclines me to bring that creature to His love.

14. "I will apply myself continually to conform and submit my will in everything to that of my Sovereign.

15. "I will refrain from dwelling voluntarily not only on any bad thoughts but on thoughts that are useless. I will regard myself as a poor servant in the house of God who ought to be submissive to all the people in the house, receiving as alms

whatever is given to me, being persuaded that whatever people give me, they always give me too much.

16. "I will, as far as possible, neither do nor omit anything through human respect, or through a vain desire of pleasing creatures; and as I have asked Our Lord not to allow anything that is the effect of His extraordinary graces to appear in me except what will bring me some contempt and confusion or some humiliation before creatures, thus I will regard it as a great happiness when all that I say or do will be despised, censured or blamed; endeavoring to do or to suffer everything for the love and in honor of the Sacred Heart of Jesus Christ Our Lord, and for His holy intentions, to which I unite myself in everything.

17. "I will study to do or say nothing except in view of procuring some glory for God, edification for my neighbor, and increase in virtue, making myself faithful and constant in the practice of the good which my divine Master will show me that He desires of me, committing no voluntary fault, or at least not pardoning myself for any, but taking vengeance on myself for all faults by some voluntary penance.

18. "I will watch over myself in order not to grant human nature anything except what I cannot legitimately refuse it and without making myself singular, which I wish to avoid in everything. Finally I wish to live without any will of my own, being attached to nothing and saying at everything that happens 'Thy will be done!'

"When I consider the great number of details in this vow which I am about to take, I am seized with such great fear of being wanting in some of them, that I would not have the courage to bind myself, had I not been reassured and strengthened by those words which were said to me in the depth of my soul: 'What do you fear, since I have answered for you and have made Myself your guarantee? The unity of My pure love will take the place of attention to the multiplicity of all these things; and be assured that this same love will make you repair all the little faults that you will commit against this vow by making you expiate them by mortifications and austerities.'

"These words gave me such confidence and assurance that, notwithstanding my great weakness, I put aside all fear and placed my whole confidence in Him Who can accomplish everything, and from Whom I hope for everything, placing no confidence in myself."

This vow shows what grace can accomplish in a generous and faithful soul, and what this same grace does in a heart inflamed with the pure love of Jesus Christ. A vow that extended to the smallest actions and to the least thoughts might appear to be very troublesome. It would have been so indeed, if the same Spirit that had prompted her to make it had not at the same time taught her a sure and easy way to practice it without scruple and without troubling her peace of heart. This means was none other than the continuous exercise of pure and perfect love of Jesus Christ.

"Whatever obligation your vow imposes on you," said our Savior to her, "of thinking at almost every moment of so many things, know that you will satisfy all by loving Me without reserve and without interruption; think and apply yourself to loving Me perfectly; pay attention only to loving Me and consequently only to pleasing Me on every occasion and in every thing; let My love be the object and the end of all your thoughts, actions and desires; breathe only My love, and endeavor so to love Me that you may love Me daily more. I assure you that, without troubling yourself about anything else, you will accomplish more by this holy exercise, than you have promised by your vow."

This is the proper explanation of those words of Our Savior: "It will be sufficient to attend to the unity of My love in the multiplicity of all these things."

Mediocre virtue usually remains in obscurity, Providence does not deign to put it to the test; but it is not so with sublime virtue; in vain does it seek to hide itself; its brilliancy will show itself, but this external light will be the result of much exercise of virtue. God, Who had destined this virtuous Sister for the most sublime sanctity, willed that her virtue should resemble that of all the Saints — that is, accompanied with humiliations, contempt and sufferings. However great the care she took to live forgotten and to lead an obscure, hidden life, her virtue was too great to remain long unknown; its brilliancy showed itself; her reputation extended far beyond the limits of the convent; she was spoken of as *the Saint*. But Providence permitted that this high esteem for her virtue should only give occasion to certain people to exercise her patience; and her extreme desire to suffer would have been fully satisfied by the great sufferings which she had to endure and which she gladly bore, if her desire for suffering had not gone on increasing day by day. We do not propose to go into detail here with this subject; but when, later on, her life is written, her historian will find plenty of material from this period of her life to enrich his history with the most sublime examples of heroic patience; he will at the same time find occasion to show forth the wonderful ways of Providence that allowed this great Servant of Jesus Christ to be so long humiliated, although everyone was agreed about her perfect obedience, her continual mortification, her extraordinary merit and especially her profound and sincere humility.

A very meritorious personage, having listened to stories about this saintly Religious from a person prejudiced against her, became of the same opinion about her at first. He even considered it his duty to try to undeceive other people who were better informed than himself and who had a high idea of her virtue. He did all in his power to discredit her; he accused her of hypocrisy; he called her a visionary infatuated with a fantastic kind of sanctity, who took pleasure in deceiving herself and who tried to deceive others by an appearance of virtue full of nonsense and illusions. The sentiments which this important person entertained about her got noised abroad and created a strange impression disturbing the minds of many. The fear which she herself had of really suffering from delusion caused her great confusion. She describes it as follows: "I feel myself afflicted in many ways, but the most painful is to regard myself as the plaything of the devil. I see that everything in me is worthy of chastisement, since I have been so miserable as not only to deceive myself, but perhaps by my hypocrisy, to deceive others as well, although I do not think that I ever intended to do so. However, I should have no more doubt about the matter after the opinion expressed by this great servant of God. I have reason to thank Our Lord for having sent him to undeceive those who have been so simple as to entertain any good opinion of me. What great obligation shall I not be under all my life to this great servant of God for having rendered me this important service of making me known to myself and to others just as I am! I can assure you that nothing gives me greater consolation than to know that creatures have been undeceived and that I can now satisfy God's justice and remain in eternal oblivion. This thought consoles me and in a moment has alleviated all my sufferings."

The devotion to the Sacred Heart of Jesus for the establishment of which God had chosen her, brought on her at first persecution that was all the more painful because it came from those very people who should have been the first to approve of it. Although their idea of her virtue was very high, she had no sooner spoken of this devotion to the Sacred Heart of Jesus, than they called her a visionary and, without even knowing the meaning of the devotion, they forbade her to speak of it, and this continued until God, Who is Master of all hearts, so changed the hearts and minds of those who put obstacles in her way, that she had the consolation of seeing this solid devotion approved of, preached and established almost everywhere a couple of years before her death.

It may be said that the amiable Savior has, in our time, united in the person of this saintly Religious all the extraordinary graces which He had, in past ages, conferred on all His greatest servants. She had the happiness of conversing familiarly with Jesus Christ frequently like St. Melchtilde and St. Gertrude. The Son of God gave her His Heart in the same manner in which He had given It to St. Catherine of Sienna, by taking hers which He purified and inflamed with His pure love. He willed to leave her, as He had left St. Teresa, a continual and sensible proof of this extraordinary grace by a pain in her side so severe that no human remedy could relieve it, and which accompanied her to the tomb. The bare enumeration of these extraordinary graces, and especially of the admirable lessons which she received from her divine Master would fill a large volume. An account of these favors, written by herself, was found after her death.

But among such remarkable favors, the truth of which we have no reason to doubt because of the visible proofs which we have for them, what seems to be the greatest and most deserving of admiration is the low opinion which she always had of herself. She believed herself to be a hypocrite, she said that she had always been deceiving people, and that perhaps she was deceived herself; she not only said that she was unworthy to live among the holy Sisters, but she conducted herself towards them in such a way as to show that she believed it. These were always her sentiments with regard to herself, and

she died with these same sentiments. Such sincere and profound humility would have robbed us of the knowledge of the
extraordinary graces which she received, had not the person
in whom she had particular confidence and whom she consulted frequently on matters of conscience obliged her, for
greater security, to write down for him an account of all the
remarkable favors which she had received from God. The extreme repugnance which she felt to do this made her put off
for a long time the execution of this request, until God had
made known to her that she was to do so and her Superior
ordered her to obey. We are then in the happy position of
learning from herself of the great graces conferred on her by
God as well as of all that concerns the devotion to the Sacred
Heart of Jesus, for the establishment of which she received
such remarkable favors. The precautions which she took to
remain forever unknown while obeying in this matter are another signal proof of the sincerity of her sentiments. Thus we
have been able to learn of some of the marvels which God has
wrought in this saintly Sister. At first we thought of publishing
her letters in abridged form, but we considered that it would
be against the designs of Providence to omit the smallest portion, for the reading over of these letters would always be pro-
ductive of spiritual good and would never cause weariness.
The following is what she wrote:

"Reverend Father, the ardent and just desire which, since
my earliest years, has always urged me to live poor, unknown,
forgotten and despised, would have prevented me from ever
writing or appearing in the parlor, if obedience, which is an
inviolable law for me, had not ordered it otherwise by not allowing me to follow my own inclination. My only consolation
is that I have the happiness to obey in writing to you.

"I confess that my divine Master conducts me on a road
completely opposed to my inclinations. I have a strange aversion for all positions of responsibility in the Community. I have
an equally great aversion for the parlor and for writing letters.
However, I was obliged to sacrifice my inclinations constantly
in these matters, and found no repose day or night until I
bound myself by vow to obey blindly in all these things, and
as far as possible not to allow my extreme repugnance to appear. In spite of all this, I experience even greater repugnance
than formerly, but I accept this cross with all the others with

which it may please my divine Savior to honor me, and I confess that if I were a single moment without suffering, I would believe that He had forgotten me and abandoned me.

"You ask me to speak out all my sentiments; alas! it is not in my power to do as you request; I must write as it pleases my sovereign Master. If you were aware to what extent He renders me powerless to say more than He wishes, you would advise me to keep silent rather than think of offering Him the smallest resistance. But amidst all the graces which I receive from His mercy, I confess to you seriously that I fear lest I may be deceiving myself and that I am deceiving those whom charity has prompted to entertain thoughts too favorable to me, and too far removed from what I really am. Do not you be among that number, but having examined before God all that I am about to tell in the strictest secrecy, I ask you to write and tell me whether I am in error; for although I have been already reassured on this point, I cannot get rid of the fear that I may be under a delusion. For several years I have had, strictly speaking, no other Director than my sovereign Master; for from the time when I commenced to know myself, He assumed such absolute dominion over my will that He obliged me to obey Him in everything, so that, in a certain sense, I could not escape from it. He Himself reproved me for my faults, even the smallest ones, with sweet severity. I then conceived such a horror for sin, that I was accustomed to hide myself in order to weep at leisure when I perceived that I had committed the smallest fault. My divine Master Himself taught me how to make mental prayer though I had never heard of it. My only pleasure was to spend whole hours on my knees before the Blessed Sacrament. I sighed constantly for some place of solitude where I might live poor, despised and unknown, and as soon as I entered Religion, I doubted not that I had found the place of retreat for which I had sighed so long. Since that time, my amiable Savior poured out His greatest graces in such profusion into the soul of His unworthy servant that I had difficulty in containing the joy and the ineffable sweetness which I felt in my heart. This joy was, however, for some time, troubled by the fear which I had that these great favors might insensibly bring me to dispense myself from my smallest duties; but this fear was soon dispelled by the promise which the divine Savior made to me that He would so adjust the great graces that He would confer on me to the spirit of my rule and to the obedience which I owed to my Superiors, that one would never be in opposition to the other.

"I have long enjoyed this sweet peace; but God permitted several people to believe that I was deceived by the Spirit that conducted me; they ordered me to resist all His inspirations, they forbade me to follow the impulses which He gave me.

"I made all possible efforts to obey, believing that I was certainly in error, but all my efforts were in vain. I then became convinced that I was abandoned by God and that I was among the lost souls, because people made me believe that it was not the Spirit of God that possessed me, and I found by experience however, that no matter what efforts I made; it was impossible for me to resist this Spirit. I was in this most terrible state of mind until my divine Master sent Father Claude de la Colombiere (now Blessed Claude) who He told me, was one of His most faithful servants and dearest friends. This saintly Director put an end to all my trouble by assuring me that it was the Spirit of God that conducted me, and he ordered me to walk without fear in the way in which it might please Him to conduct me. From that time on, I entered into this great tranquility of heart and into this sweet peace in which my dear Savior has always preserved me amidst the crosses, humiliations, and sufferings with which He has never ceased to honor His unworthy slave and in which alone I can find my consolation, my enjoyment and my repose."

Subsequently in obedience to an express command she wrote the following letter: "I am obliged to make known to Your Reverence the great graces which my Savior has granted me and of which I would wish never to think, because I never think of them without suffering extraordinary affliction at the sight of my ingratitude which, without doubt, would have precipitated me into hell, were it not that the mercy of my divine Savior and the all-powerful intercession of the Blessed Virgin, my good Mother, have disarmed the justice of God in my regard. To tell what I think, I never reflect on these great graces but I fear exceedingly that having deceived myself I may also deceive those to whom I am obliged by obedience to speak. I never cease to ask of God that He may grant me the grace to be unknown, annihilated and buried in eternal oblivion, and I regard this favor as the greatest that He has conferred upon me. For that reason, it is only under the two following conditions that I can bring myself to write to your Reverence all that follows: The first condition is that you burn my letter when you have read it; the second is that you keep all that I write an inviolable secret. My Divine Master gave me to understand that He wishes this sacrifice of me, but I do not think that He wishes that any remembrance of so wicked a creature should remain on the earth.

"I tell you this once for all and the promise which you will make to observe these two conditions faithfully will alleviate the pain I feel in writing and will preserve my soul in great peace. I trust that you will give me your views, for I do not know what to think when I consider on the one hand so many graces, and on the other, a life so little in conformity with such great benefits.

"I will tell you, then, that the Divine Savior having one day appeared to His unworthy slave said to me: 'I seek a victim for My Heart who will be willing to sacrifice herself as a victim of immolation for the accomplishment of My designs.' Then feeling myself penetrated with the greatness of this sovereign Majesty, I prostrated myself humbly at His feet and presented to Him several holy souls who would correspond faithfully with His designs. 'No, I want no other but yourself,' the amiable Savior said to me, 'and I have chosen you for that purpose.' Then bursting into tears, I replied that He knew well that I was a criminal, and that victims should be innocent; that truly I had no other will than His but that I could not make a resolution to do anything except what my Superior should order me. To this He consented. I continued, however, to resist His inspirations through the great fear which I had lest these extraordinary ways might draw me away from the simple spirit of my vocation. But it was in vain that I resisted Him, for He gave me no repose until, by order of obedience, I had sacrificed myself to all that He desired of me — which was to make me a victim immolated to all kinds of sufferings, humiliations, contradictions, pains and contempt without any other intention than that of accomplishing His designs. When with all my heart I had offered myself for this, He told me that He knew what my fears were, but He promised me (as I think I have already told you) that He would so adjust His graces to the spirit of my Rule, to the obedience due to my Superiors and to my own weakness and infirmity, that one would not run counter to the other. After this, He made me share in His graces in such profusion, that I did not know myself. So many extraordinary favors and such great benefits increased still more the fears that I had of coming under notice; this obliged me to ask of Him immediately that He would not allow anything to appear in me, except what would render me more vile and contemptible in the eyes of creatures, and it seems to me that He promised me this.

"In a retreat which I made some time afterwards my amiable Savior revealed to me the greater part of the graces which He intended to confer on me, principally those which I was to receive through the devotion to His Sacred Heart. Whereupon I prostrated myself at His feet and implored Him that in His Mercy, He would give His graces to some faithful soul that would know how to correspond to them, knowing well that I was only fit to serve as an obstacle to His designs. He then gave me to understand that it was for that reason that He had chosen me, in order that being perfectly persuaded of my own nothingness, I could not attribute to myself any of the blessings which He would confer on me, and He promised that He Himself would supply for all that would be wanting in me.

"At another time this Sovereign of my soul Who takes delight in displaying the treasures of His merits in the weakest subjects and those least suited for His great designs, having honored me by visiting me, said to me (it seems to me) that He had come to tell me how much I would have to suffer for the rest of my life for His Love and for the execution of His designs. Profoundly prostrated in His presence, I could not persuade myself that God would ever deign to render me capable of suffering anything for His love. Nevertheless, the desire of suffering for His love increased in me in such measure that I would have wished to see all the instruments of torture employed against me to make me suffer for Jesus Christ. Then my divine Savior revealed to me clearly (it seems to me) all the humiliations and sufferings which were to come on me till the hour of my death; and what consoles me still more is that He revealed this to me with such strong impressions that all these sufferings, which were then only in my imagination, imprinted themselves on me in a manner as vivid and perceptible, as if I had suffered them all. Whereupon He told me that I should fear nothing because He wished to confer a new grace on me still greater than all the others which He had already conferred on me. This favor would cause me never to lose sight of Him, always having Him intimately present to me. I regard this favor as the consummation of all the other favors that I had up to then received from His infinite mercy, for since that time I have never ceased to have this divine Savior intimately present. He instructs me, He sustains me, He warns me about my faults and He never ceases to increase in me by His grace the ardent desire of loving Him perfectly and of suffering for His love. This divine presence inspires me with such respect that, when I am alone, I am obliged to prostrate myself with my face pressed to the ground and to annihilate myself, so to speak, in the presence of my Savior and my God; especially when I think of what I am — the most wretched of all slaves, who certainly do not merit even this position of slave of Jesus Christ. Furthermore, all these graces are accompanied with an unalterable peace, an interior joy and especially an ever-increasing desire to be humiliated, despised, annihilated and overwhelmed with all kinds of sufferings in order to be a little less unworthy to be the least of the servants of Jesus Christ. But, Reverend Father, how can it be that poverty, contempt, sorrows, and humiliations have such an attraction for me that I regard them as delicious morsels for which my soul hungers unceasingly; how can it be true that these things are the marks of the Spirit of Jesus Christ, and nevertheless I suffer so little that it seems to me that I suffer nothing!

"Besides, I confess to you, Reverend Father, that this Sovereign of my soul has assumed such dominion over me that, if it is not the Spirit of God that possesses me, I would be damned in the lowest depths of hell. I tell you all this as I believe I experience it. But alas! may I not be deceived? For I assure you that whenever I reflect on myself, I discover so many imperfections and miseries and so little fidelity and gratitude for so many favors that I cannot get rid of the thought that all these great graces of which I have already spoken to you and the others which I am obliged by obedience to tell you of later on, are only the result of error and delusion. Write and tell me, Reverend Father, what you think of this and what I ought to do.

"I cannot undertake to give you all the details concerning

the extraordinary favors which my Savior has conferred on me in connection with the devotion to His Sacred Heart. The following is all that I am able to tell you to satisfy the orders of my Superiors:

On the Feast of St. John the Evangelist, having received from my divine Savior a favor almost similar to that which this Beloved Disciple received on the evening of the Last Supper, the divine Heart was represented to me as a throne all of fire with flames radiating its light on every side.

It appeared more brilliant than the sun, and transparent like crystal. The wound which He received on the Cross appeared clearly. There was a crown of thorns around the Sacred Heart and it was surmounted by a cross. My divine Savior gave me to understand that these instruments of His passion signified that the immense love which He had for man was the cause of all the sufferings and all the humiliations which He willed to suffer for us; that from the first moment of His Incarnation, all these torments and all this contempt were present to Him, and that it was at this first moment that the Cross was, so to speak, planted in His Sacred Heart, Which then in testimony of Its love for us, accepted all the humiliations, poverty and sorrows which His sacred Humanity was to suffer during the whole course of His mortal life; and in addition, It accepted the outrages to which His love was to expose Him to the end of the ages on the Altar in the Most Holy and August Sacrament.

He then gave me to understand that the great desire which He had of being perfectly loved by men had caused Him to form this design of manifesting to them His Heart and of opening to them all the treasures of love, mercy, grace, sanctification and salvation which It contains, in order that all those who would be willing to render to It and procure for It all the love and honor in their power, would be enriched in profusion with these divine treasures of which this Sacred Heart is the source; and He assured me that He takes a singular pleasure in being honored under the figure of this Heart of flesh, the image of which He wished to be exposed in public, in order, He added, to touch the unfeeling hearts of men: He promised me that He would pour out in abundance into the hearts of all those who would honor It, all the gifts with which It was filled, and that everywhere that this image would be exposed in order to be

specially honored, it would draw down all kinds of blessings;
that, in addition, this devotion was as a last effort of His love,
which wished to favor in a special manner the Christians of
these last ages by proposing to them an object and a means
which was at the same time so suitable to make men love Him
and love Him solidly.

"After that my divine Savior spoke to me (as far as I know)
these words: 'That is, My child, the design for which I have
chosen you; for this have I conferred on you so many graces,
taking special care of you from the cradle. The reason why
I made Myself your Master and Director was in order to dispose you to receive all these great graces, among which you
are to regard as the most precious that by which I reveal to you
and give you the greatest of all treasures by showing and at
the same time giving to you My Heart.' Then prostrating myself
with my face pressed to the earth, it was impossible for me to
express my sentiments in any other manner than by my silence
which I soon interrupted by my tears and sighs.

"From that time, the graces of my sovereign Master became
more abundant. The result of these great graces was, that not
being able to contain the sentiments of the ardent love which
I felt for Jesus Christ, I tried to diffuse them by my words every
time that occasion offered, thinking that others, receiving the
same graces as I had received, would have the same sentiments.
But I was dissuaded from doing so both by Father Claude de
la Colombiere and by the great opposition with which I met.

"Though these little exercises of zeal and fervor had no
result at the time, at least they procured for me the pleasure
and advantage of some humiliations and a little trial which
lasted some years.

"The time destined by my divine Savior for this great work
had not yet come. Nevertheless He Himself took care, as He
had promised me, to dispose me according to His desire for
the graces which He wished to confer on me, and this was
done by conferring on me graces still greater than those which
he had already given me.

"The first was when, after a general confession of my whole
most criminal life I had received absolution, He showed me
a robe whiter than snow which He called the robe of innocence, and clothed me with it saying, it seems to me, almost

these very words: 'Henceforth, My child, the faults which you will commit will humiliate you much but they will not oblige Me to withdraw from you.' Then for a second time He opened His adorable Heart and said to me: 'Behold the place of your eternal dwelling where you can preserve without stain the robe of innocence with which I have clothed your soul.' From that time I do not remember that I have ever gone out from this adorable Heart. I dwell there always but in a manner and with sentiments that it is not permitted to me to express. All that I am able to say is that usually I am there as in an ardent furnace of pure love.

Another time, this divine Savior commanded me to make a donation to Him of all that was in me capable of pleasing Him, of all that I could do or suffer to the end of my life and of all the good works that others might do for me.

"As obedience has always been the rule of my conduct, I did not think that I ought to make this donation, which I regarded as a kind of vow, without having obtained permission. This act of obedience pleased Him as much as the act of donation which I made to Him when I had received permission. But this sovereign Master recompensed me liberally for the gift which I had made to Him of all that belonged to me, by assuring me that His Sacred Heart would always be open in favor of all those who would pray for me. I besought Him at the same time to be no less liberal in favor of those who would give me an opportunity of suffering for Him."

On another occasion Jesus Christ appeared to her, and having lavished on her graces still greater than those hitherto conferred, said to her:

"My child, be attentive to my voice and to what I ask you to do in order to dispose you for the accomplishment of My designs. You will receive Me in Holy Communion as often as obedience permits you, whatever mortification and humiliation it may bring on you, which you will receive as a pledge of My love; in addition you will receive Holy Communion on the First Fridays of each month; and on all the nights of Thursday to Friday I will make you share in this mortal sadness, which it was My will to feel in the Garden of Olives and which will reduce you to a kind of agony more painful to support than

death. And in order to accompany Me in that humble prayer which I then presented to My Father in that pitiable state to which I was reduced, you will rise between eleven o'clock and midnight to pass an hour in prayer, prostrated with your face against the ground, in order to appease My anger by asking pardon for sinners, and to alleviate in some measure the bitter sorrow which I felt on seeing Myself abandoned by My apostles, which obliged Me to reproach them for their cowardice, telling them that they could not watch one hour with Me. During this hour I Myself will teach you what you will have to do.

"But amidst all these favors which I am conferring on you, take good care, My child, not to believe lightly every spirit and not to trust yourself to them, for the devil will try every means to deceive you. Therefore never do anything without the approval of those who are guiding you, in order that having the consent of your Superiors you will never fall into the trap which the devil lays for you, for he has no power over those who are really obedient."

This holy Sister did not fail to ask permission from her Superior to do what her divine Master had ordered her; but it was in vain that she protested that God had ordered her to do these things, it was in vain that she pressed her demand and craved that it be granted. These Communions on special days, and this hour of prayer at midnight appeared to her Superiors to be too singular to grant; they regarded these practices as unsuitable for a Community.

Besides, she had been very ill for a long time, and no medicine had been able to give her relief. One day, when she made a new demand to have her requests granted, her Superior promised to grant them on condition that she obtained from Our Lord the restoration of her health; adding that she would be able to recognize by this mark whether what passed within her came from the Spirit of God. When this humble Sister conveyed this message to Our Lord, she was cured immediately. The Blessed Virgin appeared to her, and after a long conversation with her encouraged her to persevere on the painful road which she would have to travel. These are the words which the Blessed Virgin used, and she added that she was taking her under her protection anew and that she regarded her as her beloved daughter.

This miraculous restoration of health caused great astonishment in the Community. It was no longer doubted that she was guided by the Spirit of God; permission was granted to her to receive Holy Communion on all the First Fridays in honor of the Sacred Heart of Jesus. This custom was soon followed by the whole Community and produced abundant fruit. Permission was granted to her at the same time to make the midnight hour of prayer which she had asked for and which became for her a source of blessings and merits, for during this hour she participated in a mysterious manner, as she herself states, in the agony and sorrows of Jesus Christ. She tells of this sharing in Christ's sufferings in one of her letters as follows: "My Superior granted me permission (to make this hour of prayer); I cannot describe what I suffer during this hour. It seems to me that this divine Heart pours into mine a share of the bitter sorrow of His Passion which reduces my soul to a kind of agony so painful that sometimes I seem to be on the point of death."

In another letter she writes: "Sometime afterwards this divine Savior showed me two kinds of sanctity in His Sacred Heart; one, the sanctity of love, the other, the sanctity of justice. This sanctity of justice obliges Jesus Christ to reject far from His Heart the impenitent sinner who has despised all the means of salvation that He has presented to him. Then God abandons this sinner to himself and this unhappy one becomes insensible to his own misfortune. He makes me suffer by this sanctity of justice when He is about to abandon some soul that is consecrated to Him in a special manner. The pains which I then suffer are so intense that I do not think that there is any kind of torture in this world which could equal them and it seems to me that if I listened to the promptings of my natural inclination, I would prefer to be in a blazing furnace rather than to suffer such pains as I then experience.

"The sanctity of love is hardly less painful in its way. These sufferings are to make reparation in some manner for the ingratitude and insensibility of the hearts of so many ungrateful people who make no return for the ardent love of Jesus Christ. This sanctity of love makes me suffer by the keen regret which I feel at not being able to suffer enough, and it inspires me with such an ardent desire to love Jesus Christ, and to see Him loved by the whole world, that there is no torment to which I would not gladly expose myself to make Him known and loved. It was then shown to me that these two kinds of sanctity would be continually made use of to make me suffer and this fills me with joy which I cannot express.

"Indeed, Father, it seems to me that I could not live a moment without suffering. It is true that I would have succumbed many times, were I not sustained by a special grace, and it is in order to obtain this grace that my Savior commanded me to receive Holy Communion on the First Friday of each month; or rather to repair, as far as is possible for me, the outrages which He has received during the month in the Blessed Sacrament. However, there is still another circumstance that causes me still greater sorrow than all that I have hitherto described; it is when this amiable Heart was represented to me with these words:

"I have an ardent thirst to be honored and loved by men in the Most Blessed Sacrament and I find hardly anyone who endeavors according to My wish to quench this thirst by making Me some return of love."

"At another time, it seemed to me that I saw this amiable Heart like a Sun projecting Its rays in every direction and on every heart, but in a manner differing very much according to the dispositions of those on whom these rays fell; for the souls of the lost became still more hardened as mud becomes hardened by the rays of the sun; on the contrary, the souls of the just become more pure and were softened like wax. However, when receiving these graces I always felt myself urged interiorly to make this divine Heart known. I could find no means of doing so until Father Claude de la Colombiere was sent here. During the Octave of Corpus Christi, having received in abundance the greatest favors and no longer able to resist the reproaches made to me by my divine Master Who lovingly complained of my want of fidelity to His orders and of my timidity (which was nothing else than the result of my self-love), I had finally to go to this Father and disclose to him what I had always kept hidden with such care, because it was told to me distinctly that this great servant of God had been destined to share in the execution of this great design.

"I am obliged to inform you, Reverend Father, that I cannot

tell you any more; if you knew the great torment which I suffer in writing this for you, although you have made me aware that this is necessary for the glory of the Sacred Heart of my adorable Master to Which I have sacrificed myself completely, and although my Superiors have given me an express command to write, yet if you know how much I suffer, perhaps you would think differently. I have told you all quite simply and as I believe everything took place. But once more alas! may I not have been deceived up to this, and may I not still be deceived? I know that God is sometimes pleased to confer his great favors on those who deserve them least, but do not my imperfections give me great reason for fearing that all this is but vanity and delusion? In all that passes within me I find nothing so solid as the humiliations which this has procured for me, and the happiness which I experience in suffering."

It is certain that solid virtue and consummate sanctity do not consist either in reflections such as these, or in extraordinary graces; but when all these extraordinary graces and these revelations tend only to make Jesus Christ loved more ardently and more perfectly, while they are accompanied with profound humility, continual mortification, and perfect obedience, these extraordinary graces and these revelations are certain proofs of perfect sanctity.

St. Teresa says that a certain proof of holy transport is that it causes in the soul extraordinary desires to suffer and that the soul never returns from these intimate communications with God without an ardent thirst for suffering and for being continually humiliated for the love of Jesus Christ. It is stated that Our Lord, wishing to console Blessed Angela de Foligno when she feared that her revelations and interior inspirations might not have come from the Spirit of God, spoke to her these beautiful words: "My child, the exterior, visible signs which you demand in order to know whether it is I Who speak to your heart, are uncertain, and you might be deceived by them; but I will give you one which is infallible and which the devil cannot counterfeit; it is such an ardent desire to suffer pain, labor, and humiliations for the love of Me that you will experience no less joy in opprobrium than people usually do when treated with honor."

Such signs as these have accompanied the extraordinary favors with which God has honored this holy Sister, and are proofs that she was guided by the Spirit of God. The ordinary result of these great graces was an extreme desire to suffer and to be humiliated and especially to hide carefully these gifts of God, wishing that, so far as it depended on her, no one would know about them. All these familiar communications, which she had so often with Jesus Christ, served only to make her more humble, more obedient and more mortified. The fear which constantly haunted her that she was under delusion made her regard all these great graces as means used by God in her regard to oblige her to work without relaxation to acquire solid virtue.

In her writings she tells how Our Lord came to her assistance: "As a remedy against this fear which I have constantly that there may be some illusion in the great graces and extraordinary favors which I receive continually from God, my Sovereign Master has deigned to give me certain marks by which I can distinguish between what comes from Him and what comes from the devil, from self-love, or from some other natural impulse.

"In the first place, these special graces and favors will always be accompanied in me by some humiliation, contradiction or contempt on the part of creatures; in the second place, after receiving some of these favors or divine communications of which my soul is so unworthy, I will feel my soul plunged in an abyss of annihilation and interior confusion which will make me feel as much sorrow at the sight of my unworthiness as I had received consolation by the liberality of my divine Savior, thus killing all vain complaisance and all sentiment of esteem of myself.

"Furthermore, these graces and communications whether for myself or for others, will never produce in me the least feeling of contempt for anyone; and any knowledge that He may give me of the interior state of others will not cause me to esteem them the less, however great their misery may appear to me; all this will produce in me sentiments of compassion and will cause me to to pray for them constantly.

"In the fourth place, all these graces, however extraordinary they may be, will never prevent me from obeying my Rule and obeying blindly; my divine Savior had given me to understand that He had so subjected these favors to obedience that if I should in the smallest depart from obedience, He would withdraw from me with all His great graces.

"Finally, this Spirit that guides me and that rules over me with such complete dominion urges me in particular to do these five things: (1) to love my divine Savior Jesus Christ with an extreme love; (2) to obey perfectly after the example of Jesus Christ; (3) to wish for suffering ceaselessly for the love of Jesus Christ; (4) to wish to suffer in silence without anyone perceiving that I suffer, if possible; (5) to have an insatiable hunger to receive Holy Communion, to adore the most Blessed Sacrament, to be humiliated, to live poor, unknown and despised by all, and finally to live overwhelmed with all kinds of infirmity and misery.

"This sovereign Lord of my soul has deigned in His Mercy to give this unworthy sinner these marks in order that I may know whether the graces which I receive come from the good Spirit or not; and if I be not deceived, it seems to me that all the graces which I have so far received have produced all these effects in me. For the rest I feel and I see more clearly than day that a life without the love of Jesus Christ is the culmination of all evils imaginable."

Those who knew the state of her conscience are convinced that she had arrived at consummate perfection. Her love for Jesus Christ increased day by day; she could no longer speak of anything but of the devotion to His Sacred Heart. In one of her letters she says:

"Would that I could recount all that I know about this amiable devotion, and reveal to the whole world the treasures of grace which Jesus Christ has stored up in His adorable Heart and which He intends to pour out in profusion on all those who practice devotion to It! I implore you, Reverend Father, to do all in your power to propagate it everywhere. Jesus Christ has given me to understand in a manner that leaves no doubt that it is principally by means of the Fathers of the Company of Jesus that He wishes to establish everywhere this solid devotion, and through it to make for Himself an infinite number of faithful servants, perfect friends and truly grateful children. The treasures of blessings and graces which this Sacred Heart contains are infinite. I do not know that there is any other exercise in the spiritual life which is more calculated to raise a soul in a short time to the height of perfection and to make

it taste the true sweetness to be found in the service of Jesus Christ. Yes, I say with assurance that if it were known how pleasing this devotion is to Jesus Christ, there is no Christian, however little his love for this amiable Savior, who would not begin to practice it immediately. Endeavor above all to make Religious take up the practice of it, for they will draw from it such help that they will require no other means to reestablish the first fervor and the most exact regularity in the most disordered Communities, and to bring to the height of perfection those who live in the greatest regularity.

"People who live in the world will find through this amiable devotion, all the helps necessary for their state of life, that is to say, peace in their families, solace in their labors, the blessings of Heaven on all their enterprises, consolation in their afflictions, and they will really find in this Sacred Heart of Jesus a place of refuge during their whole life and especially at the hour of their death. Ah! how sweet it is to die after having a tender and constant devotion to the Sacred Heart of Jesus Christ. My divine Master gave me to understand that those who labor for the salvation of souls will labor with success, and will have the art of touching the most hardened hearts, if they have a tender devotion to His Sacred Heart and work to propagate this devotion and establish it everywhere. Finally it is quite evident that there are none in the world who would not receive all manner of help from heaven, if they had a truly grateful love for Jesus Christ such as the love shown Him by means of devotion to His Sacred Heart."

She told Blessed Claude de la Colombiere positively when everything seemed to be against the establishment of this devotion and when there seemed to be little likelihood that it would be adopted, that even if she saw the whole world up in arms against this devotion, she would never despair of seeing it established, since she had heard Our Savior say: "My daughter, do not be cast down by so much opposition, I will reign in spite of My enemies and I will accomplish the design for which I have chosen you in spite of all the efforts which those opposed to this devotion may make." Indeed she had the happiness of seeing this promise accomplished some years before her death. She had seen a magnificent chapel erected within the enclosure of her monastery in honor of the Sacred Heart of

Jesus, and she had the pleasure of learning that this example was being followed by many other religious bodies, and that this devotion was being every day spread with wonderful fruit. It is easy to see that all this was not accomplished without little miracles. The design for which Providence had chosen her was happily executed. It pleased God to call her to a happier life, thus granting the crowning grace to the others which He had conferred on her. For more than a year she had felt the interior fire which consumed her to be more intense than formerly, and she had arrived at that sublime pinnacle of perfection, of which St. Teresa speaks, when a soul is so intimately united to God that it is no longer itself that lives but Jesus Christ Who lives in it, by its perfect acquiescence in His Orders without having any other desires or sentiments than those of Jesus Christ. Her profound humility made her at first regard this perfect tranquility of heart which a soul in this state enjoys, as a chastisement from God.

She writes to her Director: "I do not know what to think of the state in which I find myself at present. I find three desires so ardent that I regard them as three tyrants which make me suffer a continued martyrdom without giving me a moment's rest. These three desires are: to love God perfectly, to suffer much for His love, and to die in this ardent love and by the ardor of this love. But at present I find myself in a certain tranquility of heart and in a cessation of desires which astonishes me. I fear that this pretended peace may only be the result of this insensibility in which God sometimes leaves unfaithful souls, and I fear that, by my great infidelity to His graces, I may have drawn upon myself this state which is perhaps a kind of abandonment and reprobation; for I confess to you that I can no longer wish for or desire anything in this world although I see how much I am lacking in the matter of virtue. Sometimes I wish to grieve about this, but I cannot do so, it being no longer in my power, so to speak, to act. I only feel a perfect acquiescence in the good pleasure of God and an ineffable pleasure in suffering. The thought which consoles me from time to time is that the Sacred Heart of Jesus Christ will do everything for me if I allow Him to act. He will wish, He will love, He will desire for me, He will supply for all my defects."

She had arrived at this state of perfection when it pleased Our Savior to call her to Himself. There is reason to believe that she had certain knowledge of the time of her death long before she fell ill. Three months before her death she wrote to the priest before mentioned saying that it was her last letter. She told one of the Sisters of the convent that she would die the year that she died, saying that she was an obstacle to the exaltation of the Sacred Heart of Jesus Christ and to the complete establishment of the devotion. At the time she spoke, the true sense of what she said was not apparent, but it became so after her death, because her death made it possible to publish the extraordinary graces which God had conferred on her in view of this devotion: "I will die assuredly this year," she said, "in order not to prevent the great fruits which my divine Savior intends to draw from a book on devotion to the Sacred Heart of Jesus which Father (Croiset) will get printed as soon as possible." At the time she spoke, he wrote to her saying that it would be some years before he could think of publishing the book,* so she could have no knowledge of the matter from human sources.

As soon as she fell ill, she stated with certainty that she would die; her illness appeared so light that her doctors said that there was no appearance of death, but she insisted on saying that she was dying. This certainty of death made her ask for the Holy Viaticum the evening before her death; and as the Sisters said that her illness was not serious, she asked that she might at least get Holy Communion as she was still fasting. Her request was granted and she received Holy Communion with extraordinary devotion saying that she received it as Holy Viaticum, knowing that it was her last Holy Communion.

The virtues which she exercised during her illness corresponded with the high idea entertained about her perfection during life. One of the Sisters, who perceived that she was suffering terribly, offered to procure her some relief, but she thanked her saying that all the moments which remained were too precious not to profit by them; that in truth she suffered much, but that she did not suffer enough, because she found such pleasure in living and dying on the Cross that however ardent was her desire to die, she would willingly consent to remain in the state in which she was until the day of judgment, if it were the good pleasure of God, such was her attraction

---

*The first edition of Father Croiset's book was actually published in May, 1691, the year after her death.

for suffering.

Never, it seemed, had anyone shown such eagerness to die. All those who visited her during her illness admired the extraordinary joy which the thought of death caused her. But God wished to interrupt for some time this abundance of interior consolations with which she was filled, by inspiring her with such a great fear of His divine Justice that she was suddenly filled with strange fears at the sight of the terrible judgments of God. By this way God wished to purify her soul. She was seen to tremble, to humble and annihilate herself in the presence of the Crucifix and was heard to say: "Mercy, O my God, mercy." But some time afterwards all her fears disappeared, and her spirit found itself in great calm and great assurance of her salvation. Her joy and tranquility of heart appeared on her countenance. An hour before her death she called the Superioress who had made her promise that she would not die without giving her warning. She requested to get Extreme Unction and thanked her for all the little acts of kindness which she had done to relieve her suffering. She said that she was at the end of life and that nothing remained for her but to lose herself in the abyss of the Sacred Heart there to give her last sigh. After this, directing her eyes to the Crucifix, she remained calm while Extreme Unction was being administered, and having pronounced the Sacred Name of Jesus, she rendered her soul into the hands of her Creator on the seventeenth of October, 1690, at the age of forty-two, in the odor of sanctity.

The death of this saintly Religious created that impression of admiration for her piety which usually accompanies the death of the saints. One heard both in the monastery and in the town the words: "The Saint is dead." And far from feeling that horror which a corpse naturally inspires, people never tired of looking at her and remaining near her body. People said that there was a something in her face that inspired that veneration which is felt for the relics of the Saints. There was an extraordinary concourse of people at her funeral; many demanded permission to touch their beads to her body, others asked for part of her clothes; all wished to have some relic, and the veneration for her went on increasing. There is no reason for doubting that God had revealed many secret things to this saintly Religious. Blessed Claude de la Colombiere and several others saw things happen which she had predicted long before, although what she predicted was against all appearances. There was hardly any of those who were privileged to speak to her but felt themselves extraordinarily touched by her words and went away from the interview with a new resolution to love Jesus Christ more ardently.

Several people affirm that since her death they have received particular favors which they prayed for through her intercession. These are convincing proofs that she received extraordinary graces from Jesus Christ and that she had revelations which are judged to be among the number to which we can safely give credence. But we can say that the extreme love which she had for Jesus Christ, the perfect obedience, the prodigius love of suffering and the profound humility which she kept to her last breath, make her more estimable in the eyes of those who know how to value sanctity, than the greatest miracles would do.

THE MOTIVES FOR THIS DEVOTION

Chapter I

What do we mean by devotion to the Sacred Heart of Jesus, and in what does it consist?

The particular object of this devotion is the immense love of the Son of God which induced Him to deliver Himself up to death for us and to give Himself entirely to us in the Blessed Sacrament of the Altar. The thought of all the ingratitude and all the outrages which He was to receive in this state of immolated victim until the end of time did not prevent Him from operating this prodigy; He preferred to expose Himself each day to the insults and opprobrium of men rather than be prevented from testifying by working the greatest of all miracles to what excess He loved us.

This has excited the piety and zeal of many people, for when they consider how little the world is moved by this excess of love, how little men love Jesus Christ in return, and how little pains they take to be loved by Him, His faithful friends have not been able to endure seeing Him treated with such contempt day after day; they have endeavored to show their just sorrow at such treatment, and, by their ardent love, their profound respect and by special acts of homage, to testify their great desire to make reparation to the utmost of their capacity for this ingratitude and contempt.

With this end in view, they have chosen certain days of the year to recognize in a more particular manner the extreme love which Jesus Christ has shown us in the Blessed Sacrament; and at the same time to make some reparation of honor to Him for all the indignities and all the contempt which this amiable Savior has received and which He still receives every day in this mystery of love; and certainly this regret which they show at the sight of the little love which men have for Jesus Christ in this adorable mystery, this sensible sorrow which they feel at seeing Him so badly treated, these practices of devotion which love alone suggests, and which have as their sole object to make reparation as far as possible for the outrages which He suffers there, are certain proofs of the ardent love which they have for Jesus Christ and visible marks of their just gratitude.

The object and the principal motive of this devotion is, as has been already said, the immense love which Jesus Christ has for men who, for the most part, have nothing but contempt or at least indifference for Him. The end which is proposed is, first, to recognize and honor as much as lies in our power, by our frequent adoration, by a return of love, by our acts of thanksgiving and by every kind of homage, all the sentiments of tender love which Jesus Christ has for us in the adorable Sacrament of the Blessed Eucharist, where, however, He is so little known by men, or at least so little loved even by these people who know Him; secondly, to make reparation, by all possible means, for the indignities and outrages to which His love has exposed Him during the course of His mortal life, and to which this same love exposes Him every day in the Blessed Sacrament of the Altar.

This devotion consists, therefore, in ardently loving Jesus Christ, Whom we have always with us in the adorable Sacrament of the Eucharist, and in showing this ardent love by our grief at seeing Him so little honored by men, and by our acts of reparation for this contempt and this want of love. But just as in the case of even the most spiritual devotions, we have always need of material and sensible objects which appeal to our human nature, act on the imagination and memory and facilitate the practice, so in the case of this devotion, the Sacred Heart of Jesus has been chosen as the sensible object most worthy of our veneration, and at the same time most proper for the end proposed by this devotion.

In truth, even if we had no particular reasons to give to these exercises of piety the title of "devotion to the Sacred Heart of Jesus", it seems that we could not better express the particular character of this devotion than by this title; for indeed this devotion properly understood is nothing else than an exercise of love. Love is its object, love is its motive and principle, and it is love that ought to be its end. The heart of man is, says St. Thomas, in a certain manner, both the source and the seat of love; its natural movements follow and continually imitate the affections of the soul, and serve to no small extent either by their vehemence or their weakness, to increase or diminish the passions.

It is for this reason that we commonly attribute to the heart the most tender sentiments of the soul, and it is also that consideration which renders so precious the hearts of the Saints.

From what has been said so far, it is easy to see what is meant by the devotion to the Sacred Heart: by this devotion we mean the ardent love which we conceive for Jesus Christ at the remembrance of all the marvels which He has wrought to show His tender love for us, especially in the Sacrament of the Eucharist, which is the miracle of His love; we mean the keen regret which we feel at the sight of the outrages which men commit against Jesus Christ in this adorable Mystery; we mean the ardent desire which presses us to leave nothing undone to make reparation for these outrages by every possible means. That is what we mean by the devotion to the Sacred Heart of Jesus and that is what it consists in. It cannot be reduced — as some people might think at seeing this title — to merely loving and honoring by special worship this Heart of flesh like ours, which forms part of the adorable Body of Jesus Christ.

It is not that the Sacred Heart is not worthy of our adoration; it suffices to say that It is the Heart of Jesus Christ; and if His Sacred Body and His Precious Blood deserve our respect and homage, who does not see that His Sacred Heart has still more special claim to respect and homage and if we feel in ourselves such a strong attraction to the devotion to the Sacred Wounds, should we not feel ourselves still more penetrated with devotion to His Sacred Heart? What we wish to make clear is that the word "heart" is taken here only in the figurative sense, and that this Divine Heart, considered as a part of the Adorable Body of Jesus Christ, is, properly speaking, only the sensible object of this devotion and that it is nothing less than the immense love which Jesus Christ bears to us which is its principal motive.

Now as this love is altogether spiritual, it cannot be perceived by the senses; it was necessary, therefore, to find a symbol, and what symbol could be more proper and more natural for love than the heart?

For the same reason, the Church wishing to give us a sensible object for the sufferings of the Son of God, which are not less spiritual than His love, represents to us the image of His Sacred Wounds; so that the devotion to the Sacred

Wounds is, properly speaking, only a particular devotion to Jesus Christ suffering; in like manner *the devotion to the Sacred Heart of Jesus is a more warm-hearted and ardent devotion towards Jesus Christ in the Blessed Sacrament, its principal motive being the extreme love which He shows us in this Sacrament, and the principal object, to make reparation for the contempt and its outrages which He suffers in this same Sacrament.**

The Sacred Heart of Jesus has, certainly, as much relation to His love, for which we endeavor by this devotion to inspire sentiments of gratitude and love, as the Sacred Wounds have to His sufferings, for which the Church endeavors to inspire her children with sentiments of gratitude and love by devotion to these Sacred Wounds. Now if people had at all times such devotion to the Sacred Wounds of Jesus Christ, and if the Church, wishing to inspire all her children with love for Jesus Christ, unceasingly puts before their eyes these same Wounds, what ought not be the effect of the remembrance and of the image of the Sacred Heart?

We shall see later on that the devotion is not new; that several great Saints confirmed the use of it by their example. We may say that the Holy See authorized the use of it under the same title, since Clement X, by the Bull of Oct. 4th, 1674, accorded great indulgences to an Association of the Sacred Heart of Jesus in the Church of the Seminary of Coutance consecrated in its honor, and our Holy Father, Pope Innocent XII, by a special Brief, has just accorded a plenary indulgence in favor of the devotion to the Sacred Heart.

.*(The devotion to the Blessed Eucharist and the devotion to the Sacred Heart are not only two sister devotions, in reality they are only one and the same devotion. They complete each other and develop each other; they blend so perfectly together that one cannot go on without the other and their union is absolute. Not only can one of these devotions not be prejudical to the other, but because they complete each other and perfect each other, they also reciprocally increase each other.

"If we have devotion to the Sacred Heart, we will wish to find It, to adore It, to love It, and where shall we look for It but in the Blessed Eucharist where It is found, eternally living? . . . The devotion to the divine Heart infallibly brings souls to the Blessed Eucharist; and faith in and devotion to the Blessed Eucharist necessarily lead souls to discover the mysteries of Infinite Love of which the divine Heart is the organ and the symbol.") *Extract from the "Book of Infinite Love" by Mother Louise Margaret.*

It is not necessary to give here the hundred reasons which show the solidity of this devotion; it suffices to say that the immense love which Jesus has for us and of which He has given such a signal proof in the adorable Sacrament of the Eucharist, is the principal motive; that reparation for the contempt with which men have treated this love is the principal end proposed; that the Sacred Heart of Jesus, all enflamed with love for men, is the sensible object; and that a very ardent and tender love for the adorable Person of Jesus Christ ought to be the fruit.

Chapter II

The means which God made use of to propagate this devotion to the Sacred Heart of Jesus

Blessed Claude de la Colombiere, S.J., was among the persons selected by God to publish this devotion to the faithful. This great servant of God was illustrious both as Confessor of the Faith in England, and as Chaplain to the Duchess of York, afterwards Queen of England. He was celebrated for his works on religious subjects, but more celebrated for his sublime virtue. He was sent by Providence to St. Margaret Mary to assist her in her mission of establishing the public worship of the Sacred Heart of Jesus.

Having examined into the private revelations received by St. Margaret Mary he came to the conclusion after careful inquiry that those revelations were genuine and guided by divine help he consecrated himself to the Sacred Heart. The devotion was for him the means of arriving at great perfection. Convinced by his inquiry and by the great favors which he himself received that the devotion was the work of God, he regarded himself under an obligation to do all in his power to make public the treasures of grace and mercy hidden in the Sacred Heart which hitherto had been revealed only to chosen souls. The following is what he wrote in his "Journal of Spiritual Retreats", which he composed in London and which was published after his death. *(It is of great historic interest because it was the first explanation of the devotion of the Sacred Heart of Jesus addressed to the ordinary faithful):* "Finishing this retreat full of confidence in the mercy of my God, I have made a law for myself to procure by all means possible the execution of what I was ordered by my adorable Master concerning His precious Body in the Blessed Sacrament, in which I believe Him to be truly and really present. Filled with sweetness which I have been able to taste and receive from the mercy of my God without being able to explain it . . . I have come to recognize that God wishes that I serve Him by procuring the accomplishment of His desires concerning the devotion, which He has suggested to a person (St. Margaret Mary) to whom He has communicated Himself very intimately, and for the propagation of which He has deigned to make use of my weakness. I have already preached this devotion to many people in England, and have written about it in France, and have asked one of my friends to make it known in the place where he is. It will be very useful there. The great number of chosen souls which there are in this Community makes me believe that the practice of it in this house will be very pleasing to God. Would that I could be everywhere, O my God, and could publish what Thou dost expect from Thy servants and friends!

God having revealed Himself to this person (St. Margaret Mary) who, from the graces which she has received is, I believe, according to His Heart, she informed me about the revelations which she received. I obliged her to write down for me what she had told me. I have gladly transcribed the account into my "Journal of Retreats" because the good God wishes to make use of my weakness for the execution of His designs.

This saintly soul says: "Being one day before the Blessed Sacrament during the Octave of the Feast, I received from my God excessive graces of His love. When I was touched by the desire to make some return to Him and to render love for love, He said to me: 'You can give Me no greater return than by doing what I have so many times commanded you to do,' and revealing His Heart to me He said: "Behold this Heart which has so loved men as to spare Itself nothing, even to exhausting and consuming Itself, to testify to them Its love, and in return I receive nothing but ingratitude from the greater part of men by the contempt, irreverence, sacrileges, and coldness which they have for Me in this Sacrament of My Love; but what is still more repulsive is that it is hearts consecrated to Me that

treat Me thus. For this reason I ask that the First Friday after
the Octave of Corpus Christi be set apart for a particular Feast
to honor my Heart; I ask that reparation of honor be made to
My Heart, that Communion be received on that day to repair
the indignities which It has received during the time It has been
exposed on the altars; and I promise you that My Heart will
expand Itself to pour out in abundance the influences of Its
love on those who will render It this honor."

"But my Lord, to whom dost Thou address Thyself?" said
this person (St. Margaret Mary). "To a wretched slave, to a poor
sinner who by her unworthiness would be capable of hinder-
ing Thy designs. Thou hast so many generous souls to execute
Thy commands!" "Poor innocent that you are," said Our
Savior, "do you not know that I make use of the weak to confound the strong? That it is usually on the lowliest and the poor
in spirit that I show My power with greatest effect, in order that
they may attribute nothing to themselves?" "Give me then,"
said I (St. Margaret Mary), "the means to do what Thou dost
command me to do." Then Our Savior said "Address yourself to My servant" (Blessed Claude de la Colombiere), "and
tell him on My part, to do everything possible to establish this
devotion and to give this pleasure to My divine Heart: tell him
not to be discouraged by the difficulties which he will meet
because he will want for nothing; but he should be aware that
he is all powerful who distrusts himself completely, in order
to put all his confidence in Me."

Blessed Claude, who had the gift of discernment, was not a
man to believe anything lightly; but he had two striking proofs
of the high and solid virtue of this person (St. Margaret Mary)
who spoke to him to dread any illusion. Therefore he applied
himself immediately to the ministry that God had confided to
him. But to acquit himself of it solidly and perfectly, he wished
to begin by himself; he consecrated himself entirely to the
Sacred Heart of Jesus; he offered to It all that he thought capable of honoring and pleasing It. The extraordinary graces which
he received from this practice soon confirmed him in the idea
that he already had of the importance and solidity of this devotion. He had no sooner considered the sentiments full of tenderness that Jesus Christ has for us in the Blessed Sacrament in
which His Sacred Heart is always burning with love for men,
always open to pour out on them all kinds of graces and bless-

ings, than he could no longer think without grieving of the horrible outrages which Jesus Christ suffers at the hands of heretics, and of the strange contempt with which even the generality of Catholics treat Jesus Christ in this august Sacrament; this neglect and contempt, and these outrages touched him sensibly and obliged him to consecrate himself anew by this beautiful prayer which he calls the offering to the Sacred Heart of Jesus, and which will be found at the end of this book.

The voyage of this Servant of God to England, his imprisonment and his early death after his return to France, did not permit him to give further instruction on this devotion to the public. But God did not leave His work unfinished. He Himself made use of the mysterious influence of His grace to accomplish His designs. In former times He had made known to St. Gertrude that this devotion was reserved for these last ages as a means to arouse the faithful from their tepidity and cowardice; now He makes use of a humble Sister (Sister Joly) to compose a little book which though it had neither art nor design, was the means of winning over to the devotion those very persons who formerly had no relish for it, and who, without hardly knowing what it was about, had opposed it; and God made use of these very people to spread the devotion everywhere.

Thus, in less than a year we have seen this devotion happily established. The most prudent directors, doctors and prelates have praised it; preachers have preached it with success, chapels have been built in honor of the Sacred Heart, images have been engraved and painted, altars have been erected in Its honor; the Religious of the Visitation, who in this matter have been the zealous pioneers, have had the pleasure of hearing solemnly sung in their chapel at Dijon, which they had built for the Sacred Heart of Jesus, the Mass composed in Its honor. Their example has been followed with great fruit by many other Religious. This solid devotion has been spread and established with marvelous success through almost the whole of France; it has passed into foreign countries; it has gone even across the seas to Quebec and Malta, and we have reason to believe that by means of missionaries it is already spread in Syria, in India, and even in China. Finally, the universal approbation which this devotion has received, and the esteem which people of recognized merit and virtue have for it, gives us ground for hope that Jesus Christ will henceforth be less forgotten, better served and much better loved.

Chapter III

How eminently just and reasonable it is to practice devotion to the Sacred Heart of Our Lord Jesus Christ

The reasons which should induce us to love Jesus Christ do not depend on mere sentiment; people realize them according to their state of grace or holiness. It would seem that to wish to seek for motives to induce us to love Jesus Christ is to forget what we are, or not to know what He is.

It might then appear useless to give here the motives which should induce us to practice devotion to the Sacred Heart of Jesus since this devotion consists in the exercise of the love which we ought to have for Jesus Christ. However, as all men are not always in the same dispositions, and as grace in all men is not always the same, we deem it advisable to make some reflections on the three principal motives which influence us most, and by which all reasonable men are convinced.

These three motives are taken from the three things which have most influence over our minds and hearts, namely, reason, interest and pleasure. We shall endeavor to show in this chapter and the two following ones: (1) how just and reasonable the devotion to the Sacred Heart of Jesus is; (2) how much it helps towards our eternal salvation and towards attaining perfection; and (3) what sweet spiritual consolation it brings to the soul. Truly, whether we consider the sensible object of this devotion, which is the Sacred Heart of Jesus, or meditate on the principal and spiritual object which is the immense love of Jesus Christ for men, must we not feel our hearts filled with sentiments of reverence, gratitude and love?

I

THE EXCELLENCE OF THE ADORABLE HEART OF OUR LORD JESUS CHRIST

The Heart of Jesus is holy with the holiness of God Himself; from this it follows that, as all the movements of this Heart participate in the dignity of the Person Who is the cause of them, they are actions of infinite price and value, since they are actions of the Man-God; it is therefore just that the Sacred Heart be honored with a special worship since in honoring It, we honor His divine Person.

If the veneration which we have for the Saints makes us esteem their hearts so highly, if we regard these hearts as the most precious of their relics, what ought we not think of the adorable Heart of Jesus Christ? What heart has ever had such admirable dispositions, and has been so devoted to our real interests? Where could we find a heart whose movements have been so advantageous to us? It is in this divine Heart that have been formed all the designs for our salvation, and it is by the love with which the same Heart burns that these designs have been executed.

This Sacred Heart, said a great Servant of God, is the seat of all the virtues, the source of all blessings, the place of refuge for all holy souls. The principal virtues to be honored in this Sacred Heart of Jesus are: first, His most ardent love for God the Father, joined with the most profound respect and the greatest humility that human heart ever possessed; secondly, Its infinite patience in adversity, extreme sorrow for the sins with which It was laden, the confidence of a most tender son, joined with the confusion of a very great sinner; thirdly, Its most tender compassion for our miseries and immense love for us in spite of these same miseries. Finally, although all these movements of the Sacred Heart were each in the highest degree possible, It preserves unalterable tranquility because It is in such perfect conformity with the will of God that It cannot be troubled by any event, however contrary it may appear to Its zeal, Its humility, Its love and all Its other dispositions.

This adorable Heart has still, as far as it is possible, these same sentiments, and especially, It is always burning with love for men, always open to pour out on them all kinds of graces and blessings; always touched by our evils, always urged by the desire to make us share in Its treasures and to give Itself to us; always disposed to receive us and to serve as a place of refuge, as a dwelling place and paradise for us during this life For all that It finds nothing in the hearts of men but unkindness, neglect, contempt and ingratitude. Are not these motives capable of inducing Christians to honor the Sacred Heart, and

to make reparation for such contempt and for so many outrages by giving striking proofs of their love?

II

THE AMIABLE QUALITIES WHICH ARE FOUND IN THE PERSON OF JESUS CHRIST

If we apply ourselves to the study of the sacred character of
Our Lord Jesus Christ we shall find in it all that is amiable in
creatures, both those endowed with reason and those without
reason. Men are attracted to love by various motives, according
to their dispositions; some are affected by beauty, others by
great meekness; for others, uprightness that is merciful, nobil-
ity of character that is modest are charms which they cannot
resist. We see people who allow themselves to be attracted by
the virtues which are wanting to themselves, because these
virtues appear to them more admirable than those which they
themselves possess. Some others are more captivated by qualities which have more relation to their own inclinations; beautiful qualities, real virtues conquer the love of everyone. But,
says a great Servant of God, if there is a person in whom all
these qualities are united, who could refuse him his love? Now
everyone is agreed that all these qualities are found united in
an eminent degree in the adorable Person of Jesus Christ, and
nevertheless, Jesus Christ is loved only by a very small number of people.

The most dazzling beauty, says the Prophet, is only a dried-
up flower compared with the beauty of this divine Savior; it
seems to me, said St. Teresa, that the sun casts only pale shad-
ows on the earth, since I have seen in an ecstasy some rays of
the beauty of Jesus Christ. The most beautiful creatures of this
world are those which have the least defects; the most beautiful qualities in men are accompanied by so many imperfections
that, while on the one hand the former attracts us, on the
other, the latter repel us. Jesus Christ alone is perfect to a sovereign degree; everything in Him is equally amiable, we find
nothing in Him but what ought to attract all hearts to Him. In
Him we find united all the advantages of nature, all the riches
of grace and glory, all the perfections of the Divinity. We dis-

cover nothing in Him but abysses and as it were immense spaces, and an infinite extent of grandeur. In fine, this Man-God Who loves us so tenderly and Whom men love so little, is the object of the love, the homage, the adoration and praise of the whole heavenly court.

It is He Who has sovereign authority to judge men and angels. The destiny and the eternal happiness of all creatures is in His hands. His domain extends over all nature. All spirits tremble in His presence; they are obliged to adore Him either by voluntary submission of love or by sufferings forced by the effects of justice. He reigns absolutely in the order of grace and in the state of glory, and the whole world visible and invisible is under His feet. Is there not here, O insensible men, an object worthy of your homage? And does not this Man-God with all His titles and the glory which He possesses, Who loves us to such extremes as He does, merit your love? But what appears still more amiable in this adorable Savior is that He combines all these splendid qualities, this sublime excellence, with the most excessive meekness and tenderness for us. His meekness is so amiable that it has charmed his mortal enemies. "He shall be led," said the Prophet, "as a sheep to the slaughter and shall be dumb as a lamb before his shearer, and shall not open his mouth." (Isaias LIII, 7). He compares Himself at one time to a father who cannot contain his joy at the return of his prodigal son, at another time to a shepherd who, having found one sheep that had gone astray, puts it on his shoulders and calls his friends and neighbors to rejoice with him because he had found his sheep (Luke XV, 9). "Has no man condemned you?" He says to the woman taken in adultery. "Neither will I condemn thee. Go, and now sin no more" (John VIII, 11). He displays no less meekness towards us every day. It is strange what restraint one must keep over oneself in company so as to avoid shocking a friend. Men are so sensitive, that a mere display of bad humor is enough to make them forget fifteen years of kindness, and a single word said at the wrong time, sometimes breaks the greatest friendship.

It is not so with Jesus Christ. It appears incredible, but it is nevertheless true, that we get better terms from Him than from our most grateful friends. We must not even imagine that He is capable of breaking with us because of a slight act of ingratitude. He sees all our infidelities. He knows all our weakness and He endures, with incredible goodness, all the failings of those whom He loves. He forgets them, He pretends not to see them. His compassion goes so far as even to console people who are excessively afflicted by these infidelities. He does not wish that the fear we have of displeasing Him should go so far as to trouble us. He desires that we avoid the slightest faults, but He does not wish that we worry too much even about the great ones, He decrees that joy, liberty and peace of heart shall be the eternal inheritance of all those who love Him truly.

The least of all those qualities in one of the great ones of this world would be enough to gain the hearts of all his subjects. The mere narration of some of these virtues about a prince whom we have never seen and who we shall never see, makes an impression on our hearts, and makes us love even strangers, Jesus Christ is the only one in Whom all these fine qualities, all these virtues and all the grandeur, excellence and amiability imaginable, are found united, and must it be that so many reasons for loving cannot make us truly love Him? In the world, a mere nothing is often sufficient to gain our hearts. We give our hearts, we lavish them on so many occasions for a mere trifle; Thou alone, O Lord, can have no share in them!

Can we make even a little reflection on these things and not love Jesus Christ ardently, and not have at least keen regret that He is so little loved? In truth, we owe Him our hearts on several titles; and can we refuse them to Him, if we add to all these titles the immense benefits which He has gratuitously conferred upon us, and the extreme tenderness with which He has loved us and still loves us, never ceasing to give us striking proofs of His immense love for us?

III

THE VISIBLE PROOFS OF THE IMMENSE LOVE WHICH JESUS CHRIST HAS FOR US

Men are usually more affected by benefits received than by any other mark of love, either because nothing else proves so well that the love is genuine, or because nothing is so pleasing to our self-seeking human nature as a love which is useful. It is by this way that Jesus Christ has tried to engage us to love Him. He has anticipated our wishes, He has conferred upon us countless benefits, the least of which surpasses all that we could merit, all that we could expect, all that we could reasonably desire. Everyone receives these favors continuously, everyone is agreed about the excess of His love of which the same benefits are striking proofs; and nevertheless how few are those who are gained by these benefits? How few respond to His love?

From constantly hearing mention of the Creation, the Incarnation and the Redemption, we become familiar with these words and with what they signify, and yet we remain unmoved; but even the most unreasonable of men would go into ecstasies of love for another man, if he learned that he had received from him the hundredth part of the least of these favors.

As our soul depends much on our senses in its operations, we are naturally little touched by the remembrance of a Being that is altogether spiritual; thus is seems that before the Incarnation of the Word, however great the prodigies God performed in favor of His people, He was always more feared than loved by them; but finally God made Himself perceptible, so to speak, by becoming man, and this same Man has done things that go beyond anything that we can imagine to induce men to love Him. Even if He had not willed to redeem us, He would not have been either less holy, or less powerful, or less happy; nevertheless, He has taken our salvation so much to heart that on seeing what He has done and the manner in which He has accomplished it, one would say that all His happiness depended on ours; whereas He might have redeemed us at little cost, He has willed to merit the grace of our redemption by His death, even by the most shameful and cruel death on the cross; and whereas He might have applied His merits to us in a thousand other ways. He has chosen that way which involves such prodigious abasement that it has amazed both heaven and earth; and all this is done to touch hearts that are naturally sensitive to the least benefit, and to the least mark of friendship. Birth in poverty, an obscure life full of labors, a passion full of opprobrium, an infamous and sorrowful death are marvels that go beyond our comprehension and these are the effects of the love which Jesus has for us.

Have we ever formed an adequate concept of the greatness

of the benefit of our Redemption? And if we have formed a concept of it, is it possible for us to be only a little moved by the remembrance of this benefit? The sin of the first man brought great evils upon us, it deprived us of great advantages; but can we see Jesus Christ in the crib, can we look upon Him on the Cross, or in the Blessed Eucharist, without confessing that our losses have been repaired with advantage, and that the advantages of the man redeemed by the adorable Blood of Jesus Christ surpass the privileges of the man in the state of innocence?

The quality of universal Redeemer is a motive no less powerful to make us love Him. "All men," says the apostle, "died by the sin of Adam, and Jesus Christ died for all men." (Rom. V, 12-18). No one has been able to defend himself from the contagion of so great an evil and everyone has felt the effect of such a powerful remedy. This amiable Savior gave all His Blood both for the infidel who knows Him not, for the heretic who refuses to believe in Him, and for this member of the faithful who, while believing in Him, still refuses to love Him.

And if we reflect on the infinite value of His Blood! what a Savior! and what abundance of Redemption! Jesus Christ was not content with paying the debts which we had contracted, He anticipated all the debts that we might contract in the future; He has, so to speak, paid them in advance before they have been contracted. Add to this those powerful helps, those great graces, those signal favors which He lavishes on faithful souls and by which He charms and sweetens all that is hard and rough in our exile.

My God! if Thou wouldst confer on us the grace to understand this excess of mercy, could it be that we would not be moved by it and that we would not love Jesus Christ with our whole heart? How amiable is not this divine Savior for having willed to redeem us in such a difficult manner! But is He not still more amiable for having desired to deliver us in this manner without being forced to do so, but being moved to it only by His immense love and by His desire to induce us to love Him by such striking proof of His ardent love? The Eternal Father, says Salvien, knows us too well to have set such a high price on us, so that it is Jesus Christ Himself Who has fixed our price, and with His full consent has offered this excessive ransom, and after all this shall we not love Jesus?

But remark that, inexpressibly great as are all these things which Our Lord has done for our salvation, the love which induces Him to do these things is still greater than the things themselves, because it is infinite; and as if this love of Jesus would not be satisfied so long as there remained a prodigy which He had not done, He instituted the Blessed Sacrament of the Altar, that is to say, the abridgment of all marvels, that is to say, that He remains with us really and truly until the end of the ages; that He gives Himself to us in the Blessed Eucharist under the appearance of bread and wine; that He makes His Flesh and Blood the nourishment of our souls in order to unite Himself more closely to us, or rather to unite us more closely to Him.

Christians, can one be a rational being and remain unmoved by the mere narration of this prodigy? Can a person retain any sentiments of humanity and not be all on fire with love for Jesus Christ at the sight of this benefit? God making a mere man the object of His tender love and complacence, and eager to confer benefits upon him! God desiring to unite Himself to man in a manner that involves emptying Himself and immolating Himself daily, and condescending to make Himself man's daily food; and all this in spite of the indifference, the aversion, and contempt of those who never receive Him; and the coldness and even the crimes of those who receive Him often! God consenting to remain shut up in the ciborium day and night, century after century! Christians, are not these marvels signal proofs of the love which Jesus Christ has for us? Are they not motives capable of making us love Him? Ungrateful men, for whom alone these marvels are performed, what do you think of them? Does not Jesus Christ on our altars deserve to be honored by you? and does He not still show sufficient love to merit to be loved by you? "If any man love not our Lord Jesus Christ, let him be anathema." (1 Cor, XVI, 22).

"In truth," says a great Servant of God, "if anything could shake my faith in the mystery of the Eucharist, it would not be this infinite power which God shows in changing bread and wine into His Body and Blood that I would doubt; it would be rather the extreme love of which He gives proof in this mystery. How can the Body of Jesus Christ be in several places at the same time? How can He be enclosed in a space that is almost indivisible? To all that I have only to reply, that God is omnipotent; but if I am asked how can it be that God loves a creature so feeble and so miserable as man and loves him with such eagerness, with such ecstasy, loves him to the degree that He has loved him? I confess that I have no reply to make; that it is a truth that passes my comprehension, that the love which Jesus bears us is an excessive love, an ineffable love, an incomprehensible love, a love which ought to amaze and astonish any reasonable man."

I do not know whether these reflections will be capable of touching the faithful today, but I do know that in the past they have deeply touched peoples, even the most inhuman and the most barbarous; and that these peoples were heard to cry out at the bare mention of these marvels: Oh! how good the God of Christians is! how liberal He is! how amiable! Oh! who could prevent himself from loving a God Who loves us so passionately! As a result of these reflections, in order to make some return to our Savior Who has loved so tenderly, and to show Him some gratitude, the cloisters were filled with religious, and the deserts peopled with a prodigious number of holy anchorites altogether devoted and consecrated to the praise and the love of Jesus Christ.

However fitting this way of showing gratitude is, Christians of today are not asked to do so much; they are only asked not to forget altogether Jesus Christ, Who has performed the greatest of His miracles with the sole object of satisfying His extreme desire to be always with them; they are only asked to be a little less insensible to the outrages which the excessive love of Jesus Christ brings upon Him; finally they are exhorted to be at least as grateful to Jesus Christ Who loves them so constantly and Who has performed marvels in their interest that surpass their comprehension, as people of the world are to their friends — who, for the most part, are ready to sacrifice them, if their own interest demands it.

Now does not a devotion seem reasonable which tends to inspire gratitude to Jesus Christ, and which in itself properly speaking is but a continual exercise of perfectly grateful love? And is it not just that we seek means to show our tender love for Jesus Christ especially at a time when He is so little loved? He is little loved in the world where people are so little sensitive to His benefits, where they follow His counsels so little, where they decry His maxims so strongly; He is little loved at a time when people have nothing but indifference for His Person, when all the gratitude and respect which people show Him are reduced to a few prayers and a few ceremonies, which by custom have degenerated into pure routine; and finally at a time when His divine presence causes ennui and His precious Body and Blood cause aversion.

IV

THE EXTREME INGRATITUDE OF MAN TOWARDS JESUS CHRIST

Incredible as may appear, the love which the Son of God shows us in the adorable sacrament of the Eucharist, there is something which is still more astonishing: it is the ingratitude which men show in return for this love. It is astonishing that Jesus Christ should be willing to love men, but it is strange that men should not be willing to love Jesus Christ, and that no motive, no benefit, no excess of love can inspire them with the least sentiment of gratitude. We might, perhaps, be able to give some reasons why Jesus Christ should love men: they are His work, He loves in them His Own gifts; He loves Himself in loving them; but can we have any reason for not loving Jesus Christ, for only loving Him coldly, for sharing with anyone else our love for Him? Speak, ungrateful men, unfeeling men, is there anything in Him which repels you? Perhaps He has not yet done enough to merit your love? What do you think of it? Would we have dared to desire, could we have even imagined all that He has condescended to do to gain our hearts in this adorable mystery of the Blessed Eucharist? Nevertheless, all this has not been able to induce men to love Jesus Christ ardently!

What advantage did this prodigious abasement bring to Jesus Christ? It might be said that, in some degree, all the other mysteries, which are all effects of His love, have been accompanied with circumstances so glorious and with prodigies so striking that it is easy to see that, while taking care of our interests, He did not altogther neglect His own glory. But in this amiable Sacrament, Jesus Christ seems to have forgotten all advantage for Himself, and to have made it completely and entirely the Sacrament of His love. After this, who would not say that such a prodigious excess of love would at least excite an eagerness, a desire, an excessive love in the hearts of all men? Alas! it is quite the contrary, and it seems that people would love Jesus Christ more, if Jesus Christ had loved men less. I shudder with horror, O my God, at the sole thought of the indignities and the outrages which impious and wicked Christians, and furious heretics have committed against Thee in this august Sacrament. By what horrible sacrileges have they not profaned both our altars and our churches? And with what opprobrium, with what impiety, with what infamy, have they not hundreds of times treated the adorable Body of Jesus Christ? Can a Christian think on these acts of impiety without conceiving an ardent desire to make reparation for such cruel outrages by all means possible? But can a Christian live without even thinking of them?

If Jesus Christ, who had received such indignities from heretics, were at least assiduously honored, and ardently loved by the faithful, people could console themselves that their love and sincere homage would in some manner atone for these outrages. But alas! where do we find these numerous adorers eager and assiduous in paying court to Jesus Christ in our Churches? Rather do we not find our churches deserted and empty, without faithful adorers? Really, could people show more coldness and more indifference to Jesus Christ in the Blessed Sacrament than they do? Is not the small number of people found in our churches during the greatest part of the day a visible proof of the neglect and the want of love of almost all Christians? Those who approach the Altar oftenest become accustomed to our most awe-inspiring mysteries; and it may be said that priests are found who become so familiar with Jesus Christ as to treat Him with indifference and contempt! How many of them do we find who, although they daily offer up this adorable Victim inflamed with love for them, love Jesus Christ the more for it? How many of them are there who celebrate these adorable mysteries with the reverence that is a fitting expression of their faith in them?

Can we think that Jesus Christ is insensible to such treatment and can we ourselves think on this disrespectful treatment and remain insensible? And not seek every possible means to make reparation? How could anyone who reflects but a little on these truths not devote himself completely to the love of this God-Man Who ought by so many titles to possess the hearts of all men?

In order not to love Him, one must either not know Him or be worse than this unhappy demon spoken of in the life of St. Catherine of Genoa, who did not at all complain of the flames which burned him, nor of the other pains which he suffered, but only that he was without love, that is to say, wihout this love which so many souls ignore or reject to their eternal woe.

Do we remember that the Sacred Heart of Jesus in the Blessed Sacrament has still, as far as it is possible, the same sentiments as It always has had; that It is always burning with love for us, always sensibly touched by the evils that befall us, always urged by the desire to make us share in His treasures, and to give Himself to us; always ready to receive us and to serve as a dwelling place and as an earthly paradise for us in this life, and especially as a place of refuge at the hour of our death? And for all that what sentiments of gratitude are found in our hearts, what eagerness to serve Him, what love? He loves; and He is not loved; people do not even know of His love because they are not willing to receive the gifts by which He deigns to show it, or to listen to the tender and secret declarations which He wishes to make to our hearts of this love.

Is not this a pressing motive to touch the hearts of all those who have even the least sentiments of reasonableness or the smallest particle of love for Jesus Christ? This amiable Savior, when instituting this Sacrament of Love, foresaw clearly all the ingratitude of men, and He felt in advance all its bitterness in His Sacred Heart; all that, however, has not been able to repel Him or prevent Him from showing us the excess of His love by instituting this mystery.

Is it not just that amidst such incredulity, such coldness, such profanations and outrages, this God of love should find at least some friends of His Sacred Heart who will grieve for the want of love that people show Him, who feels the insults that are offered to Him, who are faithful and assiduous in paying Him court and who leave nothing undone to repair by their love, by their adoration and by every kind of homage, all the outrages to which the excess of His love exposes Him at every hour in this august Sacrament?

This is the end proposed in this devotion which consists in

honoring the Sacred Heart Who should be infinitely dearer to us than in our own heart; and this reparation of honor, these offerings, these regular visits to the Blessed Sacrament, these prayers, these Holy Communions, and all the other practices (which will be found in the third part of this book) will help to make us more and more grateful and more faithful by making us love Jesus Christ more ardently. What other devotion can we find more just and reasonable or more useful for helping us to attain salvation and acquire perfection?

Chapter IV

How the practice of this devotion conduces to our Salvation, and aids in the acquiring of Perfection

If Jesus Christ has performed so many prodigies to induce us to love Him, what favors will He not confer on those whom He sees eager to testify to Him their gratitude and their ardent love? He has loved us tenderly, says St. Bernard, and He has lavished His blessings on us when we did not love Him, even when we did not wish Him to love us. What gifts and graces will He not pour out on those who love Him and who are grieved at seeing Him so little loved?

It is sufficiently evident that the devotion to the Sacred Heart is a proof, or to express it more accurately, a continual exercise of ardent love of Jesus Christ. Besides the fact that it consists in the practice of the most holy exercises of our religion, it has a something so strong and so tender about it that it obtains everything from God; and in truth, if Jesus Christ confers such great favors on those who have devotion to the instruments of His passion, and to His Wounds, what favors will He not confer on those who have a tender devotion to His Sacred Heart?

In the preface to this book we have given reasons why prudent men should not refuse to give credence to the revelations of St. Mechtilde. This Saint gives the following account of a revelation which she received about this devotion:

"One day I saw the Son of God, holding in His Hand His own Heart, Which appeared more brilliant than the sun and

*Which was casting rays of light on every side; then, this ami-
able Savior gave me to understand that all the graces which
God unceasingly pours forth on men according to the capacity
of each, come from the plenitude of this divine Heart."*

And this same Saint, a short time before her death, declared
that having one day earnestly asked Our Lord for some great
favor for a person who had asked her to do so, Jesus Christ
said to her: "My child, tell that person for whom you are praying to Me, to seek in My Heart all that she desires; tell her to
have a great devotion to My Sacred Heart, and to ask for everything in this same Heart, like a child asking its father for everything it wants, knowing no other artifice but what love suggests
to it" (Liber Specialis Gratiae, Pt. IV, Chap. 28).

God, having revealed to this person (St. Margaret Mary Alacoque), mentioned in the second chapter, for whom Father de
la Colombiere had such veneration, the great graces which He
had attached to the practice of this devotion, told here that it
was by a last effort of His love for men that He had resolved to
reveal to them the treasures of His Sacred Heart and to give
them this devotion which would enkindle the fire of His love
in the hearts of the most unfeeling and inflame the hearts of
the least fervent with ardent love.

*"Publish this devotion everywhere," said this amiable Savior,
"propagate it, recommend it to people of the world as a sure
and easy means to obtain from Me a true love of God; to
Ecclesiastics and Religious, as an efficacious means to arrive at
the perfection of their state; to those who work for the salvation of their neighbor, as an assured means to touch the most
hardened hearts; and finally, to all the faithful, as a most solid
devotion, and one most proper to obtain victory over the strong-
est passions, to establish union and peace in the most divided
families; to get rid of the most long standing imperfections;
to obtain a most ardent and tender love for Me; in fine to
arrive in little time and in a very easy manner at the most sublime perfection."*

St. Bernard (1091-1153 A.D.) full of these sentiments never
speaks of the Sacred Heart of Jesus but as an inexhaustible
source of all blessing:

"O most sweet Jesus," he cries out, "what riches Thou hast contained in Thy Sacred Heart, and how easy it is for us to enrich ourselves when we possess in the Blessed Eucharist this infinite treasure." "It is in this adorable Heart," says Cardinal Peter Damien, "that we find all the weapons proper for our defense; all the remedies proper for the cure of our evils, all the most powerful aids against the assaults of our enemies, all the sweetest consolations to solace our sufferings, all the purest delights to fill our souls with joy. Are you afflicted? Do your enemies persecute you? Does the remembrance of your past sins trouble you? Do you feel your heart agitated by un-easiness, fear or passion? Go and prostrate yourself at the foot of our Altar; throw yourself, so to speak, into the arms of Jesus Christ, enter into His Sacred Heart, it is a sanctuary, a retreat for holy souls, a place of refuge where our souls are in perfect safety." The devout Lanspergius says: "Not only is the Sacred Heart the seat of all the virtues, but it is also the source of the graces by aid of which we acquire and preserve these virtues. Have devotion to the Sacred Heart all full of love and mercy; through It, demand all that you wish to ob-tain, by It offer all your actions because this Sacred Heart is the treasury of all supernatural gifts; It is, so to speak, the way by which we unite ourselves more closely with God and through which God communicates Himself most lovingly to us. Draw at will from this Sacred Heart all the graces, all the virtues of which you have need, and do not fear that you will exhaust this infinite treasure; have recourse to It in all your necessities; be faithful in the exercise of so reasonable and so useful a devotion and you will soon feel its effects." (Lansperg. Pharetra divini amoris).

We find still another illustrious example of all this in the life of St. Mechtilde. The Son of God, having appeared to her, commanded her to love Him ardently, and to honor His Sacred Heart in the Blessed Sacrament as much as possible. He gave her His Sacred Heart as a pledge of His love and as a place of refuge during her life, and as her consolation at the hour of her death. From this time this Saint was penetrated with an extraor-dinary devotion for this Sacred Heart, and she received such great graces from It that she was accustomed to say that, if she had to write down all the favors and all the blessings which she had received by means of this devotion, a large book would not contain them (Liber Specialis Gratiae). Those who practice devotion to the Sacred Heart in our own times receive also great graces and experience great consolation and thus confirm by their own experience the truth of the statements of those cherished servants of God.

The author of the "Interior Christian" writes: "I am resolved to depend henceforth on Providence alone without seeking either consolation or support in creatures; I ought to be like a child that, without uneasiness or fear, reposes sweetly in the arms of its mother from whom it receives a thousand caresses, a thousand kindnesses; I confess that Our Lord treats me in that manner; for without seeking elsewhere nourishment and riches for my soul, I find in His Sacred Heart, all the helps and blessings of which I have need; and I find these blessings in such great abundance, and I am so liberally enriched by them, that I am sometimes astonished, and fear that there may be negligence on my part because I receive such great graces while making so little effort."

But even though we could not adduce either authority, or examples, or particular revelations in favor of this devotion; even if Jesus Christ Himself had not explained it so frequently, should a Christian have need of elaborate reasoning to see there is nothing more solid or more advantageous for our salvation and our perfection than a devotion that has as motive, the most pure love of Jesus Christ; and which has as end, to make reparation as far as possible for all the indignities which Jesus Christ suffers in the adorable Sacrament of the Eucharist; and of which all the practices tend solely to honor Jesus Christ and to make Him ardently loved?

Can this admirable Savior, Who has done so much to gain the heart of men, refuse anything to those who themselves ask of Him a place in His heart? If Jesus Christ allows Himself to be given to those who do not love Him, if He allows Himself to be brought at the hour of death to people who have scarcely ever deigned to visit Him during their lives, people who have been insensible both to the striking proofs of love which He gives them and to the cruel outrages which He receives in the adorable Sacrament of the Eucharist, people even who have perhaps themselves treated Him with indignity, what will He not do for these faithful servants who, sensibly touched at seeing their good Master so little loved, so rarely visited and so cruelly outraged, frequently make reparation to Him for all the contempt which He suffers and leave nothing undone to repair the outrages offered to Him by their frequent visits, by their adoration and homage, and especially by their ardent love? It is therefore clear that there is nothing more reasonable, nothing more useful than the practice of this devotion, and will it then be necessary to give lengthy reasons to Christians to persuade them to take up the practice of it?

The precious advantages attached to the practice of devotion to the Sacred Heart which Father Croiset had just pointed out had been announced long before his time by the great contemplative, St. Gertrude of Saxony (1256-1302).

What St. Gertrude has written on this subject has been frequently quoted; a few words will suffice to recall it. Her historian relates that the Beloved Disciple, St. John, appeared to her on one occasion, and that she asked her heavenly Visitor how it was that he, whose head had reposed on the breast of the Savior at the Last Supper, kept complete silence about the throbbing of the adorable Heart of his Master; and she expressed regret to him that he had said nothing about it for our instruction. The Saint replied to her: "My mission was to write for the Church, still in its infancy, something about the uncreated Word of God the Father, something which of itself alone would give exercise to every human intellect to the end of time, something that no one would ever succeed in fully understanding. As for the language of these blessed beats of the Heart of Jesus, it is reserved for the last ages when the world, grown old and become cold in the love of God, will need to be warmed again by the revelation of these mysteries." (Lanspergius, Legatus Divinae Pietatis Lib. IV, Cap. IV).

Chapter V

What true sweetness and consolation is to be found in the Devotion to the Sacred Heart of Jesus

Although all exercises of devotion can fill those who practice them with interior consolation, and although there are no good works that are not accompanied by the inexpressible pleasure and joy which are inseparable from the testimony of a good conscience, and which surpass all other pleasures, it is however certain that Jesus Christ has never conferred so many favors, even sensible favors, as in the practice of the devotion which tends to honor Him in the Blessed Sacrament. The lives of the Saints are filled with examples which demonstrate this truth.

When was it that St. Francis, St. Ignatius, St. Teresa, St. Philip Neri, St. Aloysius of Gonzaga and a hundred others, have felt their hearts more than usually inflamed with love but when they approached this august Sacrament? How many loving sighs, how many sweet tears in the celebration or in the participation of this adorable mystery? With what consolation and with what torrents of delights have they not been filled. And, in truth, as there is no place where Jesus Christ is more liberal, so there is no place where He makes the sweetness of his presence and His gifts more felt. In the other mysteries He gives us His graces but in this, the first grace which He gives us, is to give us Himself really and truly.

Joy is inseparable from a feast; Jesus Christ has made a feast every day for Christians in the adorable Sacrament of the Eucharist. Are we to be astonished that He treats His friends with so much sweetness and love at this sacred banquet?

Now as the devotion to the Sacred Heart makes us true and faithful adorers of Jesus Christ in the Blessed Sacrament, and as it consecrates us in a special way to this mystery, it procures for us the greatest sweetness from it. One would say that Our Savior measures the special favors which He confers in this Sacrament by the number of insults which He has endured in it, and as there is no mystery in which He has received so many outrages, there is also no other mystery in which He fills with such sweet consolations those who do all in their power to make reparation for these outrages. As the motive of this holy practice is so pure and agreeable to Jesus Christ, we should not be surprised if the best and holiest of all masters shows such sweetness to His grateful and faithful servants, especially at a time when gratitude is rare, and when so little eagerness to serve Him and so little true love are found even in those who make a profession of loving Him.

As it is impossible to have this devotion at heart without having great love for Jesus Christ, it would be difficult not to feel in its practice that sweetness and those interior consolations inseparable from the exercise of true love; and as the mere sight of the wounds of Jesus Christ inspires us with a certain confidence in His mercy, the mere sight of His Heart inspires us with a certain sweetness and joy that can be distinctly felt, but which is difficult to describe. In truth, it is strange if one should approach Jesus Christ, be well received by Him, and not feel the same pleasure as is usually felt when one is well received by the great ones of this earth. If we do not experience this consolation, — and this is a greater misfortune than some people think — it is because of our want of love for Jesus Christ, because of our great imperfections, our little faith and a hundred other faults. But we can say that as those who have true devotion to the Sacred Heart of Jesus have none of these faults, all these caresses, all these singular favors ought to be inseparable from the exercise of this devotion.

This has been the happy experience so far of all persons who have been known to be devoted to the Sacred Heart of Jesus; and this is still the experience every day of those who imitate them; this is proof that Jesus Christ cannot refuse His sweetest caresses to the friends of His Sacred Heart. It has always been remarked that the Saints who have had most devotion to the Sacred Heart have been all filled with most signal favors, and those Saints hardly ever speak of the devotion to the Sacred Heart of Jesus without using language that lets us see the extraordinary graces and interior sweetness with which they have been filled. "O how good and sweet it is," says St. Bernard, "to make one's abode in this Sacred Heart. It is enough to bring to mind Thy Sacred Heart, O my amiable Jesus, to be filled with joy." It is by means of this devotion that St. Gertrude and St. Mechtilde received such great favors from Jesus Christ. St. Clare assures us that it was to the tender devotion which she had to the Sacred Heart of Jesus that she owed the extraordinary sweetness with which her soul was filled every time that she presented herself before the Blessed Sacrament; and St. Catherine of Siena felt herself all inflamed with the love of Jesus at the mere thought of this adorable Heart; and Jesus Christ, having appeared to St. Mechtilde, addressed these beautiful words to her: "My daughter, if you wish to obtain pardon for all your negligence in My service, have a tender devotion to My Sacred Heart, for It is the treasury of all the graces which I confer on you unceasingly. It is Itself the source of all those interior consolations and of the ineffable sweetness which I lavish on My faithful friends."

Father Claude de la Colombiere never expresses himself in any other manner on this subject, and although for many years God had led him in the paths of the most sublime perfection, not by sensible consolations, but only by a lively faith and by rude trials, nevertheless, the Holy Spirit seems to have changed His method as soon as He had inspired him with the practice of this devotion. The following quotation with reference to this subject is taken from his "Book of Retreats." "My heart expands and feels sweetness which I can taste and receive from the mercy of God, without being able to explain it. Thou art very good, my God, to communicate Thyself with such liberality to the most ungrateful of creatures and to the most unworthy of Thy servants. May Thou be praised and blessed eternally for it! I have recognized that God wished that I should serve Him, by procuring the accomplishment of His desires concerning the devotion (to the Sacred Heart) which he has suggested to a person (St. Margaret Mary) to whom He communicates Himself very confidentially. Would that I could be everywhere, O my God, and publish what Thou dost expect from Thy servants and friends!" And in another place he says: "Cease, my Sovereign, to fill me with Thy favors, I recognize how unworthy I am of them ... can I merit these ineffable graces and consolations which Thou dost shower on me without any deserving on my part? No, no, my God, it is Thou alone Who by Thy sufferings hast obtained for me all these favors from Thy Eternal Father; may Thou be eternally blessed, and may Thou fill me with evils and miseries to give me some share in Thine; I cannot believe that Thou dost love me unless Thou grant me many long sufferings."

It is thus that this holy man expresses himself in the excess of the sweetness and interior consolations which he felt in the exercise of a tender devotion towards the Sacred Heart of Our Lord Jesus Christ.

Chapter VI

The devotion which the Saints had to the Sacred Heart of Jesus Christ

As the example of the Saints is at the same time a powerful motive to urge us to the practice of a devotion which they themselves have practiced, and a salutary lesson to teach us how to practice it, we think it advisable to give here the views of those who had the tenderest love for the Sacred Heart of Jesus and who were most penetrated with this devotion.

St. Clare, who was inflamed with the love of Jesus Christ and filled with eagerness to love Him in return, believed that she could find no practice more suitable to testify her gratitude than to salute and adore, several times each day, the Sacred Heart of Jesus in the Blessed Sacrament; and by means of this devotion, as is related in her life, her soul was filled with the sweetest delights and the most signal favors.

The prayer of St. Gertrude (1256-1302) to the Sacred Heart of Jesus (to be found at the end of this book) shows the high esteem which this Saint had for this devotion. The historian of her life describing her precious death, said: "Her blessed soul took its flight towards heaven and retired into the Sanctuary of the Divinity; I mean," he added, "into the adorable Heart of Jesus, Which this divine Spouse in an excess of love had opened to her."

St. Mechtilde (1240-1298) was so penetrated with the devotion that all day long she could speak only of this adorable Heart of Jesus and of the singular favors which she received from this devotion. This amiable Savior gave her His Heart as a pledge of His love and to serve her as a place of refuge where she would unceasingly find sweet repose during life, and inexpressible peace and consolation at the hour of death.

St. Catherine of Siena loved this devotion to an extraordinary degree; she made an entire donation of her heart to her divine Spouse and she obtained the Heart of Jesus in exchange; from that time on, she endeavored to live and act only according to the movements and inclinations of the Heart of Jesus Christ.

St. Elzear writing to St. Delphine says: "You are troubled about my health, you wish to have news of me. Go often and pay court to our amiable Jesus in the Blessed Sacrament, enter into His Sacred Heart and you will get news about me there, because you will find me always there, it is my ordinary dwelling place."

The words of St. Bernard not only express his own beautiful sentiments about this adorable Heart, but show that this devotion to the Sacred Heart was known and practiced before the time of St. Margaret Mary. He writes in his book "Vitis Mystica": "O sweetest Jesus, what riches Thou hast stored up in Thy Sacred Heart! Can it be that men are indifferent to the loss which they suffer by the neglect and indifference which they show to this amiable heart? As for me, I will spare no pains to gain It and possess It. Henceforth I will consecrate to It all my thoughts; Its sentiments and desires shall be my sentiments and desires. I will give everything to possess this precious treasure. But what need have I to buy It since It is truly mine? Yes, I say with assurance, the Heart of Jesus is mine, since It belongs to my Master, and does not what belongs to our Master belong also to all His members? Henceforth this Sacred Heart will be both the Temple where I shall never cease to adore Him, and the Victim Who I shall unceasingly offer to Him; and the Altar on which I shall offer my sacrifices, on which the same flames of divine love with which It burns, will consume mine; in the Sacred Heart I shall find a model to regulate all the movements of mine, a source of wealth with which to pay all my debts to divine justice, and an assured place of refuge where I shall be protected from shipwreck and storms. I will say with David: 'I have found my heart to pray to my God' (II Kings VII, 27); Yes, I have found this Heart in the adorable Eucharist when I have found there the Heart of my Sovereign, of my Friend, of my Brother, that is to say, the Heart of my amiable Redeemer. And after that who will prevent me from praying with a confidence and obtaining all that I shall ask? Come, my brethren, let us enter into this amiable Heart never again to go out from It. My God, if we feel such consolation at the bare remembrance of this Sacred Heart, what will it be when we love It with tenderness, what will it be if we enter into It and make our dwelling there always? Draw me completely into this heart, O my amiable Jesus. Open to me this Heart which has so many attractions for me! What! does not this open breast leave an entrance open for me, and does not the open wound of this Sacred Heart invite me to enter there?" (Vitis Mystica, Cap. III).

The famous Lanspergius (+1538), well known for his works which are full of unction and solid piety, writes in the Chapter on "The Exercise of the Devotion to the Sacred Heart of Jesus" of his "Epistolae Paroeneticae," as follows:

"Take care to excite yourself by frequent acts of constant devotion to honor the amiable Heart of Jesus, all full of love and mercy for us; it is through It that you must ask for all you wish to obtain; it is by It and in It that you must offer to the Eternal Father all that you do, because the Sacred Heart is the treasury of all supernatural gifts and of all graces. It is, so to speak, the way by which we unite ourselves more closely to God, and by which God Himself communicates Himself more liberally to us. That is why I advise you to put in the places where you pass most often some pious image on which the Sacred Heart is represented, the sight of which will constantly remind you of your holy practices of devotion towards this Adorable Heart, and will urge you always to love it more ... When you feel yourself touched with a more tender devotion you can kiss this image with the same sentiments with which you would truly kiss the Sacred Heart of Our Lord Jesus Christ. You should endeavor to unite yourself constantly to the Sacred Heart, wishing to have no other desires, no other sentiments than those of Jesus Christ; persuading yourself that His Spirit and His Sacred Heart will, so to speak, pass into yours, and that of the two hearts there will be no longer two but one. Draw at will from this amiable Heart all imaginable blessings, you will never exhaust It. Besides, it is proper, it is even necessary to honor with a special devotion the Sacred Heart of Our Lord and Savior Jesus Christ which should be for you a sanctuary in which you can take refuge in all your necessities, and from which you can draw the consolation and all the helps of which you have need. For even if all men should abandon you and forget you, Jesus will be always your faithful Friend; He will keep you always in His Heart, put your trust in Him, rely on Him; others may deceive you and indeed do deceive you; the Sacred Heart of Jesus is the only heart that loves you sincerely; It is the only Heart which will never deceive you."

The author of the book entitled "The Interior Christian"

writes: "The Sacred Heart of Jesus is the center of men; when your heart is distracted and dissipated, you must bring it gently to the Heart of Jesus Christ and offer to the Eternal Father the holy dispositions of this adorable Heart, and unite the little which you do to the infinite amount which Jesus Christ accomplishes, thus, while doing nothing yourself, you shall do much through Jesus Christ; this divine Heart of Jesus will henceforth, devout soul, be for you an Oratory; in It and by It you will offer all your prayers to God the Father, if you wish them to be pleasing to Him; It will be your school in which you will learn the sublime science of God, which is so contrary to the opinions and wretched maxims of the world; It will be your treasure where you will go to get all that is necessary to enrich you; purity, pure love, fidelity; but what is most precious and most abundant in this Treasure are humiliations, sufferings and an ardent love of the greatest poverty; and learn that the esteem and love of all these things is a gift so precious that it is found only in the Heart of a God made man, as in its first Source; other hearts, however holy, however noble they may be, have this gift more or less in the measure that they go and draw out of this treasury, I mean, out of the Heart of Jesus Christ."

Finally, we may remark that not only all the Saints of the Church who appear to have been filled with the greatest graces, have had for Jesus Christ a most ardent and tender love, but there is scarcely one of those who have had for Jesus Christ this extremely tender love but has had also a singular devotion to His Sacred Heart.

Those who have read the life of St. Francis of Assisi, the works of St. Thomas, the works of St. Teresa, the lives of St. Bonaventure, of St. Ignatius, of St. Francis Xavier, of St. Philip Neri, of St. Francis de Sales, of St. Aloysius of Gonzaga, will be able to remark the tender devotion which these saints had for the Sacred Heart of Jesus.

Indeed, we find examples of great devotion to the Sacred Heart of Jesus (prior to the time of St. Margaret Mary) not only in the lives of the great saints but of many of God's chosen servants living in the world. Armelle Nicholas, a humble peasant girl, who died recently (1671) in the odor of sanctity is a case of this. In her life written under the title: "The Triumph of Divine Love," we read the following:

"Whenever I met with any affliction from creatures, I always had recourse to my amiable Savior, Who immediately filled me with sweet consolations. You would have thought that He feared that I should be in any way troubled, so careful was He to console me in all pains and afflictions. Very often He would show me His open Heart in order that I might hide myself in It, and at the same moment I would find myself enclosed in It with such great assurance of safety that all the efforts of hell seemed to me to be but weakness. For a long space of time I could neither see nor hear except in the Sacred Heart, so that I used to say to my friends: if you wish to find me, do not seek me anywhere else but in the Heart of my divine Love, for I do not stir from It either day or night; It is my sanctuary, my place of refuge against all my enemies."*

From "The school of the pure love of God open to the learned and unlearned by a poor uneducated girl, a peasant by birth and a servant by condition commonly called 'The Good Armelle,' who died recently in Brittany, 1671," by a Religious who knew her.

THE MEANS OF ACQUIRING THIS DEVOTION

Chapter I

The dispositions which are necessary in order to have a tender devotion to the Sacred Heart of Jesus

All the dispositions necessary for this devotion may be reduced to four: a great horror of sin, a lively faith, a great desire to love Jesus Christ, and, for those who wish to taste the real sweetness of this devotion and draw all the fruit from it, interior recollection.

FIRST DISPOSITION

A Great Horror of Sin

As the end of the devotion to the Sacred Heart is none other than a very ardent and tender love for Jesus Christ, it is evident that to have this devotion one must be in the state of grace, and have an extreme horror of all kind of sins incompatible with this love. The Sacred Heart being the source of all purity, not only can nothing sullied ever enter It, but nothing except what is extremely pure is capable of pleasing It. Whatever we may say or do for His love or for His glory, if we do not live in the state of grace, we are devoid of supernatural merit. The Heart of Jesus gives entrance only to souls extremely pure, His Sacred Heart cannot endure sin; the smallest fault, the least stain, causes It a kind of horror.

But on the contrary, great innocence and purity give assured access to the Sacred Heart. Jesus loved St. John in a particular way and why? Because his singular chastity had made him worthy to be loved with a singular love. He was loved in a special way, says St. Cyril, because he had extreme purity of heart. All those who aspire to true devotion to the Sacred Heart are so many souls who aspire to the quality of being the beloved of the adorable Savior; and the practice of this devotion properly speaking consists chiefly in a more tender and intimate love than that which the generality of the faithful have for Him. As soon as a soul begins to be little concerned about avoiding deliberate venial sins, intending to preserve itself only from mortal sin, besides the fact that it is in great danger of soon losing its innocence and the grace of God, it may not expect to taste the inexplicable sweetness which usually fills those who love Him truly and without reserve.

It is then evident that whoever undertakes to practice true devotion to the Sacred Heart of Jesus, should at the same time resolve to do all in his power to acquire a purity of heart much above that of Christians of ordinary virtue.

It is true that the practices of this devotion are means to acquire this extreme purity.

II

SECOND DISPOSITION

A Lively Faith

The second disposition required is a lively faith. Languid faith will never produce great love. Jesus Christ is little loved, although everybody is agreed that He is infinitely amiable; this is so because people do not believe as they should in the great marvels by which He testifies the greatness of His love. What will people not do to welcome a man who is thought to be powerful at court? What assiduous attention, what ceremony, what respect will be shown to a man who is believed to be a king, even though he may be disguised under the rags of the poorest of men? What would not people do in the presence of Jesus Christ on our Altars, what assiduous attention, what respect, but above all, what love would they not show in the presence of so amiable a Redeemer, in the presence of our King, of our Judge, disguised under the lowly species of bread, if they sincerely believe with firm conviction and lively faith that He is there present? The bones of the Saints inspire a certain respect; the mere reading about their virtues gives rise to a certain veneration and love for their person, because people do not doubt what they have heard or read; and yet the living Body and Blood of Jesus Christ whole and entire, present on our altars, even the sight of marvels which He performs to show His extreme love, inspires people with hardly any respect, and much less love! People never find the time long enough in presence of those whom they love; how does it come that a quarter of an hour before the Blessed Sacrament wearies them so much? A play at a theatre, a profane representation, always finishes too soon even if it has lasted three hours; a Mass, in which Jesus Christ is really and truly offered in sacrifice for our sins, appears to some people insupportably long if it lasts a half an hour, although they know well that the play is a fable, that the actors are not at all what they represent, that the whole action is completely useless to them, while on the contrary they profess to believe that the Sacrifice of the Mass contains the same Victim as that of Calvary, that there is nothing that can be more useful to them than this most august and most holy act of our religion.

Jesus Christ remains among us much in the same manner as He lived at Nazareth among His kinsmen; they did not recognize Him as a Prophet, they showed Him no honor, and He worked no miracles among them; as in the case of the people of Nazareth, our want of faith in Him and our bad dispositions towards Him, prevent us from experiencing the wonderful effects which He operates in the souls of those whom He finds well disposed. Whence comes it that people deplore the wickedness of the Jews, that they feel themselves so indignant against them for having treated our Savior with such disrespect that they were not willing to recognize Him? It is doubtless because they believe in the truth of His Divinity; and whence comes it, however, that they are so little touched by the neglect with which they themselves treat Jesus Christ in the Blessed Sacrament where so few people visit Him; and by the outrages which He suffers in it at the hands of those very people who make profession of recognizing Him? It is assuredly because the faith of Christians on this point is very languid. Lively faith is therefore a necessary condition to acquire this ardent love for Jesus Christ in the Blessed Sacrament, to feel oneself touched by the outrages to which the excess of His love exposes Him, and in fine to have a real devotion to His Sacred Heart. For this it is necessary to lead a pure and innocent life. We should animate our faith by our assiduous attention and especially by our profound respect before the Blessed Sacrament, and by every kind of good works; we should pray much; we should often ask God for this lively faith; we should, in fine, behave like people who believe, and we shall soon feel ourselves animated with this lively faith.

III

THIRD DISPOSITION

A Great Desire to Love Jesus Christ Ardently

The third disposition is a great desire to love Jesus Christ ardently. It is true that one cannot have a lively faith and live in innocence without at the same time being inflamed by very ardent love for Jesus Christ, or at least having an ardent desire to love Him. Now it is evident that desire of loving Jesus Christ ardently is an absolutely necessary disposition to have this devotion, which is itself a continual exercise of this ardent love. Jesus Christ never gives His love except to those who desire it passionately; the capacity of our heart is measured by the greatness of its desires; all the Saints agree that the most proper disposition to love Jesus Christ tenderly is to have an ardent desire to love Him. "Blessed," says the son of God, "are they that hunger and thirst after justice, for they shall have their fill" (Matt. V. 6). It is necessary that the heart be purified by this ardent desire in order to be inflamed by the pure flames of divine love. This ardent desire not only disposes our hearts to be inflamed with the love of Jesus Christ; it induces the amiable Savior to enkindle in our hearts this sacred fire. Let us truly desire to love Him, for it may be said that this desire is always efficacious, and it is unheard of that Jesus Christ has ever refused His love to those who desire it.

Could anything more reasonable be insisted on? Could anything easier be asked for, since there is no Christian who does not at least claim to desire to love Jesus Christ? If, then, it is true that this desire is so proper a disposition for acquiring an ardent love for Jesus Christ, what is the reason that so few people love Him ardently, although all flatter themselves that they have this disposition, and although Jesus Christ is ready to give His love to those who are well disposed? It is because our hearts are altogether occupied with self-love. What we call the desire to love Jesus Christ is in truth only a mere speculative inclination, only a sterile knowledge of the obligation that we are under to love Him. This is an act of the understanding and not of the will. This knowledge is common to all those who are not ignorant of the benefits for which they are indebted to Him and passes today for a real desire with all those who think themselves in good conscience, provided that they have some specious pretext for deceiving themselves.

To convince ourselves that we have not a real desire to love Jesus Christ, we have only to compare this pretended desire with all the other desires that we really have. What care, what eagerness people show when they have a passionate desire for something! They are altogether occupied with this desire, they think of it, they constantly speak of it, they are always busy taking measures to accomplish it, they even lose their sleep over it. What similar effect has our pretended desire to love Jesus Christ produced in us? Has the fear of not having this love given us much pain? Does the thought of this love occupy us much? We scarcely love Jesus Christ at all; and we deceive ourselves when we flatter ourselves that we eagerly desire His love.

The true desire of loving Jesus Christ comes too near true love not to have similar effects; self-love may vainly use all its artifices to convince people of the contrary, but it will never be true that we desire to love Jesus Christ ardently, so long as we love Him so little.

There is a great danger that these kinds of sterile desires to love Jesus Christ which we sometimes feel, are only some little sparks of a fire that is nearly extinct, or real marks of the lukewarmness in which we live. But if we have not this ardent love for Jesus Christ, let us at least once in our life, make some serious reflections on the obligations which we have of loving Him and it is certain that they will give rise to at least a true desire to be inflamed with this ardent love.

IV

FOURTH DISPOSITION

Interior Recollection

The fourth disposition which we must have for this devotion, especially if we wish to taste all its sweetness and derive from it all its advantages, is interior recollection. God does not make His presence felt where there is turmoil, *"non in commotione Dominus"*; a heart completely unguarded, and a soul in continual exterior distraction, and occupied with a thousand superfluous cares and useless thoughts, is hardly in a state to listen to the voice of Him Who communicates Himself only to a soul, and Who speaks only to a heart, in solitude. "I will lead her into the wilderness and I will speak to her heart." (Osee, Chap. II, 14).

Perfect devotion to the Sacred Heart is a continuous exercise of love for Jesus Christ; it cannot, therefore, exist without recollection. Jesus Christ communicates Himself in a more particular way to the soul by means of this devotion; the soul must, therefore, be in peace; it must be disengaged from the distractions and the tumult of exterior things, and be in a state to listen to the voice of our amiable Savior, if it wishes to taste the singular graces which He confers on a heart that is free from all that can trouble it and is occupied only with God.

This interior recollection is the foundation of the whole spiritual edifice of souls, so that without it progress towards perfection is impossible. It may be said that all the graces which a soul not established on this foundation receives from God, are like characters formed on water, or figures printed on sand. The reason for this is that in order to advance towards perfection, one must necessarily unite oneself more and more to God; now without interior recollection, one cannot unite oneself to God, Who will make his sojourn only in peace of spirit, and in the retirement of a soul not dissipated by different objects nor troubled and distracted by exterior occupations. St. Gregory remarks that when Jesus Christ wishes to inflame a soul with His divine love, one of the first graces He gives it is a great attraction for interior recollection.

It may be said that the commonest source of our imperfections is the want of recollection and of vigilance over ourselves. This is what stops so many people on the road to perfection, this is what causes the soul to find scarcely any relish for the holiest exercises of devotion. A man with little interior life is never devout. "Whence comes it," says a holy man, "that so many religious, so many devout people who have such good desires, and who seem to do all that is necessary to become saints, nevertheless, draw so little fruit from their prayers, their

Communions and their spiritual reading; and that after practicing all the exterior exercises of the spiritual life for so many years, they can hardly see any profit from it? Whence comes it that Directors who conduct others on the road of perfection remain themselves in their ordinary imperfections? How many zealous men, how many workers who labor with such ardor for the salvation of souls, how many people who give themselves to good works, suffer nevertheless from the violence of their passions, are always subject to the same faults, make hardly any progress in prayer, pass their whole life in a certain langor without ever tasting the ineffable sweetness of peace of heart, and are always uneasy, terrified by the thought of death and disheartened by the smallest accident? Does not all that come from their negligence in guarding their heart and keeping themselves in recollection? These people abandon the care of their interior and give themselves too much to the exterior. This causes an infinite number of faults to escape their attention, a thousand unconsidered words, sallies of ill humor, unregulated movements, actions purely natural. This would not happen to them if they had an actual intention to regulate their interior conduct, and if they guarded themselves a little in their activities, to prevent their passions which find their nourishment in this external activity, from being strengthened all the more dangerously, because the passions disguise themselves under the specious appearance of zeal and virtue.

We must then confess that interior recollection is so necessary for the perfect love of Jesus Christ and for progress in the spiritual life that a person will advance only in proportion as he gives himself to this exercise; it is by this means that St. Ignatius, St. Francis de Sales, St. Teresa, St. Francis Xavier and St. Aloysius of Gonzaga have arrived at the height of perfection; if we do not take care to keep ourselves recollected at the time of action, we shall draw little fruit from even our best actions. Let us keep silent if we wish to hear the voice of Jesus Christ; let us keep our souls away from the tumult and the embarrassment of exterior things in order to be able to find liberty to converse longer with Him, to love Him ardently and with tenderness.

The devil knows only too well the great advantages to be derived from this interior peace and guard over the heart; accordingly he uses all his cunning to make people give up this interior recollection. Whenever he despairs of making them leave off their exercises of devotion and their good works, he endeavors to make them concentrate all their attention on exterior works to the detriment of their devotions, and to induce them to leave their entrenchment where they were, so to speak, protected from all his darts. When a soul gives way to that satisfaction found in a large number of exterior actions, pleased with the illusion that it is doing much for God, it becomes dissipated and insensibly loses its union with God, and that sweet presence of God without which one may work much and accomplish little. A dissipated soul is like a stray and wandering sheep that is soon devoured by the wolf. Such a person may think that it will be easy for him to return into himself, but besides the fact that this presence of God is a grace that is not always at his disposal, he scarcely finds himself in a state to rid himself of the hundred exterior objects which occupy him, he has lost the taste for spiritual things by the too long sojourn which he has made in a strange country. The remorse and anxiety which he feels as soon as he pays some attention to himself causes this interior recollection to become a torture for him; he is dissipated and he loves dissipation.

My God, what loss does not a soul suffer that allows itself to be completely immersed in exterior things; what inspirations, what graces does it not render useless, and of what favors does it not deprive itself by the want of recollection?

To avoid this evil, we should take great care to keep ourselves always in the presence of God and to preserve the spirit of recollection in all our exterior occupations; it is necessary that while the mind works, the heart be in repose and remain motionless in its center, which is the will of God, from which it should never separate itself. To acquire this interior recollection which is assuredly the gift of God, but which God never refuses to those who ardently desire it and who take the means to obtain it, we must accustom ourselves to reflect much on the motives which should animate us in everything which we do. Before beginning an action, let us look and see that it is in order, that it is pleasing to God, and that it is for Him that we do it; during the action let us lift up our minds from time to time to Our Lord and renew the purity of our intention. It is a sign that we perform an act for God, if we leave it off when necessary without pain, if we continue it without uneasiness or chagrin, and if we are not angry when we are interrupted. But the surest and most efficacious practice to preserve this interior recollection in our greatest exterior occupations is to represent to ourselves Jesus Christ in His occupations. Let us represent to ourselves the manner, the modesty, the exactness with which He acted when on earth; the attention which He expended to acquit Himself perfectly of all that He did; and the tranquility and sweetness with which He nevertheless acquitted Himself. What a difference in His manner of acting and ours! If something which we are obliged to do displeases us, what false reasons we allege to dispense ourselves from it, what artifices to put it off, with what languor, what indifference we do it! If it is according to our inclination, we feel a kind of joy which at once causes dissipation of soul. The very fear of not succeeding makes us uneasy and vexed. Let us then keep Jesus Christ before us as our model; we must constantly look on Him, if we wish to keep ourselves in interior recollection and to increase continually in His love.

When we say that to keep ourselves in this interior recollection, the soul must not be too much occupied with exterior things, we do not mean that the occupation in exterior things which are of obligation is a hindrance to interior recollection; one can be very recollected in action; the greatest Saints who have received the most communications from God, and who have been consequently the most recollected, have often been those most occupied with exterior works. Such have been the Apostles and Apostolic men who have given themselves up to the salvation of their neighbor; and thus it is an error to think that the greatest exterior occupations are obstacles to interior recollection; provided that it is God Who puts us in these employments, these employments are the most proper means to keep us united continually with God. We must give our mind only to these exterior occupations but not our heart.

We must absolutely choose one of two things, said a great Servant of God, either to become interior men, or to lead cowardly and useless lives, lives filled with a thousand vain occupations, none of which will ever lead us to the perfection to which God calls us; and if we do not take great care to preserve ourselves in interior recollection, far from accomplishing the designs of God, we shall not even know what His designs are, and shall never arrive at the height of sanctity and perfection which our state demands.

A man who is not recollected goes wandering about without finding his repose anywhere, and seeks all sorts of objects with avidity, without being able to satisfy himself with any of them; whereas if he gave himself to recollection he would enter into himself and would find God there; he would taste God Who, by His presence, would fill him with such an abundance of blessings that he would no more go to seek elsewhere objects to fill the void of his desire. We can remark this every day in recollected souls. We may sometimes imagine that the love which they have for solitude and the pain which they feel by being distracted is an effect of melancholy; it is nothing of the kind; it is because they taste God within themselves; and the ineffable sweetness with which they are filled makes them judge the amusements and pleasures found in the world to be so stale and disgusting that they look upon them with horror. Once a person has tasted what God and spiritual things are, all that belongs to the contagion of flesh and blood appears insipid.

What marvelous advantages are derived from the interior life once a person is established in it! It may be said that it is only a person of this kind who tastes God and feels the sweetness of virtue. I do not know whether it is the effect of interior recollection, or the reward for the care taken to keep oneself always united with God; but it is certain that an interior man possesses faith, hope and charity in such a sublime manner that nothing is capable of shaking him in his belief; he insensibly finds himself above all human fear, he remains always in the same state of mind, always immovable in God. He takes occasion to raise himself up to God from everything which he sees or hears. In creatures he sees only God, as those who have looked at the sun for a long time always imagine that they see the sun, no matter what objects they may look on afterwards.

It must not be imagined that this interior recollection makes people idle or encourages negligence. A truly interior man is most active; he does more good and renders more service to the Church in a day than a hundred others who are not interior men will be able to render in several years even though they may have much more natural talents than he has. This is true not only because dissipation is an obstacle to the fruits of zeal, but also because a man who is not recollected, even though he may be very active is, at best, a man who works for God, while in the case of an interior man, it is God Himself who works through him; that is to say, that a man who does not live in interior recollection may have God as the motive of his actions, but temper, self-love and the natural man will usually have the largest share in his good works, while a recollected person always attentive to God and to himself, always on his guard against sallies of the natural man and the artifices of self-love, acts for God alone and according to the inspiration and the guidance of the Spirit of God. The very difference between an interior man and one who is not, is sufficient to give us an esteem for recollection. In an unrecollected man, there is a certain dissipated air which obscures the most brilliant acts of virtue, which has something repellent about it, which lowers the esteem we had for his piety and causes his words to have hardly an unction; and on the contrary, what a favorable impression is created by the modest air, the sweetness, the peace which appears on the face of a truly interior person, and the reserve, the silence, the continual guard over himself! Does not all this inspire us with veneration and love for virtue? It is indeed difficult to be for long recollected and not to be truly devout, since it is certain that want of devotion usually comes from want of recollection.

The means to acquire this interior recollection and to keep the precious gift when once acquired, are to take great care: (1) to avoid eagerness in all that we do, and to undertake nothing that would interfere with the full performance of all our exercises of devotion; (2) never to let our heart be so distracted by unnecessary occupations that it becomes sterile for prayer; (3) to watch over ourselves constantly and to keep ourselves in such dispositions that we are always in a state to pray; (4) to render ourselves masters of our actions, lifting ourselves up above our employment, holding our heart disengaged from the trouble and embarrassment ordinarily caused by works of zeal for souls, application to study, care of family, commerce with the world, business cares and diverse occupations; always regarding the employments of our state of life as means towards our last end. (5) Retreat and silence are efficacious means to be recollected; it is difficult to find a person who speaks much who is really recollected. (6) Interior recollection is not only the mark of great purity of heart; it is the recompense for it. "Blessed are the pure of heart; because they shall see God." (Matt. V, 8), that is to say they walk constantly in His presence. In order to render the exercise of the presence of God easier, we may make use of some signal which recalls it to us such as the sound of the clock, the beginning and end of each action, entry into our room and leaving it, the sight of an image, the arrival of a person and other similar things. Reserve and modesty in everything which we do is a great means to become interior if we take care to propose as our model the modesty and sweetness of Jesus Christ. (7) Frequent reflection is a great help to a person who wishes to be recollected; so also is the thought from time to time that God is in the midst of us or rather that we are in the midst of Him, and that everywhere we are, He sees and hears us and touches us, whether we are at prayer, at work, at table, or engaged in conversation; so also is the making of acts of faith in the presence of God; being as modest when alone as when in company.

In fine, interior recollection is a gift of God; we should often pray to Him for this gift, and pray to Him for it as a necessary disposition to love Jesus Christ ardently; this motive renders all our prayers efficacious. Devotion to those Saints who have most excelled in the interior life can help us much to obtain interior recollection, such are the Queen of All Saints, St. Joseph, St. Anne, St. Joachim, St. John the Baptist, St. Aloysius Gonzaga, etc.

Chapter II

The obstacles which prevent us from deriving all the fruit we should from the devotion to the Sacred Heart of Jesus

As this devotion to the Sacred Heart of Jesus is extremely useful, easy, reasonable and solid, there are few really virtuous people who do not approve of it, few who do not practice it, but all do not feel this ardent love for Jesus Christ, nor this true sweetness which Jesus Christ makes those whom He loves experience, although these singular favors are the fruit of devotion to His Sacred Heart. Everything which prevents souls from making progress in virtue is an obstacle to the great graces which this devotion procures for us, and these obstacles which few people surmount, dry up the source of these great graces, and are the reason why God communicates Himself intimately only to few people.

People have been long complaining that they no longer feel in the practices of devotion the heavenly sweetness which the Saints have tasted, and which, although they are only the trappings of sanctity, nevertheless have served much to form Saints. Some people experience only dryness, lukewarmness, and aversion for the exercises of piety. They find no consolation or sweetness in prayer, no feeling of devotion either at Communion or Mass; they experience coldness and ennui in all that should cause the greatest pleasure and excite eagerness. What do people do? They try to console themselves with the thought that sanctity does not consist in this sensible devotion. It is true that one can be a great Saint and never have had this sensible devotion; but when we are everyday so cowardly and imperfect, we have reason to believe that it is in punishment of our cowardice that God does not grant us these interior consolations and spiritual sweetness, which would help much to make us more courageous and more perfect.

The way of perfection today is not different from that by which the Saints have walked; they all confess that it is not possible to imagine greater pleasure than that tasted in the service of God; that they are filled with such sweetness that the greatest labors are delights, that they do not know what disrelish or melancholy is, that what appears most repulsive causes a pure and perfect joy that cannot be troubled by the most vexatious occurrences. They assure us that the most terrible trials which God sends them have their sweetness and consolation; that nothing but sin can trouble the peace which they enjoy, and that God Himself inspires them with such great confidence in His mercy that their own faults cannot trouble their peace.

These are not merely the sentiments of a few people, they are the experiences of all the true servants of God, of all times, of every age and quality, of every country and of every walk of life; and these experiences of heavenly sweetness have been confirmed at the hour of their death, which is the time when people are most sincere. What reason could we have to imagine that people so wise, people universally recognized to be upright and virtuous would either wish to deceive us, or that they were themselves deceived? Can, then, any reasonable person, doubt the truth of a fact so well established, when there is such a very great number of irreproachable witnesses who all speak with like uniformity during such a long succession of centuries? Whence comes it, then, that among such a great number of people who in our time make profession of piety, and appear to walk in the footsteps of these Saints, so few are found who receive the same graces? The reason, doubtless, is that there are few whose virtue is really solid. Holiness does not, it is true, consist in these sensible devotions, but it is nonetheless true that this interior joy and this peace which all the accidents of life cannot trouble, that this perfect submission to the will of God, this sweet confidence in His mercy which are characteristic of sensible devotion, have always been the inheritance of the Saints and are still the privilege of all true servants of God.

We have already seen what great sweetness is found in the devotion to the Sacred Heart of Jesus, that is to say, that the fruit of this devotion is a very ardent and very tender love of Jesus Christ accompanied by interior joy, heavenly consolations, sweetness and unalterable peace which surpass all understanding, and all which are gifts inseparable from the perfect love of Jesus Christ. We are going to consider what are the obstacles which prevent people from reaping this fruit. All these obstacles may be reduced to four: great tepidity in the service of God, self-love, secret pride, and certain passions which people have not taken care to mortify from the beginning of their conversation. From these four heads as from four fatal fountains, proceed all those faults and imperfections which stop so many souls on the road of piety, which shipwreck the finest projects and the most generous resolutions, and finally which render unfruitful the holiest practices of devotion.

FIRST OBSTACLE

Tepidity

As the devotion to the Sacred Heart of Jesus is a continual exercise of ardent love of God, it is evident that tepidity, the great obstacle to the ardent love of God, is also a great obstacle to acquiring true devotion to the Sacred Heart or deriving any profit from it. Although the Son of God has an infinite hatred for sin, He has not a hatred for the sinner; He calls him, He seeks him, He has compassion on him, but His divine Heart cannot endure a tepid soul: "I would that thou wert cold or hot," says this amiable Savior, "but because thou art luke-warm, and neither cold nor hot I will begin to vomit thee out of My mouth" (Apocalypse III, 15, 16). The Heart of Jesus seeks pure souls capable of loving Him; the Sacred Heart is always liberal, It desires souls which are in a state to receive Its favors, and which have the dispositions necessary for arriving at the degree of perfection to which He destines them; these dispositions are not found in a soul that lives in tepidity.

A tepid soul is in a state of blindness caused by the passions which tyrannize over it, by the continual dissipation in which it lives, by the multitude of venial sins which it commits, and by the withdrawal of the graces of Heaven brought on it by its own resistance. This blindness brings about the formation of a false conscience, causing people even those who frequent the Sacraments to remain for many years in serious venial sins, hidden or disguised by passion, because these people have neither the will nor the courage to correct them.

We sometimes see souls of Religious or of seculars who make a profession of piety, that nourish secret aversions, envenomed jealousy, dangerous attachments, a spirit of bitterness and murmuring against superiors, self-love and pride which influence all their actions, and other faults of this nature, in the midst of which they live tranquilly, persuading themselves, or trying to persuade themselves, that there is nothing very criminal in all this, and seeking for reasons to excuse faults which nevertheless God condemns as serious sins and which they themselves will condemn at the hour of death when passion will no longer prevent them from seeing things as they are in themselves.

What renders this state more dangerous and what compels Jesus Christ to reject a tepid soul from His Heart, is that it is, in a certain sense, desperate, because tepidity is rarely ever cured. As sins committed by a tepid soul are not gross and scandalous, such as excite horror in a timorous soul, but are often purely interior, and take place only in the heart, they escape the attention of a lax conscience, or of a soul not attentive to itself. Thus as it does not know the greatness of its evils, it takes no pains to remedy them; whereas a great sinner is more in a state to be touched by his disorders, and to conceive a horror for them because he knows them. It is in this sense that Our Savior says that it is better to be cold than tepid.

The most solid practices of devotion are useless to a person who is in this unhappy state, whether it be that he has lost all relish for them because of the little fruit which he derives from them, or because too great familiarity with these holy exercises breeds contempt. Even the great and terrible truths of salvation, which by their novelty and force strike terror into the hearts of the greatest sinners, make scarcely any impression on the tepid because they have been so often and so fruitlessly appealed to.

As soon as a person begins to live in tepidity, he seeks himself in everything, he continually looks for what will give pleasure, he surpasses the sensual in seeking his own comforts, and his self-love, not being weakened by being bestowed on exterior objects, concentrates itself on himself and applies itself entirely to thinking out a lax, comfortable life. It is easy to see that a soul in this state, insensible to the most terrible truths of salvation, and still more insensible to the striking proofs of the love which Jesus Christ has for us, is too far from the dispositions necessary for the devotion to the Sacred Heart of Jesus Christ to draw any fruit from it.

The marks by which a person can recognize whether he is in this dangerous state of tepidity are the effects which it usually produces on the tepid soul: (1) great negligence in all spiritual exercises; prayers without attention, confessions without amendment, Communions without preparation, without fervor and without fruit; (2) continual dissipation of spirit which is scarcely ever attentive either to itself or to God, but which becomes engrossed indifferently in all kinds of objects and occupies itself with a thousand trifles; (3) a perverse habit of doing all one's actions without any interior spirit, but by whim or custom, and of taking no pains to prevent passion, self-love and human respect having their share; (4) sloth in acquiring the virtues proper to one's state; (5) disgust for spiritual things and particularly indifference to the great virtues; in the state of tepidity the yoke of Jesus Christ begins to feel heavy, the exercises of piety become a burden, the maxims of the Gospel about hating oneself, love of the Cross and of humiliations, the necessity to do violence to oneself and to walk in the straight path, appear inconceivable; the continual exercise of modesty, mortification and interior recollection are found to be insupportable; the lives of solidly virtuous people are regarded as unhappy and the practice of virtue almost impossible: (6) insensibility of conscience to little things; a person is no longer affected by his ordinary infidelities or by his relapses; he easily allows himself to commit all kinds of deliberate venial sins.

But how it ought to be feared that this want of delicacy of conscience, this facility to relapse into the same faults and to confess them without correcting them, this negligence, this contempt for little things, this indifference for great virtues, this infidelity in the exercises of piety, this repeated loss of fervor, may not be visible marks of a dying faith and of charity that is almost extinct! How it should be feared that this state of tepidity may not insensibly lead to that of hardness of heart and insensibility!

This unhappy state is all the more dangerous because people do not know it sufficiently, nor fear its fatal effects. Thus, those who have no taste for the devotion to the Sacred Heart and those who practice it but derive no fruit from it, have reason to fear that their tepidity is the obstacle which causes these effects.

As the fatal cause of this unhappy state often comes from deep-seated self-love, the means given in the following chapter to kill or at least mortify this self-love will serve as a remedy for tepidity, since true mortification and fervor are inseparable.

What has been said about tepidity is taken from the Spiritual Retreat of Father Nepveu, S.J. The following additional reflections will be found useful.

(1) It is strange that many religious who have left all for God should prefer to deprive themselves of great graces and consolations rather than sacrifice little things which stop them on the road to perfection and prevent them from tasting the holy joy which is the lot of fervent servants of God.

(2) It is no less strange that people who have made great sacrifices to assure their salvation and merit a happy death, sometimes die with regret and trouble, and this for want of a little more generosity.

(3) What is it that hinders us? Persons in Religion have frequently good desires, but because of cowardice, such as people of the world would not think Religious capable of, they fail to put them into practice. We have sometimes begun to serve God well; at those times, were we endeavoring to deceive people? If God had been the true motive of our conversion how comes it that with such a motive we do not persevere?

(4) Truly, either the Saints have done too much or we do not do enough to be Saints; but you will say, a person would have to be a Saint to live as the Saints have lived; let us rather say: we must make ourselves Saints, and it is only by living as the Saints have lived that we can do so.

(5) People never think that it is too early to begin to work, or too late to continue, when there is a question of amassing riches, which after all must be left to others; or of gaining a vain reputation in the world; but when there is question of gaining heaven or acquiring eternal happiness they think that it is too soon to begin in youth and too late when old age comes. Then again, some people of good natural talents or of gifted mind and quick wit, think that they cannot be expected to resign themselves to lead a perfect life. As a matter of fact, great natural qualities, so far from being an obstacle to sanctity, have at all times been helps towards arriving at the most sublime virtue.

(6) What an error it is to imagine that there is any age or state not suitable for great virtue! What answer can those people give who imagine that such is the case, when it is pointed out to them that there have been great numbers of Saints in every age and in every walk of life, and that they have become great Saints in every kind of condition and employment? Not only will the example of these Saints be brought in judgment against us one day, but our zeal for worldly interests will be made to condemn us; when we plead our age or employment or condition of life as an excuse for our tepidity and cowardice, we shall be reminded that we worked and suffered more in the service of the world at the same age, employment and state of life, than God asked us to do for heaven.

(7) No one would dare to say, or would be satisfied that people believe about him, that, after ten years spent in the study of human sciences, he would deem himself happy if he knew as much as he did after the first six months; yet we find peo-

ple who make a profession of piety, and even some whose principal employment is to become perfect, who, after ten or even twenty years' study and practice of the sublime science of salvation, are not ashamed to say, and are content that people believe, that they would esteem themselves happy if they were as fervent and mortified and holy as they had been after the first six months of their perfect conversion. They endeavor to divert their thoughts from this fact by all kinds of dissipation and by the insipid pleasures of their cowardly life, but when these people come to the end of their life how great will be their remorse at the hour of their death!

(8) Are we really convinced of the truth of the doctrines of our holy Religion? If we do not believe them, we are doing too much, but if we really believe them, we are certainly doing too little. What is the truth about the matter? We talk about our eternal salvation, about our immortal soul, about the length of eternity! Is it true that we are in the world for the sole purpose of saving our souls? Is it true that Jesus Christ became man and died to save us, and that salvation is the only affair which merits all our attention, and which depends on the attention which we pay to it? Is it true that if our salvation is lost all is lost; and that whoever puts himself in danger of failing in this all-important affair is risking the loss of everything, and that a life of tepidity is one of the chief causes of failure to secure salvation? Is it true that eternity is at stake? Could God have been deceived when He said that everything else is of no consequence? Could God have made a mistake in directing all the cares of His Providence to this end? Could God, Who understands everything, and Who is the Alpha and the Omega of everything be indifferent about the loss of our souls? Why so many tears, such cruel remorse in hell, if the good which the damned have lost, required such little effort to be gained, and why do people shudder at the thought of eternity, if it is of little consequence to be eternally miserable? But does this carelessness in avoiding this supreme evil show that it is feared as it should? And is not a life of tepidity and indifference a sign of carelessness about the loss of salvation?

(9) If we reflected frequently in this manner, we would be ashamed of leading a tepid life and of being cowardly in the service of God, and we would soon begin to love Jesus Christ. But alas! even though we make such reflections and are touched

by them, a moment later we seek to distract ourselves as if we
were angry at seeing ourselves as we are and at being touched
by our state, "like a man beholding his own countenance in a
glass . . . presently forgot what manner of man he was" (James
I. 23, 24).

II

SECOND OBSTACLE

Self-Love

It is only too true that people who are not influenced in
their action by self-love are very rare, and that the difference
between spiritual people and those who are not so, is that in
the latter self-love acts without disguise, while in the former
it is less visible and somewhat better disguised. If people
wished to take the trouble to examine into the true motives of
the most of their actions which they think have least defects,
they would discover that self-love puts on a hundred disguises
and prevents the fruit of their actions, because it is the most
powerful motive.

Self-love dictates that the practices of virtue to be adopted
are those which give us least trouble and suit our tastes best.
The specious pretext of preserving health, which most people
imagine to be indispensable for God's glory, occupies the mind
completely with a thousand little worries. We take care of ourselves and spare ourselves; almost all kinds of mortification are
regarded as indiscreet or unsuitable for our age or state of life.
Good inspirations and desires which God sends at intervals to
labor to acquire perfection are treated as delusions; we try to
persuade ourselves that God does not demand such high sanctity from us, although He has given us great graces, or placed
us in a state which demands the highest sanctity. We flatter
ourselves that we really wish to leave all and undertake everything as soon as the will of God is manifested to us; but it is
in vain that God makes His voice heard by His inspirations, by
the advice given by our Director or Spiritual Father, by the
lights which we receive in meditation, by the examples which
we see and which we approve of; we refuse to recognize the
will of God when it contradicts our self-love; the reason is

that, in truth, it is not the will of God that we take as the rule of our conduct, but our own inclination and our own self-love, which we wish to be the rule instead of the will of God.

Why is it that there are people who are never so uneasy, so gloomy, so sensitive, as at the times when they seem to be most recollected and most eager to make themselves perfect? The reason is that the lights which they receive in prayer, and the inspirations which God sends them disturb them because they are at variance with the self-love with which they are filled. These people, it appears, wish as a prerequisite condition for making a serious effort to acquire sanctity, either that the road of perfection have nothing difficult, or that God fill them with exterior sweetness and consolation before they make the first step on that road; however, although the life of these people appears to be fairly well regulated and their conduct seems irreproachable, they crawl along in this languid state all their lives without ever correcting themselves of a single fault.

It would almost appear better not to have certain virtues of which we are so proud; at least we would then recognize our want and misery; but the little virtue which we have appears to serve only to make us more imperfect every day. We content ourselves with a mere external rule, with natural or affected modesty, with apparent virtue which is the fruit of education, rather than of grace; and because we see that we are protected against reproaches which people of more careless lives draw upon themselves, we imagine that we have much virtue because we do not show many faults.

People draw up plans of devotion according to their humor, natural bent, or caprice. They find only too easily faint-hearted, obliging Directors to approve of the system upon which their whole life turns; and that is why they are unmoved either by the example of others, or by their own reflections, or by the truths which touch even the greatest sinners. We need not then be astonished if these people, so full of self-love, are always seeking their own conveniences; under the pretext that they are willing to leave all, they do not wish to sacrifice anything; and if they deprive themselves of something, it is usually in order to make themselves important in their own eyes by this pretended mortification and to enjoy quietly a hundred other things which they have more at heart and which they will not sacrifice. Most usually they act according to their natural dispositions and inclinations; they love only those for whom they have a liking, they refuse nothing to their senses, and if they mortify themselves in something, it is in what causes them least pain or when this act of mortification brings them honor. We wish to do good works but we wish to have the satisfaction of choosing those which we do. Hence comes our repugnance for the smallest obligations imposed on us by our state of life, while we find an attraction for more troublesome occupations, provided they are of our own choice, or give us an excuse for dispensing ourselves from the most ordinary obligation of our state of life. We regard sickness in others as a visitation or as a gift of God, but God no sooner sends that gift to ourselves than we become disturbed, melancholy, impatient and gloomy; it is not the sickness that produces that effect on us, but in sickness we appear as we really are, because we have neither the motives nor the means to disguise our self-love such as we had in health.

From this same source of self-love comes those sterile desires, those fantastic projects on which naturally proud people feed, and on which self-love nourishes itself. Certain grandiose projects are proposed by them which are to be executed after a certain time, and forthwith, as if their conversion and sanctity were assured, they take no further trouble to correct their imperfections. Though they are persuaded that mortification is absolutely necessary for holiness, they refuse the little crosses that present themselves under the pretext that they are too light, but really because they are at hand, and they sigh for great crosses only because they are far away. Nevertheless they feed on these vain imaginations, they rest content with this respectable exterior, with these good works which give them pleasure, and with those practices of devotion to which they are generally faithful; and intoxicated with vain insipid praise which flatterers give, full of the idea of virtue which is possessed only in name, they are found without merit at the end of a long life, and often they have no more laudable sentiments than to be as good as they had been at the beginning of their conversion.

These are the effects of self-love from which very few people are exempt. How much we are to be pitied if we nourish within ourselves an enemy that is all the more dangerous because he is cunning, and because we are not on our guard against him?

Now, it is evident that Jesus Christ will never recognize as true friends of His Sacred Heart people who are completely attached to their own ease and who, loving only themselves, give Him such grudging service. He Himself has told us so expressly when He depicted the character of His true servants. In vain, He says, will people flatter themselves that they are My disciples because they have left their possessions and their friends, if they do not renounce themselves and even their lives. We must, then, do violence to ourselves, we must wage war against our passions and destroy or at least mortify our self-love, if we wish to be His true disciples. There is no true love of Jesus Christ where there is no real mortification.

III

THIRD OBSTACLE

Secret Pride

Secret pride is no less an obstacle to the love of Jesus Christ, in fact there is no greater obstacle to perfection, and consequently to the ardent love of Jesus Christ than the spirit of vanity by which most people are dominated. Other enemies are overcome or weakened by the practice of virtue, but vanity feeds on this very practice. Even our victories are weapons which the devil makes use of against us, profiting by them to inspire us with pride. It may be said that of all the vices there is none which has stopped more souls on the road of piety, none which has brought down more souls from the heights of virtue and plunged them into tepidity and even into licentiousness. From this spirit of vanity comes the immoderate desire to appear important, and the extreme eagerness to succeed in everything that we do. It is in vain that we endeavor to find reasons to assure ourselves that we are seeking only the glory of God; we have only to listen to the voice of our conscience to know that it is for our own glory that we are laboring; this inordinate fear that we may not succeed, this sadness and discouragement when we have failed, this joy and exultation when we are praised and honored, are so many visible proofs that deep-seated vanity is the motive of our actions.

This same spirit infiltrates into the exercise of the greatest virtues; virtuous people try to be mortified, obliging, honest, civil and charitable, but they are very pleased when their virtues are known, because, as they say, their neighbors will be edified. From this same source most faults proceed. People are easily puffed up by the idea of virtue which they do not really possess, and which would be destroyed by this vain glory, if they possessed it. People like to recount their adventures, they have some personal experience to give to illustrate all topics of conversation, and one would think that when a person has acquired some reputation for virtue, he is at liberty to sound his own praises on every occasion. Pride makes people wish to be popular, to possess the esteem and affection of everyone, with the result that they prefer to dispense themselves from their obligations rather than to disoblige anyone, and what is still more strange, they try to cover this ambition and vanity under the specious pretexts of honesty, charity and even of helping others to be virtuous, vainly endeavoring to persuade themselves that it is necessary to act in this manner in order to make virtue less difficult for others. What! Does true virtue derive its charm from the faults and imperfections of others? People try to please God and man at the same time, and in doing so both displease God and often fail to please men.

From the same source spring delicacy on points of honor, cooling of friendship, grief resembling envy though not so malicious, secret pain at the success of others. The success of others is always attributed to some accident; people try to minimize it, they speak coldly about it, and if anyone becomes enthusiastic about it they call them flatterers. The reason of all this is that we are all full of vanity and pride; we are sensitive to the least offensive word, to the smallest suspicion of contempt; we think ourselves at liberty to dispense with certain duties of courtesy towards others, but we will not pardon others if they are wanting in what we claim to be our rights. And through a still more ridiculous illusion, some people imagine that the honor of God Whom they serve, and of the great virtue which they flatter themselves that they possess requires that they parade their wit and talents and their good qualities, natural and supernatural, before everybody; and if after that, anyone has not all the esteem and veneration for them that they expect, they think themselves justified in believing that he is a person of no virtue, a libertine who has no regard for merit, and no esteem for virtue.

These are not all the evil effects on this secret ambition; there is also the love of display, eagerness for applause and praise for everything which they do. You will find some who labor much for God but who are always telling everybody how much they labor; you will find them always worrying, always in a hurry, fatigued, overwhelmed with work; you would think that they are inviting everyone to have compassion on them for their overwork. The truth is that vanity plays a large part in their overwork; they think themselves very important, in fact indispensable, and wish to be regarded as such. Pride insinuates itself into all their actions, even those which should conduce most to humility. People sometimes like to distinguish themselves in the practice of certain virtues, and even in the exercise of good works, but is there not danger that it is less for God that they labor, than because they attract great attention to themselves? Finally, the excessive sadness and discouragement which they experience after some relapse into their old faults is not the result of delicacy of conscience as some people imagine, but of secret pride which makes people think they are greater saints than they really are.

Finally, some people pass for pious and think themselves so, who are guided by mere worldly prudence disguised under the name of common sense; to smother any qualms of conscience, they bring everything under that rule of so-called common sense which they have made for themselves. It is even according to this false rule that they judge of spiritual things, divine operations, and marvels of grace, approving of only what suits their caprice; they limit the action of the grace of God in themselves and others according to the maxims of human prudence, and, by a strange blindness, which is the punishment of proud people, they think that they are only following reason when they are going away more and more from the Spirit of God.

And after all this, they are astonished that they have neither spiritual consolation nor sentiments of devotion after ten or twenty years spent in the exercise of virtue and the practice of so many good works. They complain that they are making no advance, that they are still imperfect, that the frequent reception of the Sacraments is without fruit, and that they feel no devotion. The secret pride which they nourish at the bottom of their hearts dries up the source of the greatest graces, and is the cause why people who appear to be so wise, so regular, so reserved, who have lived with such honor, who have been proposed as an example of honest people in the world, and who, according to all appearances, should be laden with spiritual treasures, arrive at death with their hands empty of good works; self-love, petty ambition and secret pride having taken away or corrupted all. It is this worm which causes the tallest oaks of the forest to wither, this leaven which sooner or later corrupts the mass, or swells it up and fills it with wind.

It is evident that the love of Jesus Christ cannot be found along with a vice which is so opposed to it. How could this divine Savior Who made humility the first of the beatitudes, the foundation of the spiritual life, the first step on the road of virtue — how could He Who invites His followers to learn of Him because He is "meek and humble of Heart," be loved by those who resemble Him so little? This sincere humility of spirit and heart constituted the distinctive character of Jesus Christ; it is therefore impossible for us to be animated by His Spirit, and dwell in His Sacred Heart, unless we have this true spirit of humility.

IV

FOURTH OBSTACLE

Some Unmortified Passion

The fourth obstacle, or the fourth source from which those defects arise which prevent or smother the love of Jesus Christ and consequently devotion to His Sacred Heart, are certain unmortified passions which are spared and which, sooner or later, will be the fatal cause of some great evil.

Most people who wish to give themselves to God and who, consequently, declare war on all their vices, behave much like Saul in the war which he undertook by the command of God against Amalec. God had ordered Saul to exterminate all the Amalcites and to destroy all that belonged to them without sparing anything. Saul exterminated the people but, touched with compassion, he spared the king and kept for sacrifice whatever was most precious in the camp. But this disobedience cost Saul his kingdom and was the cause of his reprobation and ruin (I Kings XV, 3-23).

Many people follow the example of Saul in the war which they undertake against their vices; may God grant that they do not share his fate! They are quite persuaded that God wishes them to sacrifice all their passions, and that He cannot allow them to spare any vice; they consent in appearance, they make war on all their passions, but somehow there is one predominant one which they spare, there is something which they regard very dear and very precious which they will not touch, and in order to get over any scruple, they find some pretext for sparing this enemy, they kill the spirit of the world in themselves, but they are very pleased to see it live in their children; they dress very modestly themselves, but they like to see their daughter sumptuously adorned; they give up gambling but they frequent the gatherings; they moderate their outbursts of anger, but they spare their secret ambition and jealousy which they cannot bring themselves to destroy; they mortify this external display, this worldly air which seems incongruous in people who make profession of loving Jesus Christ, but they retain the liberty of passing whole hours in useless visits and conversations; and under the fine pretext of making themselves amiable to everyone in order to gain them for Jesus Christ and of making virtue attractive and easy to practice, they insensibly do just like everyone else and retain only the name, only a vain idea and a little outward appearance of virtue.

Some who are more generous break the great ties which attach them to the world; they leave their parents and their possessions, and they even give up their liberty, submitting themselves to the yoke of religious obedience, but they take no trouble to break the lesser bonds, that is to say, the thousand little attachments which retard their progress in virtue. And of what advantage is it if the bonds which attach us to creatures are small, if they are manifold? One bond even though small is sufficient to prevent advance in virtue unless it be broken.

Finally, there are generous souls who resolve to conquer all obstacles and who make serious efforts, but who will not go against their natural bent; they spare some failing that is in harmony with their inclination; and this one enemy spared, this one unmortified passion, this one fault which they will not correct, this one bond which they will not break, makes them limp along all their lives, and prevents them from arriving at this high perfection to which they are called: "Therefore, the Lord hath rejected thee from being king" (Kings I, XV, 23). A small leak will sink a great ship and a small defect will ruin the finest edifice in time; a single spark will cause a great fire; death is often caused by the neglect of a slight illness, and a single defect is sufficient to spoil an otherwise beautiful painting.

We are sometimes astonished at seeing people who have grown old in the exercises of piety, really spiritual people and very mortified, who have, however, great imperfections which they condemn in others but which they will not correct in themselves. The explanation is that they become familiar with their own faults, they spare them all their life, they act according to their natural inclinations and are easily carried away. They are constantly praising themselves, always for some good motive, and under some specious pretext; in fine, they neglect to become perfect when they are young and they find themselves very imperfect when they grow old.

These are the great obstacles to the pure love of Jesus Christ and consequently to the devotion to the Sacred Heart. These are the sources of so many imperfections which are only too often found in people reputed to be spiritual; imperfections, however, which do great harm to real piety by the false idea which they give of the devotion. Solid piety condemns all these faults wherever they are found. True love of Jesus Christ will not endure these imperfections, this secret pride, this self-love; the defects which come from these three baneful sources are not found in those who possess true love; nevertheless, without this pure, genuine love for Jesus Christ, there is no solid devotion, no perfect virtue.

My God! cried a great Servant of God, what disorder, what turmoil! At one moment people are gay, at another sad; today, they are gracious to everyone, tomorrow they will be like a hedgehog that nobody can touch without getting pricked; it is a visible proof that there is little virtue, that the natural inclinations are getting free rein, and that the passions are not mortified; a truly virtuous man is always the same. Is there not danger that if we do good occasionally, it is more as the result of whim than of virtue?

Chapter III

Means for surmounting the obstacles that prevent us from deriving fruit from the devotion to the Sacred Heart of Jesus

Tepidity, self-love, pride and the indulgence of our predominant passion are, as we have seen, the principal sources of our imperfections, and the greatest obstacles which prevent us from deriving the fruit which we should from the devotion to the Sacred Heart of Jesus. While our love for God is still feeble and languid, within us we nourish dangerous enemies; and without, we have the devil tempting us, the world alluring us, and occasions of sin and bad example all around us. We must therefore be on our guard and close the doors of the senses against the enemies that lay siege to us, otherwise they will become masters of our hearts.

"It is strange," says a great Servant of God, "how many enemies we have to fight as soon as we resolve to become holy. Everything seems to declare war against us; the devil by his artifices, human nature by the opposition that it offers to our good desires, the praise of the good, the mockery of the wicked, the solicitations of the tepid, the example of those who pass for virtuous and who are not so; if God visits us, vanity is to be feared, if He withdraws from us, we become timid; discouragement may succeed to great fervor; our friends take advantage of our former intimacy with them to tempt us, and we fear to displease those who are indifferent to us. Indiscretion is to be feared in fervor, sensuality in moderation, and self-love in everything.

What, then, are we to do? Sanctity does not consist in being faithful for a day or a year, but in persevering in it and increasing it until death. We must make use of the means which all the Saints employed, and which Jesus Christ Himself assures us, are the most proper to weaken and destroy this self-love and this secret pride which are the sources of these obstacles. These means are: mortification and humility. We must therefore be resolved to become truly humble and perfectly mortified or renounce the idea of acquiring the perfect love of Jesus Christ.

I

FIRST MEANS

True Mortification

Mortification is a necessary disposition for the true love of Jesus Christ; this was the first lesson that Jesus Christ Himself gave those who wished to be His disciples; without mortification no one can expect to be a true follower of Him. "If any man," says He, "will come after Me, let him deny himself and take up his cross daily and follow Me" (Luke IX, 23). And again He says: "If any man come to Me, and hate not his father, and mother, and wife and children and brethren and sisters, yea, and his own life also, he cannot be My disciple" (Luke XIV, 26). Accordingly, all the Saints had this distinguishing mark of perfect mortification. When people praised the virtue of anyone in the presence of St. Ignatius, he would ask: "Is that person truly mortified?" By that he wished to intimate that true mortification is inseparable from true piety, not only because virtue cannot exist long without general and constant mortification, but also because without mortification there can be no true virtue.

There are two kinds of mortification: the one, exterior, which consists in bodily austerities; the other, interior, which consists in repressing all inordinate affections of the mind and heart; both kinds are necessary to attain perfection, and one cannot continue to exist long without the other. Fasting, vigils, the use of the hairshirt and other such macerations of the body, are powerful means to become truly spiritual and really perfect; when used with discretion, they help wonderfully to strengthen our human nature, which is cowardly when there is question of doing good but very eager to do evil; they are of great assistance also to repel the attacks and avoid the snares of our common enemy, and to obtain from the Father of Mercies the helps necessary for the just, especially for beginners.

Sanctity, it is true, does not consist in exterior penances, and they are not incompatible with hypocrisy; it is not so with interior mortification; it is always a certain mark of true piety, and so is more necessary than exterior mortification, and no one can reasonably be dispensed from it. This is the violence

which we must do to ourselves in order to possess the kingdom of heaven. Not everyone can fast or wear a hairshirt, but
there is no one who cannot be silent when passion prompts
him to reply or vanity to speak; there is no one who cannot
mortify his human nature, his desires, and his passions. That
is what is understood by this interior mortification by which
a person weakens and conquers his self-love, and by which he
gets rid of his imperfections. It is in vain that we flatter ourselves that we love Jesus Christ if we are not mortified; all
the fine sentiments of piety and the practices of devotion are
suspect without perfect mortification. We are astonished to
see ourselves so imperfect and to find, after so many exercises
of piety and so many Holy Communions, that all our passions
are still alive and continue to excite our hearts: can we not
see that want of mortification is the source of all these revolts?
We must, then, if we wish to conquer this self-love by which
all the passions are nourished, resolve to exercise generous
and constant mortification.

Is it not enough to mortify ourselves in some things, for some
time; we must, as far as possible, mortify ourselves in everything and at all times, with prudence and discretion. A single
unlawful gratification allowed to human nature will render it
more proud and rebellious than a hundred victories gained
over it will have weakened it. Truce with this sort of enemy is
a victory for him; "Brethren," said Saint Bernard, "what is cut
will grow again, and what appears extinguished will light again,
and what is asleep will awake again." To preserve the interior
spirit of devotion, the soul must not be dissipated with exterior
distractions, and as the Prophet says, must be surrounded on
all sides by a hedge of thorns. Now, if we omit to do that, it
will be for us the cause of tepidity, back sliding, and want of
devotion. When we mortify our disordered inclinations in one
thing, we generally make up for it by some other satisfaction
which we allow ourselves. During the time of retreat, we are
recollected, but as soon as it is over we open the gates of the
senses to all kinds of distractions.

The exercise of this interior mortification, so common in the
lives of the Saints, is known by all who have a real desire to be
perfect. In this matter we have only to listen to the Spirit of
God; the love of Jesus Christ makes people so ingenious, that
the courage and energy which they display and the means of

mortifying themselves with which the Holy Spirit inspires even the most uncultured people, surpass the genius of the learned, and can be regarded as little miracles. There is nothing which they do not make an occasion to contradict their natural inclinations; there is no time or place which does not appear proper to mortify themselves without ever going beyond the rules of good sense; it is enough that they have a great desire to see or to speak, to make them lower their eyes or keep silent; the desire to learn news, or to know what is going on, or what is being said, is for them a subject of continual mortification which is as meritorious as it is ordinary, and of which God alone is the Witness. The appropriate word, a witticism in conversation, can bring them honor, but they make it the matter of a sacrifice. There is hardly a time of the day but gives opportunities for mortification; whether one is sitting or standing, one can find a place or an attitude that is uncomfortable without being remarked. If they are interrupted a hundred times in a serious employment, they will reply a hundred times with as much sweetness and civility as if they had not been occupied. The ill-humor of a person with whom we have to live, the imperfections of a servant, the ingratitude of a person under obligations to us, can give much exercise for the patience of a person solidly virtuous. Finally, the inconveniences of place, season or persons, suffered in a manner to make people believe that we do not feel them, are small occasions of mortification, it is true, but the mortification on these occasions is not small, and is of great merit; and it may be said that great graces, and even sublime sanctity, usually depend on the generosity with which we mortify ourselves constantly on these little occasions. Exact fulfillment of the duties of one's state and conformity in all things to community life without regard to one's inclinations, employment, or age, involve that continual mortification which is not subject to vanity but which is in conformity with the spirit of Jesus Christ.

If occasions for exterior mortifications are wanting, those for interior mortification are ever at hand. Modesty, recollection, reserve require mortification; honesty, sweetness and civility may be the effects of education, but are more usually the result of constant mortification. Without this virtue it is difficult for a person to be always at peace, to be self-possessed, to do his actions perfectly, and be always content with what God wishes.

SECOND MEANS

Sincere Humility

"Jesus Christ," says St. Augustine, "does not say to us: 'Learn of Me to work miracles,' but, 'Learn of Me because I am meek and humble of Heart' (Matt. XI, 29), in order to show us that without humility there can be no true piety." People are sufficiently persuaded of the necessity of this virtue; the difficulty is to know in what true humility consists. Many think themselves truly humble if they have a low opinion of themselves, but they are not pleased when others have the same opinion of them. It is not enough to know that we have no virtue or merit; we must believe it, and be satisfied when others believe it. The first step towards acquiring this virtue is to demand it constantly from God; then to convince ourselves of our imperfections by frequent and serious reflection on ourselves. The remembrance of what we have been, and of what we might have become without the grace of God, are powerful helps to keep us humble. Really good people think little about others, but pay attention to themselves. Really humble people are not scandalized because their weakness is perfectly known to themselves: they see themselves so near the precipice, and fear so much to fall in, that they are not surprised that others do fall in. The less one speaks of oneself, the more one is in conformity with true humility. An affected claim to have a low opinion of ourselves is often for the purpose of making people praise us. The truest mark of humility is to cherish those who despise us, not to avoid the humiliations which present themselves, not to take pleasure in vain thoughts and projects about the future which serve only to nourish secret pride, never to speak in praise of ourselves, never to complain of what God permits to happen to us, or wish to be pitied, not to be troubled about our falls; to excuse the faults of our neighbor, to defer in everything to others, to distrust ourselves in our undertakings, and to have a low esteem of what we accomplish; finally, to pray much and speak little.

When we know that we are miserable, we do not mind being despised, because we know it is just. A humble man always thinks he is justly dealt with, however badly he may be treated; he says that those who maltreat him are right and that they are of the same opinion as God and His angels. A man who has deserved hell should find that contempt is due to him. We do not mean to say that we should receive humiliations with sensible pleasure, for contempt is naturally disagreeable; but not to complain, to be silent when despised, to thank God for contempt and pray for those whom He has permitted to humiliate us, whatever repugnance it may cost us, are certain marks of true humility. We have, says St. Paul, enemies within and without who lay traps everywhere for us; love of humility and abjection, of a hidden and obscure life, is a great remedy for such evils. We shall have no peace if we do not forget ourselves; if we wish to be perfect, we must forget even our own spiritual interests, in order to seek only the pure glory of God.

III

THE JOY AND SWEETNESS WHICH ARE INSEPARABLE FROM THE EXERCISE OF HUMILITY AND MORTIFICATION

We have seen that there can be no true devotion without universal, generous and constant mortification, and true humility. But is it possible to speak of continuous mortification and humility without frightening those who desire to love Jesus Christ ardently? Will they not immediately cry out against such a dreary prospect? Can they envisage a life filled with crosses without being deterred? Is it not an unhappy sort of life to be continually acting contrary to our natural inclinations, allowing our senses only bare necessities, forbidding them everything else, and living in retirement and silence without seeking the applause of the world or being concerned about its contempt? But it is just those people who live in this manner who assure us that they are perfectly happy. The world says that this kind of life is insupportable; but Jesus Christ Himself tells us that it is sweet, easy, and full of joy and consolation. St. Francis de Sales calls this kind of life: "the sweetness of sweetness"; St. Ephrem, while living a life of great mortification, being filled with interior consolations, cried out: "It is enough, O my God, it is enough; Thou dost overwhelm me with Thy benefits, moderate Thy liberality, if Thou dost not wish me to die; for the ineffable consolations which I experience in Thy service are

capable of causing my death." St. Francis Xavier, writing from
Japan to the Jesuits in Europe, said: "I am in a country where
I lack all the comforts of life, but I experience such interior
consolations, that I am in danger of losing my eyesight from
weeping for joy." All the saints give a like testimony; surely
so many millions of holy men and women whom we admit to
be wise and sincere, have not conspired to tell us something in
contradiction to what they have thought and experienced!

But if the continual exercise of mortification makes people so
unhappy, as worldlings contend, how is it that the happiest
people that we can find are those who are the most mortified?
How is it that we find no people in the world who are perfectly
content and perfectly happy but those who are most mortified?
If a mortified life itself does not produce this unalterable joy,
by what artifice do these people keep themselves all their lives
in perfect peace of mind and tranquility that no accidents of
life can disturb? And if it is by dissimulation, how is it that the
people of the world, who know so well the art of dissimulation,
have not been able to hide their worries and disappointments
although they pass the most of their lives in pleasure and
amusement? Virtue alone, says St. Augustine, although it has
an austere appearance, possesses the power of making people
taste real happiness; there is no perfect happiness in this world
except for those who labor seriously to sanctify themselves.
Being exempt from the sway of the most cruel passions which
tyrannize over the wicked, they experience greater sweetness
in life and less worry; being under perfect submission to the
will of God, they enjoy profound calm and peace such as the
world cannot give. This sweet repose of conscience is the
ordinary fruit of virtue; generosity with God ensures a large
share of this holy joy, while niggardliness in His service diminishes it to the vanishing point.

Language fails us to describe this secret unction with which
God sweetens the yoke of His law, these happy moments when
He makes holy souls feel His divine presence, this sweet hope
which makes them taste in advance the joys of heaven, these
rays of light which allow them to see the vanity of the world in
its true colors, and these consoling tears which they sometimes
shed at the foot of the crucifix, in which are to be found a
pleasure more pure, more exquisite than in the most delightful
feasts of the world. These pleasures and these interior conso-

lations which surpass our understanding are mysteries hidden from tepid souls; for them all this is a strange language; but, says St. Augustine, give me a fervent soul, a truly humble and mortified person, a heart penetrated with the love of Jesus Christ, and he will understand what I say. It is true that although a person be perfect, he is not always insensible to all the accidents of life; afflictions may cause the just some mental suffering, but they cannot make him disconsolate; his virtue always comes to his relief. Although there are no crosses in evidence on the broad road followed by the tepid, everything will contribute to produce them; while if crosses are met with on the narrow way trodden by those who love Jesus Christ ardently, heaven and earth will eagerly combine to render them sweet, and the Son of God Himself will deign to assist in carrying them, and making the burden light. Finally, the very thought of death terrifies worldlings while it consoles and even rejoices the virtuous. At the hour of death when things appear in their true colors, do we ever find people who regretted that they had been mortified, that they had led a perfect life?

Assuredly, perfect mortification must have attractions that we know not of, because we are not perfectly mortified. Our cowardice will allow us to do only as much as will make us feel the pain, but not sufficient to taste the sweetness. It would appear that we are distrustful both of what the Saints tell us, and of what Jesus Christ Himself has promised us. We would wish to be paid beforehand, and we are ignorant of the fact that, in this matter, it is only the first step that counts, that is to say that the whole difficulty consists in making up our mind to become mortified. Taste, says the Prophet, and then you will see. In this the eyes deceive us, we should judge only by the taste. Those who had seen the Promised Land only from afar, were terrified and said that it devoured its inhabitants, but those who had been there said quite the contrary: that it was "a land flowing with milk and honey" (I Numbers XIII, 28). A great Servant of God gives this advice: "'Make this perfect sacrifice for a whole fortnight; the object sought after, namely, God's peace and consolation must be of very little value if it is not worth this experiment; if after a fortnight's continuous and perfect mortification, you experience none of the sweetness that others have experienced, I will allow you to say that those who love Jesus Christ truly, are traveling by the wrong road and that the yoke of Christ is heavy."

We have reason to be astonished that people find difficulty in believing that happiness can be found in continual mortification, when they see every day so many people in the midst of all kinds of amusements unhappy and discontented. If there are invisible sufferings, is it not possible that there are secret consolations? Blessed Claude de la Colombiere, with the permission of his Superiors, had made a vow to observe all the rules of his Order and, in particular, he had bound himself to practice continual mortification in all things. What will those people, who regard the three vows of the religious life as an insupportable burden, think of the life of this great Servant of God? Will they not think that it must have been very unhappy? The following, however, is what he himself wrote in his Journal of Spiritual Retreats, where, after the example of these holy men who are always making plans for further advance in virtue, he recorded the sentiments with which God had inspired him, and the graces which He conferred on him, in order to remind himself of his obligation of thanking God for these favors, and of stimulating himself to love God daily more: "On the sixth day," he writes, "when I was considering the particular vow which I had made, I found myself filled with great gratitude to God Who gave me the grace to make this vow; I had never before sufficient leisure to consider it properly. I experienced great joy at seeing myself bound with a thousand chains to do the will of God. The thought of this obligation, far from terrifying me, filled me with intense joy; far from being made a slave by it, I felt that I have entered the Kingdom of Liberty and Peace.

"When I am alone with myself," he continued, "I feel myself, through the infinite mercy of God, enjoying a liberty of heart which causes me incomparable joy. Nothing, it seems to me, is capable of making me unhappy. I feel no attachment to anything, at least at these times. But this does not prevent me from feeling the promptings of nearly all the passions; however, a moment's reflection is sufficient to calm them.

"I have often tasted great interior joy from the thought that I am in the service of God; I have realized that this is worth infinitely more than the favor of kings. The occupations of people of the world appear despicable to me in comparison with our occupations in the service of God. I feel myself raised above all the kings of this world by the honor that I enjoy in belonging to God.

"I feel an increasingly great desire to be attached to the observance of my Rule; the practice of it causes me the greatest pleasure; the more exact I become in the observance of it, the more I seem to enter into the enjoyment of perfect liberty. This exact observance is certainly not burdensome to me; on the contrary, this yoke makes me feel lighter. I regard this as the greatest grace which I have ever received during my life."

We can have no doubt that this great Servant of God practiced continual mortification in all things after he had made a vow to do so. Even during his last illness, when he was unable to remain in bed, he was seen to pass several hours each day on an armchair without leaning back for support, thus persevering until death in mortifying himself in all things. This mortified life, however, filled him with so many consolations, and such interior joy that he confessed that he indeed experienced them but that it was impossible to describe them.

"The sight of Jesus Christ," he says, "makes me love the Cross so much that I do not think I could be happy without it. I look with respect on those whom God visits with humiliations and adversity, of whatever nature they may be; these are, doubtless, His favorites; in order to humiliate myself, I have only to compare my lot with theirs when I am enjoying prosperity.

"The following words never come to my mind, but light, peace, liberty, consolation and love seem to enter along with them; they are: simplicity, confidence, humility, entire abandonment, no reserve, the will of God, my Rules."

The experience of this great Servant of God shows us that it is not only the Saints who have preceded us who have found such sweetness and consolation in the exercise of universal, constant mortification, but that people with whom we live experience the same thing as soon as they are generous enough to mortify themselves continually.

Chapter IV

The particular means of acquiring this perfect love of
Jesus Christ and this tender devotion to His Sacred Heart

FIRST MEANS

Prayer

Besides the obstacles which we must avoid, and the dispositions which we must have in order to acquire the perfect love
of Jesus Christ and a tender devotion to His Sacred Heart, it is
fitting that we should suggest here the means which are most
proper for this end.

The first means to obtain a tender devotion to His Sacred
Heart is prayer. We may well be astonished that Christians are
not all powerful, that they have not all that they desire, since
they have an infallible means of acquiring all that they ask, and
since this means consists in merely asking.

There is nothing to which Jesus Christ has so often solemnly
pledged Himself as to hear our prayers; but of all prayers there
is none so agreeable to Him as that by which we ask for His
love. He has bound Himself strictly to grant this love to all
those who ask for it, but even if He had not bound Himself to
grant this love, this request for His love would bind Him to
grant it.

Jesus Christ has done all that we can imagine, even more
than we could imagine, to induce us to love Him. It depends
on Him to grant us this love; dare we think that He will refuse
it to us if we ask it of Him? But it must be that this love is little
esteemed, since it is asked for so little. You are astonished that
you do not love Jesus Christ ardently, since this love is so just
and so conformable to reason; but you should be still more
astonished if you loved Him without praying for this love, since
it is the greatest of all God's gifts.

Of all the means for obtaining the love of Jesus Christ, there
is none more efficacious than prayer, and there is none easier.
Nevertheless, this means is very much neglected. It might be
said that the very motive that Jesus Christ uses to induce people to adopt this means, frightens people away from it: He
said: "Ask and you shall receive." If you ask, you are sure to

be heard.

We are afraid that if once we were heard, our love would drive us to become more recollected, more devout and holier than we wish to be; we fear that if we loved God ardently that we would have nothing but disgust for all that we formerly loved, and for what we still love: in a word, it seems that we fear that we could not help loving Jesus Christ. But, O my Savior, pay no attention to these first sentiments which we detest as soon as we perceive them: "Give us only Thy love and Thy grace and with this we are rich enough." How we would be disgusted with everything else, if opening to us Thy Sacred Heart Thou wouldst make us once taste the sweetness that is found in loving Thee. Let us pray for this love often: it is impossible to pray for it perseveringly and not obtain it. It is an easy and efficacious means and in this matter it may be said that the very asking obtains for us this love.

And let us not fear that by making either excessive or pressing demands for His love, we shall offend Jesus Christ either by our indiscretion or our importunity. On the contrary, the reason why we obtain so little from God, is that we do not ask enough, and do not ask it with enough vigor and constancy. It is Jesus Christ Himself Who has given us as an example to be followed by us, the parable of the man who obtained his request by his very importunity (Luke XI, 5). We obtain little because we ask too little. We should ask for nothing less than His love, for a tender, generous, ardent, perfect love; and we should ask for this love with eagerness and importunity. Since Christ has promised so solemnly not to refuse us anything that we ask, we may be sure that He will not fail to keep His promise.

It often happens that we do not know what we ask for. We would do wrong to Jesus Christ, and we would show that we do not trust Him, if, when we ask for His love, we were to doubt that we would be heard, especially if we ask for it sincerely and eagerly. It can happen that Jesus Christ, in order either to punish us or humble us, or to give us opportunities for greater merit, may leave us with certain faults and imperfections from which we ask to be delivered, but if we sincerely and perseveringly ask for His love, we shall never be refused; on the contrary, we shall be granted more than we ask for.

O my Savior, Thou has said: "I am come to cast fire on the

earth, and what will I, but that it be kindled?" (Luke XII, 49). On whom does it depend that I be all inflamed by it? O my Savior, grant me Thy love, this will henceforth be my daily prayer. I will make this prayer morning, noon and night, at rest and at work; I will make it every hour, and I will never cease to say: "Give me Thy love, O Lord, and Thy grace and with this I am rich enough."

SECOND MEANS

Frequent Communion

The second means to acquire this perfect love is the frequent reception of the Sacraments; that is to say, frequent Communion. It is sufficient to know what is meant by receiving Holy Communion, to understand that there is no surer means to be in a short time inflamed with love for Jesus Christ than to receive Communion frequently. It is not possible to carry fire in one's bosom and not be inflamed by it. Divine love has lit a great furnace on our altars in the adorable Sacrament of the Eucharist, and it is by approaching this sacred fire that all the Saints have been inflamed by a most ardent and tender love for Jesus Christ. The love by which they burned on receiving Holy Communion appeared even on their faces. How many times has it been necessary in the depths of winter for the Saints to endeavor to cool the heat communicated to their bodies by the ardor of their Divine love! At such times the very name, the very image of Jesus would be sufficient to make them go into ecstasies, and we may regard it as certain that the great love which the early Christians had for Jesus Christ was the effect of Holy Communion which they received daily.

Those who with proper dispositions receive Holy Communion daily or frequently, experience the admirable effects of frequent Communion. They love Jesus Christ ever more and more; their love increases in the measure in which they nourish themselves often with this Bread of Angels, and far from feeling satiety from the frequent reception, their hunger for it grows sensibly in the measure in which their love for Jesus Christ becomes more ardent.

All the other Sacraments are the effects of the love of Christ for men; they are all calculated to awaken in us love for the Divine Savior; but the Sacrament of the Altar, as St. Bernard says, is the love of loves: it is the effect of the greatest of all the loves which Jesus Christ has had for men, and at the same time the most fertile source of that most ardent and tender love which man should have for Jesus Christ. Everything in this mystery helps to inspire and increase this ardent love; both the gift which is given to us, the manner in which it is given, and the end for which it is given. Jesus Christ gives us His adorable Body and His precious Blood which become the food of our souls. In truth, who will be able to enkindle this divine fire in the hearts of men, if this heavenly nourishment does not do so. But the gracious manner in which Jesus Christ gives us this gift urges us no less to love Him. For four thousand years, this Divine Savior, the long-expected of the people of Israel, the desired of all nations, the desire of the eternal hills, had made men pray for and eagerly solicit Him to come to the world. But here He Himself prays men, urges them, even does violence to them to oblige them to receive Him. Compel them, He says in the Gospel, to take part in the feast which I have prepared for them. "Compel them to come in, that My house may be filled" (Luke XIV, 23).

Love is impatient, it is the enemy of delay, it knows neither cessation nor moderation. But what does our Savior desire to attain by means of such loving advances? He desires to make Himself loved by men; He gives them His Body and Blood in order to gain their hearts; it is expressly to gain their hearts, to take them from them without their being able to prevent Him, that He makes Himself their food. "Your great intention in Holy Communion," says St. Francis de Sales, "should be to advance in the love of God, to strengthen and console yourselves by it, for you should receive with love that which love alone causes Jesus Christ to give you. In no action can our Divine Savior be considered more loving and more tender than in this in which He, in a manner, annihilates Himself, and reduces Himself to food, in order to penetrate our souls and unite Himself intimately to the heart and to the body of the faithful." (Introduction to the Devout Life, Part II, Chap. XXI).

We admire the fervor of those pure souls who never approach the Altar without increasing sensibly in the love which they bear to Jesus Christ and being inflamed by it. These ardors of divine love have become strange only by becoming so rare. But, is it not a more surprising prodigy to see that Communions are so frequent, and that these kinds of wonders happen so rarely? Your sins, your relapses, your weaknesses cause you pain; you really desire to correct them, to conquer this repugnance, this tepidity; to break this attachment, which is the only thing which stops you on the road to piety. You would wish to love Jesus Christ ardently, you recognize that only those who love Him perfectly are perfectly happy, and, nevertheless, after two thousand Holy Communions you find yourself so imperfect, so tepid; you do not love Jesus Christ the more for them.

You have been saying Mass daily for years, you have received the adorable Body and the Precious Blood of Jesus Christ thousands of times, and, nevertheless, you are still fighting against an imagination, a phantom, a trifling thing which prevents you from belonging completely to God, and from tasting the peace and sweetness that is found in His service: perhaps you find even less love for Jesus Christ every day.

"What!" cries Blessed Claude de la Colombiere, "Is it heretics or infidels who speak thus? Can a Christian who nourishes himself daily with the Body of Jesus Christ wish for anything and not get it? Who can ever be made to believe that a God offered as the price of the graces asked for, is not capable of obtaining them? Or that Jesus Christ Who has instituted this mystery for the sole purpose of making Himself loved, will ever refuse His love to him to whom He gives Himself without reserve or limitation?"

But if this misfortune does happen; if we see that while receiving Holy Communion frequently, or even daily, while saying Mass every day, we seem to draw no fruit from this Sacrament, that we do not mend our faults, that we abuse the privilege of Holy Communion, that we do not love Jesus Christ more for it, that we feel always the same tepidity, the same weakness, should we leave off Holy Communion? Should we cease saying Mass every day? No, but we should regulate our lives, and rid ourselves of our vices and faults which prevent us from profiting by our Communions and Masses. The fault does not come from the fact that we receive Communion too often, but that we receive it badly. Any kind of nourishment is useless if it is taken in a wrong way. If a person finds that what he eats is useless to him, what course should he take: eat nothing at all or take the necessary precautions to profit by what he eats? Suppose a man, by some bodily or mental excess, prevents the nourishment which he takes from being digested in his stomach and becomes ill. If all the doctors in the world and all the Medical Academies were assembled to consider his case, could a single doctor be found who would order this sick person to take no more nourishment? Certainly not; the man must eat, but he must do so with the necessary precautions; he must be less indiscreet, less imprudent. But, you may say, if he does not eat, the food will not get corrupted in his stomach! Yes, but he will die of weakness: his great agitation of mind will not prevent the process of digestion because his stomach is empty, but it will soon exhaust his strength and even cause his death. He will not die of indigestion but of weakness. In a word, only a fool would forbid him to take the food by which he lives, to deliver him from his malady.

It is easy to apply this example to those who derive no profit from their Holy Communions. These people have great reason to fear that their lives are badly regulated, that their consciences are not pure, that their faith is too weak, or that their confessions are wanting either in sincerity, or in sorrow, or in resolution of amendment. You are bad; then correct yourself as soon as possible in order to communicate frequently. You are imperfect; receive Communion often in order to amend yourself.

The Son of God calls this adorable mystery our daily Bread, to show how frequent the reception of It should be. He summons to His Banquet the poor and the blind, in order to teach us that no matter in what poverty a person may find himself, no matter what infirmities he may have, provided that he is still alive, he should not make any difficulty about eating this Bread of Life.

The little fruit which the majority of people, and especially priests, draw from frequent Communion makes us sometimes doubt whether it is proper to receive Communion so often. No better reply could be given on this subject than the reply of St. Francis de Sales which is as follows:

" 'I neither praise nor blame anyone for receiving Holy Communion every day, but I advise and exhort everyone to receive Holy Communion every Sunday, provided they have no affection for sin.' These are the words of St. Augustine; like him, I neither positively praise nor blame anyone for receiving Holy Communion every day, but leave that to the discretion of the Spiritual Director of the person who seeks guidance on this point; for the dispositions required for such frequent Communion being very select, it is not good to recommend it to everyone indiscriminately; and because this disposition, although select, is found in many good souls, neither is it right to turn away people indiscriminately and dissuade them from it; therefore, this matter should be dealt with according to the interior state of each one in particular. It would be an act of imprudence to advise such frequent Holy Communion for all without distinction, but it would also be an act of imprudence to blame anyone for it especially when a person is following the advice of some worthy Director. St. Catherine of Siena gave a very apt reply, when the objection was raised against her practice of frequent Communion, that St. Augustine neither praised nor blamed daily Communion. 'Very well!' said she, 'since St. Augustine does not blame this practice, I beg of you not to blame it either, and I shall be satisfied.'

"But, Philothea, you see that St. Augustine exhorts and counsels people very strongly to receive Holy Communion every Sunday; do so then whenever possible. Since, as I presume, you have no sort of affection for mortal sin, nor any for venial sin, you have the true disposition which St. Augustine requires; indeed, you have even better, since not only have you no affection for committing sin, but you have no affection for sin; accordingly, when your Spiritual Father permits, you can, with profit to your soul, receive Holy Communion even oftener than every Sunday.

"If worldlings ask you why you receive Communion so often, tell them that it is to teach yourself how to love God, that it is in order to purify yourself from your imperfections, to deliver yourself from your miseries, to console yourself in your afflictions, and to gain a support in your weakness. Tell them that two classes of people ought to receive Communion frequently: the perfect, because being well-disposed, they would be very wrong in not approaching the source and fountain of perfection, and the imperfect in order to be able to aspire justly to perfection; the strong in order that they may not become weak, and the weak in order that they may become strong; the sick in order that they may be cured, and the healthy in order that they may not fall into sickness; and that for yourself, being imperfect, feeble and sick, you have need of frequent Communion to keep united with Him, Who is your Perfection, your Strength and your Physician. Tell them that those who have not much wordly affairs ought to receive Communion often because they can do so conveniently, and that those who have much worldly affairs ought also to receive Communion often because they have need of it, just as a person who has to labor much, and who has many cares should eat solid food and eat often. Tell them that you receive the Blessed Sacrament often in order to learn how to receive It well, because a person cannot do well a thing in which he has not often exercised himself. Receive Holy Communion, therefore, as often as possible, relying on the advice of your spiritual director. Believe me, hares become white in winter time in the mountains, because they neither see nor eat anything but snow; by dint of adoring and eating Beauty, Goodness and Purity Itself in this Divine Sacrament you will become all beautiful, all good and all pure."

This is the advice which St. Francis de Sales gives to all those who have a real horror of mortal sin, and an ardent desire for salvation. The desire for frequent Communion is usually found in all those who have a lively faith and a real love for Jesus Christ; on the contrary, it is only too well established that when people give themselves up to the pleasures of the world, and when their love for Jesus Christ grows cold, they have no longer any desire for Holy Communion. Thus there is no need to advise people steeped in vice to keep away from the Holy Table; they do that sufficiently themselves; those corrupted souls, plunged in disorder are never found eagerly desiring this Bread of Angels which is the delight of pure souls and of all those who truly love Jesus Christ.

The following extract from the decree on daily Communion issued by the Sacred Congregation of the Council, and published by order of His Holiness Pius X on December 20, 1905, shows the great similarity of the teaching on frequent and daily Communion found in this chapter and that of the decree:

"Our Savior Jesus Christ Himself repeatedly insisted in the clearest terms on the necessity of being frequently nourished with His flesh and of drinking His blood, particularly when He said: 'This is the bread that came down from Heaven. Not as your fathers did eat manna and are dead. He that eateth this bread shall live forever' (John VI, 59). By this comparison between the Bread of Angels and ordinary bread, the disciples could easily understand that, as bread is the daily nourishment of the body, and as manna had been the daily sustenance of the Jews in the desert, similarly the souls of Christians were to be nourished daily by the Bread of Angels and have their strength renewed by It. Furthermore, when He orders us in the Lord's Prayer to ask for our daily bread, we are to understand by that, as nearly all the Fathers teach, that the bread that was to be received each day was not so much the material bread which nourishes the body, but the Eucharistic Bread. Accordingly, His Holiness, in the solicitude and zeal that animates him, greatly desiring that Catholics be urged to receive Holy Communion frequently and even daily, has entrusted the Sacred Congregation with the charge of examining and defining the above question.

"The Sacred Congregation of the Council, in a plenary session on December 16, 1905, has submitted this question to careful examination and after weighing diligently and maturely the reasons on both sides, it has drawn up and issued the following decree:

"(1) Frequent and daily Communion, inasmuch as it is extremely desired by Our Lord, Jesus Christ, and by the Catholic Church, should be made accessible to all the faithful, of whatever class or condition they may be, so that no one who is in the state of grace, and approaches the Holy Table with a right and pious intention, should be prevented from doing so.

"(2) A right intention consists in approaching the Holy Table not through habit or vanity, or from human motives, but in order to please God and become more intimately united to Him by charity, and, by virtue of this divine remedy, to combat all faults and infirmities.

"(3) Although it is very desirable that those who receive Communion frequently and daily be exempt from at least fully deliberate venial sins, and have no affection for them, nevertheless, it is sufficient that they have no grave sin, and have a firm purpose of never committing any in the future. With this firm and sincere purpose of the soul, it is impossible that those who receive Communion every day should not free themselves from venial sins also, and gradually from all affection for these sins.

"(4) Although the Sacraments of the New Law produce their effect *ex opere operato* (of themselves), the extent of these effects will be in proportion to the perfection of the dispositions of those who receive them. Catholics will, therefore, take care to make a diligent preparation before Communion and a fitting thanksgiving after, according to each one's strength, condition and duties.

"(5) In order that frequent and daily Communion be made with greater prudence and merit, it is important that each one ask the advice of his Confessor. Let the Confessor, however, take care not to deprive anyone of frequent and daily Communion who is in the state of grace and approaches with a right intention."

(A decree of the Sacred Congregation of Indulgences has declared that people may gain the indulgences attached to frequent Communion without the obligation of weekly or fortnightly Confession).

(See Chapter VI, Part III on Holy Communion).

THIRD MEANS

Visits to the Blessed Sacrament

The third means to acquire this perfect love of God is to visit the Blessed Sacrament often. Friendship is preserved and increased among men by frequent visits and conversations; it is by this means that we shall gain and increase the friendship of Jesus Christ. As His object in remaining on our altars is to be continually with us, judge what must be His sentiments of affection for those whom He sees often with Him. There is nothing which gains the Heart of Jesus more than frequent visits and frequent acts of adoration in His presence; it is usually at this time that He pours out His graces in greatest abundance, and it may be said that, of all His gifts and favors which He gives at these visits, the most usual is the incomparable grace of His love.

There are visits of courtesy, and there are visits of pure love; if a person is wanting in paying visits of courtesy, it is a fault; but it is on the occasion of visits of pure love that singular favors are conferred.

The days of the great Feasts, the time of Sunday Mass and of the Divine Office are, with regard to Jesus Christ, visits of duty and courtesy such as are paid to the great ones of the world; a person is remarked if not found with the crowd; but the visits which are made at certain hours of the day when Jesus Christ is rarely visited and when the greater part of people forget Him, are visits of friends. It is at those times more than any others, that Jesus Christ converses more familiarly with His favorites, that He communicates Himself more intimately to them, that He opens to them His Sacred Heart, that He pours out on them the treasures of His grace by inflaming them with His divine love. And whether it be that the indifference of those who forget Him at those times, renders more precious the fidelity of those who visit Him, it is a fact that all the Saints have experienced that there is no more infallible means of obtaining in a short time this great love of Jesus Christ, than to visit Him often in the churches, especially at those hours of the day when He is honored so little and visited so rarely. In the Third Part of this book,* a method of making those visits will be sug-

---

*See Part III, Chap. IV for method of visiting the Blessed Sacrament.

gested, and an explanation given as to why many people profit little from their visits to the Blessed Sacrament. It is sufficient to say here that, provided people make these visits with a lively faith and consciousness that it is Jesus Christ Whom they are visiting, these visits will be found to be an infallible means of obtaining in a short time a perfect love for Jesus Christ.*

FOURTH MEANS

Fidelity in Acquitting Ourselves Exactly of the Practices of this Devotion

The fourth means is fidelity in acquitting ourselves exactly of the practices which Jesus Christ has revealed to be pleasing to Him and to be most proper to honor His Sacred Heart and to inflame us in a short time with His ardent love. These practices are visits to the Blessed Sacrament including the Holy Hour, certain prayers, Communions made more frequently and with greater fervor, and all this for motives which are found in the first chapter of the Third Part of this book.

Those who, through some false idea of virtue, treat as trifles all practices of devotion which appear to them to be too easy, and who have little esteem for those practices which do not give them sufficient opportunity to distinguish themselves, will, perhaps, not show much eagerness for these because they contain nothing very extraordinary. They imagine that what everyone is able to do is not an efficacious means to become what few people are in effect. Without examining the true cause of this illusion, might we not give them a reply like that given to Naaman who had similar ideas: If something very difficult were proposed to you to do in order to obtain so great a favor, you should not refuse to do it; for a much stronger reason, you should at least try whether this means proposed by our Divine Lord Himself is efficacious, since it costs so little.

It is true that we should depend especially on perseverance and exactness in carrying out perfectly those practices. This fidelity is usually what is most agreeable to God and most meritorious in these exercises of devotion, because it is always the surest mark of great love. It is much better to do less and

*See Part III, Chap. IV for method of visiting the Blessed Sacrament.

to be more constant. Our good works are more perfect when they are less accompanied with self-love. People who are constantly changing either their practices of devotion, or the time of these practices are, assuredly, people who are acting only by the movement of their own will, for what other motive could they have for these changes?

It is then properly in perseverance that this generous fidelity consists, which is the most certain mark of great love for Jesus Christ. If we consider seriously what we do for God, however great our work may seem, we shall see that it is, after all, very little; but in another sense we can truly say that it is not a little thing to pay no heed either to the disposiion in which we find ourselves, or to our present sentiments, or to the hundred other specious pretexts which present themselves every day, and which our natural inconstancy represents as legitimate reasons for changing, or at least for interrupting the practices of this devotion. Whether we are sad or in good humor, whether we are full of energy or fatigued, whether we are in peace or troubled, to be always constant and to carry out towards Jesus Christ certain little duties imposed on us by our love and gratitude for Him, is to be truly faithful to Him, is truly to love Jesus Christ.

FIFTH MEANS

A Tender Devotion to the Blessed Virgin

The fifth means by which we may in a short time become inflammed with ardent love for Jesus Christ, is to have a tender love for the Blessed Virgin who has such absolute power over the Sacred Heart of her Divine Son. There is no doubt but that the Blessed Virgin is, of all creatures, the one who has loved Jesus Christ most, who has been most loved by Him and who desires most ardently that He be perfectly loved. She is the mother of perfect love, it is to her that we should address ourselves in order to be inflammed with that love. The Sacred Hearts of Jesus and Mary are too comfortable and too closely united to each other to allow us entry into one without having the entry into the other, with this difference that the Heart of Jesus suffers only souls exremely pure to enter into that Sanctuary, while the Heart of Mary purifies, by means of the graces she obtains, those souls that are not pure, and puts them in a state to be received into the Heart of Jesus.

Although all the other means of obtaining this ardent love of Jesus Christ are easy and efficacious, this latter means appears to many to be the easiest. Few people have the dispositions necessary to be inflamed by this Divine love, but there are few who cannot obtain these dispositions through the intercession of the Blessed Virgin. Even sinners should not despair; Mary is the hope of sinners, the refuge of all unfortunates, the resource of everyone. Jesus Christ grants to her easily what we, of ourselves, are unworthy to receive. St. Bernard says: "Because you were unworthy to receive the gift, it was given to Mary that you might receive through her whatever you wish to have." Almighty God has established her as the dispenser of His graces; according to St. Bernard, He has resolved to grant none which do not pass through her hands. If we have a tender love for Mary, we will be soon inflamed with an ardent love for her Son. It is a sign that one does not really desire the love of the Son, when he does not feel a tender love for the Mother; and without a very tender love for the Blessed Virgin, one need never expect to get entrance into the Sacred Heart of Jesus Christ.

Thus, it has been remarked that there was never found anyone who had indifference for the Blessed Virgin, who had not at the same time aversion for Jesus Christ. It is even from this aversion for Jesus Christ that indifference and aversion for the Blessed Virgin comes. Jesus Christ said: "He that hateth Me, hateth the Father also" (John, XV, 23), and, for the same reason, might we not say that there has never been a heretic in the world who has not been an enemy of the Blessed Virgin, because there has never been one who has not hated Jesus Christ. All the works which these heretics have composed tend equally to extinguish the love for the Mother and the Son. Has there ever been one of these hidden enemies of Jesus Christ, bent on destroying the most proper means of loving Jesus Christ, who has preached devotion to the Blessed Virgin? — or rather who has not tried by all possible means to destroy this solid devotion in the hearts of the faithful?

This truth has been very forcibly expressed by one of the greatest and most zealous Prelates of his time, the illustrious Archbishop of Malines, in a Lenten Pastoral which our Holy

Father, Pope Innocent XII, praised very highly in a letter which he wrote to him. This Pastoral Letter, which is full of the spirit and zeal which animated saints like St. Charles Borromeo and St. Francis de Sales, might pass today for a masterpiece of this kind of writing, whether we consider it from the point of view of the beautiful instruction which it contains and the sound moral lessons which it inculcates, or from the point of view of the solidity of the doctrine enunciated. The following is how this great Prelate expresses himself with reference to the false zeal of those who, far from urging all the faithful to practise devotion to the Blessed Virgin, endeavor to decry it:

"Catholics are very much scandalized to see how some people endeavor in an underhand way to throw discredit on devotion to the Blessed Virgin. Catholics have imbibed this devotion with their mothers' milk; their teachers have explained and recommended it to them; hence, they are scandalized at seeing disrespect shown to images of Our Lady, at pilgrimages being derided, at people using the worn-out anti-Christian witticisms which Erasmus made on this subject; at people in private conversations, and even in anonymous publications, attacking sodalities established in honor of the Blessed Virgin; however, they are edified by the conduct of those who stand up in defence of these pious and holy practices which they have received from their ancestors, and they are determined that, today, as in the time of their ancestors, devotion to Our Lady be the distinguishing mark by which a Catholic is recognized from a heretic.

We earnestly recommend devotion to the Blessed Virgin to everybody; we wish that you exert all your energy to make this devotion better known and more widely practised; that people go and pay homage to shrines of the Blessed Virgin, especially at those where miracles have taken place; that her images be carried in processions, that candles be lighted before them and hymns and litanies and prayers be recited; that people speak with respect of Congregations and Confraternities erected in her honor, as well as of the privileges and immunities granted by Popes to them; that people be urged to enter these Confraternities where they exist, that they be established in places where there are none, and that they be reestablished wherever they have been abolished. Let all know that to show disrespect fo any of these practices, much more to condemn them or seek to abolish them, is to wound us in the apple of our eye.

We inherit these tender sentiments of piety for the Blessed Virgin from our ancestors, and we have preserved them in spite of the rage of the heretics who surround us. I desire with all my heart that they take root more and more in the hearts of the faithful. We feel ourselves urged on by the advice and example of several holy men, whom it is not necessary to mention by name, because it can be said that, in every age, all those who have been remarkable for extraordinary sanctity, have given striking proofs of their devotion to the Blessed Virgin.

The faithful should not be misled by the hollow arguments given by heretics and other enemies of devotion to Mary; these allege that honor paid to the Mother will interfere with the rights of the Son. The faithful are not so poorly instructed as not to know what they owe to the Son, and that it is only out of respect for Him that they pay honor to His Mother. All Catholics are agreed that it is for love of the Son that they honor the Mother, or rather that in the Mother they honor this Divine Son Who will rigorously avenge every insult to His Mother. The Saints tell us so frequently and the deplorable fall of many Christians makes us see this truth with our very eyes. When people relax their devotion to the Mother, insensibly, devotion to the Son diminishes and often becomes extinguished.

The zeal of St. Charles Borromeo to propagate devotion to the Blessed Virgin can be seen in the accounts of the various Councils held under this authority at Milan; for, both his addresses at these Councils and the Statutes drawn up, are so many enduring monuments showing forth his ardent devotion to the Queen of Heaven.

The books of the saintly Bishop of Geneva are full of the same sentiments, and the example of his life is also a testimony in favor of this devotion. He makes it his glory to belong to the Confraternity of the Holy Rosary of which nearly all the people of the town were members. St. Anselm, St. Bernard, St. Norbert and a host of others were equally remarkable for their devotion to Mary. Let the Pastors then listen to these Saints, let them make them models to be imitated by themselves and their flocks.

Truly, it is rare to find Catholics without a tender love for Mary, and without some special devotion to her. We can say that in our days devotion to the Blessed Virgin is universal, and it will always remain true that devotion towards the Mother will be condemned only by the enemies of her Son. Let us who desire to obtain ardent love for the Son, use all our endeavors to love the Mother tenderly, and let us be persuaded that it will be by means of the Mother, we shall find easiest access to Jesus Christ and that we shall be received into His Heart.

For the same reason, we should have a singular devotion to the Holy Family, because Our Lady and St. Joseph, who loved Jesus Christ more ardently and tenderly than all others, can help to obtain for us this tender love and to procure an entrance into the Sacred Heart over which they have such influence.

SIXTH MEANS (1)

Special Devotion to St. Aloysius of Gonzaga

The sixth means, which we propose and which God has already indicated by favors granted, as very suitable to obtain a tender love for Our Lord Jesus Christ, is devotion to St. Aloysius of Gonzaga. This Saint, who was of noble family, was remarkable for the innocence and sublime perfection of his life.

It is certain that in heaven the Saints exert their influence on behalf of those who love and honor them on earth, and that most usually the grace which they obtain for them is the virtue in which they themselves excelled and which in a manner constituted their character. The following words, that were written by St. Aloysius with his own hand, bear out this statement: "As men on earth are naturally inclined to render service to those who have the same tastes as themselves, in the same way the Saints in heaven employ with pleasure their influence with God in favor of those who have a particular attraction for this same virtue, and who work efficaciously to acquire it."

Now, since the devotion to the Sacred Heart of Jesus in the exercise of the interior life and of constant union with God, was the distinctive mark of the character of St. Aloysius of Gonzaga, we may be sure that he will interest himself in a particular manner in favor of those who have this devotion at heart. Several persons have already been fortunate in experiencing the powerful effects of his intercession in this respect.

It might be said that one could not be truly devoted to him without feeling a tender love for Jesus Christ. Devotion to him invariably inspires a high esteem and love for the interior life. There are few Saints that could be more universally proposed to all classes of people than he, to serve as a model to arrive easily at high and solid virtue in the exercise of the common life.

If we were to judge by his exterior actions, we should find nothing very extraordinary in his life, for he died very young, he never occupied any high position, he was never distinguished for any remarkable achievements, but rather always took extreme care to remain hidden. Nevertheless, the sublime degree of glory to which he has been elevated must have been the recompense of great merit, and this great merit must have been the fruit of his extreme purity of heart, of his practice of the interior life and of the continual presence of God, of his ardent, tender love for Jesus Christ, and finally of his consummate perfection, which he acquired in a few years by the great love and tender devotion which he always had for the Sacred Heart of Jesus Christ in the Blessed Sacrament. It was not without a special Providence of God that this faithful servant of Jesus Christ, died as he had predicted and desired, on the day that was destined for the Feast of the Sacred Heart of Jesus to Which he had always such great devotion.

It was in this adorable Heart that he must have received from his earliest years the gift of sublime contemplation and of continual tears, tears so abundant especially after the Consecration at Mass, that his garments were moistened with them. From that same source came the great tranquility of heart, which he preserved unaltered amidst all the events and occupations of his life; finally, it was from the Sacred Heart (as the Historian of his life tells us) that the Holy Spirit filled his soul with such ardent love and such sweet consolations, that his face seemed all on fire, and his heart seemed to be trying to leave its place, so violently did it beat. It was in the Sacred Heart that he united himself so intimately with God that, when he was obliged for some reason to turn his attention away, his heart experienced a pain similar to that which a person feels when one of his members is dislocated, as he himself testifies when he says: "I am forbidden to concentrate my attention on God, lest this application of my attention cause me headache, but the effort which I make not to think of God causes me more effort than the application itself, for I have made it a habit; thus it is no longer a labor for me but sweet repose."

But to form some idea of the sublime glory which he enjoys in heaven, and which may be said to be the fruit of his interior life and of the ardent and tender love which he always had for the adorable Heart of Jesus Christ, one has only to read the testimony given of it by St. Magdalen de Pazzi. The author of her life gives the following account of it: "On April 14th, 1600, St. Magdalen de Pazzi, being in one of these ecstasies which were customary to her, saw in Paradise the glory of St. Aloysius of Gonzaga; and being amazed at what appeared to her most extraordinary she began to speak slowly, allowing an interval to elapse between her words:

"Oh! How great is the glory of Aloysius, son of Ignatius! I could never have believed it if Our Lord had not shown it to me. It seems to me that there can be no glory in heaven equal to that of Aloysius — I repeat it! Aloysius is a great Saint. We have Saints in our Church (those whose relics were in the Monastery Church) who have not received such glory as their reward. I wish I were able to go all through the world and proclaim that Aloysius, Son of Ignatius, is a great Saint; I would wish to be able to tell about the glory which he enjoys, in order that God might be glorified by it. He has been elevated to this high degree of glory because he lived an interior life. Who could explain the value and advantages of the interior life? It is incomparably superior to the exterior life. While Aloysius was on earth, his eyes were always turned towards the Divine Word. Aloysius was a hidden martyr, because whoever knows Thee, my God, knows Thee to be so great and so amiable to behold that he cannot love Thee as much as he desires, and knows that far from Thy being loved by creatures, they offend Thee. He was a martyr because he endured voluntary suffering. Oh! How great was Aloysius's love for God on earth! That is why he enjoys God in heaven in a great plenitude of love. When he was on earth, he was constantly discharging arrows of love into the Heart of the Word; now that he is in heaven, these arrows return to his own heart and remain there, because the acts of love and charity which he elicited then are now a cause of extreme joy."

It is easy to recognize in this portrait a true and perfect lover of the Sacred Heart of Jesus Christ; those who wish to acquire true devotion to this Divine Heart and to obtain a tender love for Jesus Christ, the gift of an interior life and of the continual presence of God, should practice devotion to that great Saint, who will soon make them feel the sweet effects of his intercession with Jesus and Mary, whom he loved so ardently and tenderly and by whom he was so tenderly loved.

For this reason, the Religious of the Monastery of Anges, at Florence, besides practicing devotion to St. Aloysius every day, celebrate his feast most solemnly each year to obtain, through his intercession, this interior recollection, this continual union with God, this ardent and tender love for Jesus Christ, and this perfect devotion to His Sacred Heart.

The following two miracles confirm what Father Croiset has said about devotion to St. Aloysius; the first occurred on February 3rd, 1765, a few days after Pope Clement XIII had confirmed the decree of the Congregation of Rites authorizing the public worship of the Sacred Heart of Jesus.

A Jesuit novice named Nicholas Celestini was dying; his life had been despaired of by his physicians. A picture of St. Aloysius of Gonzaga having been placed before him, St. Aloysius appeared to him and said to him: "The Lord grants you your life in order that you may apply yourself to the pursuit of perfect virtue, and that during your life, you endeavor to propagate devotion to the Sacred Heart of Jesus, which is most pleasing in heaven." This miracle was declared to be authentic by the ecclesiastical authorities, and contributed greatly to the spread of the devotion to the Sacred Heart.

The second miracle occurred at Rome. An orphan of about twelve years of age, living in a house that had been founded by St. Ignatius, was suffering from epilepsy, and was subject to such violent fits that he had to be held during them. This child had a great devotion to St. Aloysius, and was accustomed to say a Pater, Ave and Gloria every day in honor of him. One day, during one of his violent fits, St. Aloysius appeared to him holding an image of Our Lady in his hand. The boy recognized him, called him by name and bowed his head in sign of respect. St. Aloysius said to him: "You will be cured, but on condition that you recite daily a Pater, Ave and Gloria in honor of the Sacred Hearts of Jesus and Mary, and that you urge others to do the same." The child promised to do so and was immediately cured.

SIXTH MEANS (2)

Devotion to St. Margaret Mary and to Blessed Claude de la Colombiere

All that Father Croiset has said about devotion to St. Aloysius of Gonzaga constituting a means of acquiring the perfect love of God and true devotion to the Sacred Heart of Jesus, applies with greater force to St. Margaret Mary Alacoque and to Blessed Claude de la Colombiere.

St. Margaret Mary was chosen by Our Lord Himself to be the apostle of this devotion to His Sacred Heart. She lived consumed with an intense desire to see the Sacred Heart of Jesus known, loved and honored on earth. When she realized that her mission was accomplished, that the revelations of the love of the Sacred Heart were being published to the whole world by the priest whom Our Savior had given to her as a helper, she desired equally to die in order that her presence on earth might not be a hindrance to the spread of the devotion..

While she lived, she had a vision of Blessed Claude in heaven; in that vision she saw that he had acquired more glory in heaven by his work in spreading devotion to the Sacred Heart of Jesus than by all the rest that he had done, and that he had been given charge of the propagation of the devotion on earth.

Who can doubt that St. Margaret Mary, also the beloved disciple of the Sacred Heart, now that she is in heaven, is using all her influence for the spread of this devotion, and that these two chosen apostles will eagerly come to the assistance of all those who pray to them to obtain an ardent love for Jesus Christ and true devotion to His Sacred Heart?

SEVENTH MEANS

A Day's Retreat Each Month

The seventh and last means of acquiring and preserving this ardent love of Jesus Christ is so useful and necessary that, without it, it may be said that the other means proposed will be found weak and insufficient. However sincere our resolution to love Jesus Christ ardently may be, we have need to renew from time to time the considerations which caused us to adopt it. We can recommend no better means of renewing these salutary considerations, and with them the fervor which is their ordinary effect, than to make a day's retreat each month.

We do not intend here to go over all the advantages to be derived from this practice, which conduces to a fervent Christian life by inspiring us with a great horror for sin and an ardent love for Jesus Christ. A book recently published entitled, "A Spiritual Retreat for a day each month," gives all necessary information about the necessity of such a retreat, the advantages which can be derived from it, and an easy way to make it This pious practice cannot be too much recommended to all classes of people, as a means both to preserve themselves in innocence, and to make fresh progress in virtue.

That Jesus Christ is infinitely worthy of our love seems to us to be self-evident; we are ashamed and angry with ourselves for not loving Him. How is it, then, that we love Him so little? Is it because we refuse to acknowledge the infinite obligations we are under of loving Him? It does not appear so: the reason is rather that we forget His benefits. The tumult of the world, the cares connected with our material wants, the dissipation by which the soul is wholly engrossed in exterior things, prevent us from thinking often on the great mysteries which would inspire us with sentiments of gratitude; we should, from time to time, after the example of our Divine Savior, retire at least for some hours into solitude in order to rekindle this half-extinct love of Jesus Christ by serious meditation. That is the end which we propose, and the fruit which we expect to reap from this monthly retreat.

We can find solitude in our own house: we can even make this monthly retreat without interrupting our business, or dispensing ourselves from any of the duties of our state. It is sufficient that we withdraw for the day from unnecessary distractions and cancel unnecessary visits, in order to examine ourselves and see whether there is any point in which we have relaxed the practice of virtue; whether we acquit ourselves punctually of the duties of our state; whether we have gained greater love and gratitude for Jesus Christ; whether we have made some progress in virtue; what fruit we have drawn from the reception of the Sacraments.

No more efficacious means could be proposed to make constant progress in virtue. Only one day each month is asked for; the most convenient day can be chosen. Indeed, we must confess that we have little love for Jesus Christ, if we refuse to consecrate one whole day each month to Him.

(At the end of the Third part of this book will be found meditations for the First Friday of each month as well as meditations for each Friday of every month. These meditations should make the practice of this monthly recollection easy.)

THIRD PART

THE PRACTICE OF THIS DEVOTION

Chapter I

For what motives and with what sentiments we should practice this devotion

As the holiness and merit of our actions depend on the motive for these actions and the spirit in which they are performed, the practice of this most holy devotion to the Sacred Heart will not bear its proper fruit if it is not aminated by the motive which is essential to the devotion. This motive, as has been already explained, is to make reparation, as far as is in our power, by our love and adoration and by every kind of homage, for all the indignities and outrages which Jesus Christ has suffered in the course of the ages and which He still suffers daily at the hands of wicked men in the Blessed Eucharist. It is with this spirit and these sentiments that we should perform the practices which are here proposed.

For the convenience of the reader we bring together here at the beginning of the Third Part of the Book all the principal considerations which are calculated to excite in us these sentiments. This will involve the repetition of part of what has already been written, but it will, we trust, make it easier for the reader to grasp the essential features of this devotion, and render its practice more fruitful.

In order to excite in ourselves the sentiments proper to the practice of this devotion, let us first consider seriously and attentively the divine liberality with which Jesus Christ has treated men in this Sacrament of His love, and the poor return of love which they make to Him. Let us represent to our minds the eagerness with which He offers this heavenly nourishment: "With desire have I desired to eat this Pasch with you, before I suffer" (Luke XXII, 15), and the little relish, nay even the aversion with which it is received. His love is excessive, it is without bounds, but truly could the ingratitude with which men receive this greatest pledge of His love go any further? If we had been given the choice to ask from Jesus Christ the most signal mark of the love which He bears us, could we have ever imagined such a miracle, and even if we had imagined it, would we have ever dared to ask for it or hope for it?

However, this miracle has been performed; Jesus Christ has chosen this extraordinary way to show the excess of His love. After doing everything for us and giving us everything in order to show us how much He loved us, He gave us His Own Body and Blood, He gave us Himself whole and entire in the Blessed Sacrament of the Altar, and if He had anything better or more precious He would have given it to us also. There is neither place which repels Him, nor man however miserable that disgusts Him, nor time which obliges Him to defer His gift. Nevertheless, this marvelous condescension, this prodigious gift, this stupendous love which has amazed both heaven and earth, has not been able to protect Him from the ingratitude and outrages of men. The first distribution of Holy Communion at the Last Supper was dishonored by the most horrible of all sacrileges, and this horrible sacrilege has been followed during the ages by all the outrages and profanations which hell could invent. Not only have people lost all respect for Jesus Christ on our Altars, not only have they treated Him as a mock king and ridiculed His Divinity, not only have they pillaged, demolished and burned the churches where He had condescended to remain constantly for the love of men, and the altars on which He immolated Himself every day for them; not only have they broken, melted down, and profaned the sacred vessels which have a thousand times served for the dread Sacrifice of the Mass; but they have even dragged on the ground and trampled under foot His adorable Body in the consecrated Hosts and — what should horrify devils, and even monsters worse than devils — they have pierced these consecrated Hosts with knives thousands of times. The precious Blood, which had so often flowed from these consecrated Hosts thus profaned, only increased their rage and fury. History records that wicked men have, at one time, cut these consecrated Hosts in pieces; at another, that they have thrown them into the flames; at another time — as if their sacrilegious hands and abominable hearts were not places sufficiently impure — they have given them to the most impure animals; finally, they have made them serve the most execrable uses, and Thou, O my Savior and my God, hast endured all these outrages, the very thought of which makes me shudder!

Behold to what the love of Christ has exposed Him! Behold the gratitude of men for such a stupendous favor! There is no man, however vile or abject, that would have been treated with such contempt, there is no criminal that would have been treated with such indignity, or for whom less compassion would have been felt if men saw him so ill-treated. Can it be that Jesus Christ is the only one to the outrageous treatment of Whom we are insensible? What wrong has He done by loving us to excess? If it be a crime to love us too much (may God pardon the expression!), should this fault of loving us too much draw down on Jesus Christ the hatred of those who are not willing to recognize His love? Should we take occasion of this excessive love to forget Him, to have no respect in His presence, to be insensible to the insults offered to Him? It is true that the greatest part of these outrages are the effect of the rage of heretics; but, O my Savior, how many Catholics there are who treat Thee scarcely less insultingly! Abomination penetrates even into the Holy of Holies, it is difficult to say which of the two treats Jesus Christ with greater impiety and ingratitude, the heretic who profanes our Churches in which he believes that Jesus Christ is not really present, or the Catholic who, while making profession of believing, presents himself before Jesus Christ with so little respect.

People discuss news and business matters even at the foot of the Altar, and must we confess, O my God, to the shame of our age, that there are even Catholics who are guilty of abominable and impious conversation in church? The conduct themselves better in the presence of a mere ordinary man than they do in the presence of Jesus Christ; children are allowed liberties in the church which are forbidden in their homes. The sacred vestments for the Holy Sacrifice of the Mass are sometimes not so rich as the clothes of many of the faithful. Many churches, through the negligence of those in charge, are less clean than the houses of any well-to-do family. Some people assist at Mass as they would at a profane show, but perhaps with less attention to the celebration of the adorable Sacrifice than they give to a profane representation. After a perfunctory genuflection, they sit down and often talk. Behold the homage, the gratitude, the return of love which Jesus Christ receives from a large number of Christians!

By their sublime dignity, priests are raised above the rest of men; their position and their ministry oblige them to approach nearer and oftener to Jesus Christ by Whom they are singularly loved. But do all priests love Jesus Christ ardently, and are they all perfectly grateful for being raise by their ministry above the angels themselves? Do their lives correspond with their sublime dignity? Jesus Christ has, in His mercy, distinguished them from the rest of the faithful, but do they by their virtue and their lives of faith distinguish themselves from the rest of Christians? Alas! one would say, from seeing some priests at the altar, that the adorable Body of Jesus Christ which they hold in their hands is a vile instrument used to perform some cold ceremonies; and as they often have nothing but indifference for Jesus Christ, the time spent at this adorable Sacrifice seems irksome. Tepid priests often pass from some profane occupation to the Altar, and from the altar to profane occupations. To see them, a person would think that the Mass is an empty function which, by force of habit and constant repetition, they have learned to perform skillfully and almost by instinct. They are as little touched when the hold the Body of Christ in their hands as when they hold the Missal. There is a negligence, a coldness and insensibility which show the little esteem which they have for this adorable Body, or, at least, the incomprehensible blindness in which they live.

If we pass from the ministers of the Lord to the rest of the faithful, we shall have scarcely less reason to deplore their want of faith. There are those who communicate often, but among this number there are many who receive little fruit from their Communions because of the want of preparation and lack of devotion in receiving Jesus Christ. We have even to add to the contempt which Jesus Christ receives from those who love Him little or not at all, the indifference and coldness shown to this amiable Savior in the Blessed Eucharist by those who make profession of loving Him; of whom He Himself expressly complained. Few visits are made wtih more weariness or less eagerness, than the visits of the tepid to Jesus Christ in this august Sacrament. A hundred false reasons are found to dispense people from visiting Jesus Christ in the Sacrament of His love, and if they are bound by their state of life to visit Him, are there not many who accustom themselves to do so with a minimum of respect? Some enter the church as they would enter an ordinary house, and present themselves before the Blessed Sacrament as they would before an image. There is a lack of modesty and reverence in the posture adopted, the eyes are allowed to wander, faith or respect is shown but a little, and hence little fruit is gained from the visit.

Behold, O Lord, how people repay Thee for the greatest of all benefits! We feel ourselves forced to say again that Jesus Christ would not have been treated so disrespectfully if He had loved us less. If He retained in the Blessed Sacrament that majestic air which makes Him dreaded by the very demons, if He punished immediately every outrage, He would certainly be more respected; but He would also be more feared; however, our amiable Savior Who wished to draw us by love cannot resign Himself to be feared. He prefers to expose Himself to the indignities of impious, rather than by pardoning no act of irreverence to drive away a single one of His children. It would appear that he prefers to endure these outrages from the impious rather than, by condign punishment of these offenses, lessen the confidence of the good in His mercy by the terror that this punishment would inspire. This excess of goodness, which alone should attract the love and respect of all men exposes Him every day to new contempt and makes Him every day less respected.

What can touch our hearts if this will not? We are touched by the ill-treatment given to a man whom we do not know, to a mere stranger; we have compassion on a wretch if we see him ill-treated; is it only to the outrages offered to Jesus Christ that we are insensible? Is it only to Jesus Christ that we are indifferent when we see Him despised, outraged and treated with contempt by men in the Blessed Sacrament? Can we find an outrage that has not been done to Him, an indignity that He has not suffered, a place in the world where He has been spared? And all that for being too amiable, for loving too much! He has, indeed, loved us to excess, but must this excess of love freeze the hearts of those whom He has loved so much? Truly, if we retain some sentiment of humanity, can we reflect on the conduct of so many impious, so many ungrateful ones, whose number perhaps we increase, without our hearts being pierced with sorrow at seeing Jesus Christ so much forgotten, so little loved, so unworthily treated? Can we rest satisfied with mediocre gratitude? Can we restrain ourselves from doing all in our power to make reparation for all this ingratitude by our profound adoration, our gratitude and our love?

The Church has, it is true, instituted a solemn Feast on which Jesus Christ in the Blessed Sacrament is borne with pomp and triumph to make reparation of honor for the numberless injuries which He has received in the adorable Eucharist; but has not this Feast become another occasion for new outrages on the part of evil Christians by the irreverences which they, during the Octave, commit in the presence of the Blessed Sacrament? For this reason, our amiable Savior has Himself chosen the Friday after the Octave as a second special Feast on which His Sacred Heart can find true adorers by finding perfect friends. The first Feast referred to is the Feast of Corpus Christi, the second is the Feast of His Sacred Heart. The love which He has for us triumphs in the first, the love which we have for Him ought to triumph in the second. In the first Feast, the Church shows in a solemn manner to what extreme Jesus Christ loves; in the second, we should protest in the face of heaven and earth how sincerely we love Jesus Christ.

For this reason, all those who have a tender love for Jesus Christ should celebrate this feast of the Sacred Heart of Jesus with great solemnity, and with great care. By this Feast, He wishes to distinguish His dearest friends who love Him with a generous, grateful and tender love from those who love Him only in appearance, and are too cowardly to make any sacrifice for Him. He wishes that the former, penetrated with regret for the insults which He receives in the Blessed Sacrament, and really touched with sorrow at the sight of so much ingratitude, should make a solemn act of reparation to Him, endeavor to recognize His love, and show Him theirs by an act of gratitude, consecrating all this day to honor His Sacred Heart. These are the sentiments we should have when practicing this devotion. It is with these sentiments and animated by this motive that we ought to receive Holy Communion, visit the Blessed Sacrament, pray, and perform all our good works of devotion, if we wish to receive in abundance the great graces which follow the practice of this devotion.

Chapter II

The Practice of the Devotion to the Sacred Heart of Jesus for Every Year

Although God should be the motive and the end of all our actions, and although every day of our lives belongs to Him by a hundred titles, nevertheless, it is His wish that certain days of the year be specially consecrated to Him. The Old Law had its great solemn festivals; in like manner, the Church has established special Feasts which she celebrates with great solemnity. Thus, while we know that we are bound to love Jesus Christ on all days, we also know that it is His wish that a day be set apart for the external manifestation of this love. As He had a Feast established to honor His Sacred Body in the Blessed Eucharist, and another Feast to honor His Precious Wounds, so He has designated a day for honoring His Sacred Heart. The Feast of Corpus Christi is celebrated by exposition of the Blessed Sacrament and by solemn processions arranged with great magnificence. The Feast of the Sacred Heart should be marked by the outward expression of the most sincere and ardent love for Jesus Christ in the Blessed Sacrament.

Although it has been told elsewhere how Jesus Christ chose the day for this Feast, as this is the subject treated of in this chapter, we shall repeat the account briefly.

When one day during the Octave of Corpus Christi, St. Margaret Mary Alacoque, under the inspiration of a very special grace, was filled with the desire to make some return to our loving Savior by giving love for love, the Son of God Himself appeared to her and said: "You cannot give Me a greater return of love than by doing what I have so often demanded." Then He revealed to her His Sacred Heart and said: "Behold this Heart Which has so loved men even to exhausting and consuming Itself to testify to them Its love; and in return I receive from the generality of men nothing but ingratitude through the contempt, irreverence, sacrileges and coldness which they show Me in the Sacrament of My love; but what is still more painful to Me is that there are hearts consecrated to Me that treat Me thus. For that reason I demand that the First Friday after the Octave of Corpus Christi be set apart for a special Feast to honor My Heart; that, on this day, reparation be made to It with special solemnity, that the faithful receive Holy Communion in reparation for the indignities which It has received on the Altars; and I promise that My Heart will expand to pour out in abundance the treasures of Divine love on those who render It this honor."

We see by these words what we should do on the day of this Feast and the advantages and graces promised to those who celebrate it. Now to be sure that we shall infallibly receive these great graces which Our Savior promises, the greatest of which is the supreme gift of His divine love, this Feast-day must be really spent in honoring the Sacred Heart of Jesus. The following method of occupying the day will, we trust, be found useful.

The celebration of the Feast should commence on the Vigil, namely, on the last day of the Octave of Corpus Christi. A portion of this day might be occupied in reading some chapters of this book, especially the first, second and third chapters of the first part, and the first chapter of the second part, in order to remind ourselves of the motive we should have, and of the dispositions and sentiments which should animate the various exercises of the day. The greater part of the time should, if possible, be spent in profound recollection before the Blessed Sacrament. This time could be employed by reciting Vespers and Compline of the Feast, the Rosary, the Litanies and any other prayers which each one's devotion might suggest. In the evening an hour or a half-hour might be spent in reading over carefully and reflecting seriously on the first chapter of the third part. This reading or consideration might take the place of meditation and would serve to prepare us for the celebration of the Feast on the morrow. We should endeavor as far as possible to spend the rest of the day in silence, interior recollection being a necessary disposition for this devotion. Before retiring to bed, it would be well to spend a quarter of an hour in reflecting on the object of the Feast of the Sacred Heart of Jesus and the motive which we should have in celebrating it; we could consider how reasonable it is to love Jesus Christ ardently and as far as is in our power, to make reparation to Him, for the outrages which He suffers in the most amiable of His mysteries from those who refuse to love Him. We should then tell our Divine Savior of our desire to spend the rest of the night at the foot of the altar, if we were able, and ask our

Angel-guardian to supply for our absence and resolve to show the sincerity of this desire, by our diligence on the following morning in rising is good time and going to the church. We should endeavor to keep ourselves in these good sentiments, and if we should awake during the night, we should immediately adore Jesus Christ in the Blessed Eucharist and renew our desire to go and pay Him homage.

We should, if possible, consecrate the whole of the Feast-day to honoring the Sacred Heart of Jesus in the Blessed Sacrament, put off to some other time all unnecessary business, and deny ourselves all useless amusement, for the smallest moments of the day are infinitely precious. On rising in the morning, we should prostrate ourselves to adore Jesus Christ, accompanying this act of adoration with all the sentiments of which a heart inflamed with love is capable; offering Him all that we are to do in honor of His Sacred Heart to requite His love and His benefits. Those who have the happiness of having Jesus Christ under their roof should hasten on that day to pay Him the first visit; those less favored should hasten to visit Him as soon as possible. Confession should be accompanied with greater and more perfect sorrow than ordinarily at the thought of our own ingratitude and our own want of reverence, and we should accuse ourselves, at least in general, of any irreverence committed.

Then we should prepare for a very fervent Holy Communion, because this Communion is a Communion of reparation, in the first place for the faults of our own Communions, and then for the sins of others. Our profound respect before Jesus Christ should be a visible proof of our desire to repair our past want of reverence. The ardent love, tender devotion and lively faith with which we receive Holy Communion should be a mark of our sincere desire to make reparation in some manner for the coldness, incredulity and irreverence with which so many receive Communion. Touched by sensible regret at seeing Jesus Christ so little loved and even so much insulted in the Blessed Eucharist, we should receive Him as a God irritated by man's sins Whom we wish to appease, as a Savior rejected by the multitude Whom we accept as our King, as a Spouse disgusted by man's indifference Whom we wish henceforth to love perfectly. Penetrated with most tender and affectionate sentiments, we should approach the Holy Table with great modesty and profound humility. As the Feast of the Sacred Heart is the Feast of the Infinite Love of Jesus Christ, love should inspire each one with sentiments and affections proper to this Feast of Love.

Immediately after Holy Communion, compare the excessive love of Jesus Christ with your own extreme ingratitude; prostrate yourself humbly at His feet, humble in mind and with a heart pierced with sorrow at the sight of so many outrages which Jesus receives, make a fervent act of reparation which will be the expression of the sentiments of the grief and sorrow of your heart. Then make the act of Consecration to the Sacred Heart of Jesus and offer yourself without reserve to Him. The rest of the day should be spent in recollection; the whole or at least a large part of the morning being passed before the Blessed Sacrament, while the whole day should be spent in good works and especially in making frequent acts of love to Jesus Christ according as each one's devotion suggests.

On the evening of the Feast, make the meditation marked out for the day, but if a person's condition, disposition or employment does not permit him to do so, he can at least read it with attention and spend a few moments in silence reflecting on the sentiments of love which it has suggested. At some convenient time during the day, the Office, the Rosary and the Litany of the Sacred Heart may be recited, some chapters of this or other books on the Sacred Heart can be read; and in general, each one should do all in his power to show Jesus Christ that he really loves Him, and eagerly desires that He be known and loved by all.

As Religious have the inestimable privilege of having Jesus Christ in their own houses, they should show him extraordinary love and homage on the occasion of the Feast of His Love by passing before the Blessed Sacrament all the time that they are not occupied. People in the world should spend more time than usual in visiting Our Lord, and both they and Religious should endeavor to make with great fervor at least five visits for the following intentions:

The *first* visit should be to thank Jesus Christ for the infinite love shown in instituting the Blessed Eucharist; the *second,* to thank Him for all the times we have received Holy Communion, and for all the special blessings that we have there received; the *third,* to make acts of reparation for all the outrages which

He has received from infidels and heretics; the *fourth,* to make reparation as far as is in our power, by our profound respect and by every kind of homage, for the irreverences, impieties and sacrileges which our Savior has endured from Catholics; the *fifth,* to adore Jesus Christ in spirit in all the churches whether in town or country where the Blessed Sacrament is kept, but where the generality of people neglect It, where It is badly kept, rarely visited or universally forgotten.

As the love of Jesus Christ is the principal motive of all these practices of devotion, many people, in order to make themselves more pleasing to Jesus Christ, add a number of other good works suggested by their love and tending to the same end. Some people on this day visit all the churches of their neighborhood where the Blessed Sacrament is kept, or at least a number of them, and endeavor by their fervor and reverence to make reparation for the profanations and contempt which Jesus Christ has suffered. Others get some poor people to go to Confession and Holy Communion on this day, and entertain them and give them alms. Many people accompany these practices of devotion with some austerities; all, in general, should endeavor on this day to do all their actions with a lively faith, great fervor, singular devotion and very ardent love for Jesus Christ.

Chapter III

The Practice of the Devotion to the Sacred Heart of Jesus for Every Month, for Every Week, for Every Day, and for Certain Hours of Each Day

Although it will not be necessary to mark out for a person who loves Jesus Christ fervently certain exercises for each day and each hour, because whoever loves much, as St. Augustine says, is never without giving proofs of his love, it will however be useful to mark out certain times more suitable for showing this love in a special manner. That is what we shall endeavor to do in this chapter.

I

THE PRACTICE OF THE DEVOTION TO THE SACRED HEART OF JESUS FOR THE FIRST FRIDAY OF EACH MONTH

The First Friday of each month was designated by our Savior Himself as a day to be consecrated to honoring His Sacred Heart. The devotional practices for the First Fridays are practically the same as those indicated for the Feast of the Sacred Heart. Preparation for the celebration of the First Friday should begin on the Vigil, by reading the first chapter of the third part of this book, or of some other suitable book, and by passing some time on Thursday evening before the Blessed Sacrament. On rising the following morning, all the actions of the day should be offered to Jesus Christ and consecrated to His Sacred Heart. Those who are observing the First Friday should hasten to make an early visit to the Church, where the presence of Jesus Christ in the tabernacle will help them to excite in themselves regret for the outrages and indignities which He has suffered in the Blessed Eucharist, and sentiments of love for Him. At Confession, they should accuse themselves of all faults committed in the presence of our amiable Savior in this adorable Mystery, and of all negligences in receiving Him in Holy Communion and in visiting Him. They should endeavor to have the same dispositions and the same motives in their First Friday Communion as on the day of the Feast; and then they should recite the Act of Reparation and the Act of Consecration with all possible devotion and with the sentiments of a person who loves Jesus Christ tenderly and who is deeply grieved at seeing Him so little loved. They should endeavor to keep themselves in these sentiments for the rest of the day. If possible, the Litany of the Sacred Heart, the Beads and the Office should be recited during the day; and in the evening an hour or a half-hour's meditation made on the subject indicated for the month. The five visits recommended for the day of the Feast of the Sacred Heart should be made if possible, and for the same intentions; in case five separate visits are not possible, a single visit for these five intentions could be made. To the ordinary good works performed each day, an alms-giving or penance should be added, with the motive of making reparation to the best of our ability for the outrages which Jesus Christ has suffered and still suffers daily in the Blessed Sacrament. During the day we should reflect frequently on the sentiments which we should have at the sight of our own ingratitude, and the admirable dispositions which the Sacred Heart still has in our favor. To carry out these exercises perfectly, it is evident that silence, retirement from unnecessary distractions, and interior recollection are necessary. We should visit the Blessed Sacrament during the day oftener and with more respect and devotion than on other days; and during the whole day we should excite ourselves to love Jesus Christ with a continuous, fervent love; this can be done without interrupting our ordinary duties, or necessary employment. We should pray our Divine Savior to open to us His Sacred Heart and grant us the grace to pass the rest of our days in that furnace of love.

Besides these exercises of piety, love for our neighbor, which is the ordinary effect of true love for Jesus Christ, will oblige those who practice the devotion to the Sacred Heart to pray for all those whom the same love unites in a particular manner in the Sacred Heart. Priests who practice this devotion will say Mass each month for all those who have devotion to the Sacred Heart of Jesus, offering the Divine Sacrifice for the wants of those chosen souls, asking our Lord to increase their number and inflame daily more and more with the fire of His divine love the hearts of those who truly love Him. Besides the merit derived from this act of charity, those who practice devotion to the Sacred Heart of Jesus may be assured of the additional advantage of getting each month the special prayers of a great number of the most virtuous people who love Jesus Christ most ardently. *This charity should be extended to all the souls in Purgatory who, during their lives, practiced devotion to the Sacred Heart of Jesus, and should prompt all true adorers of this Sacred Heart to offer their Communions and get the Holy Sacrifice of the Mass offered for them.*

As the object of this devotion is to make our Savior Jesus Christ ardently and perfectly loved, and to make reparation for the outrages offered to Him in the past as well as for those which He daily receives in the Blessed Eucharist, it is evident that it is not attached to certain days in such a way that it cannot be practiced on other days. Jesus Christ merits our love at all times, but alas! He is despised and outraged in the Sacrament of His love at all times, and so people should at all times make reparation to Him. Those who are prevented from attending the First Friday devotions of each month can choose any other day as early as convenient, and endeavor to carry out on the day chosen these devotions; the first Holy Communion which they receive in the month can be offered for the same intentions as the First Friday Communion.

II

THE PRACTICE OF THE DEVOTION TO THE SACRED HEART OF JESUS FOR EACH WEEK

The Friday of each week is also a day on which we should pay special honor to the Sacred Heart of Jesus; it was on this day that our loving Savior gave the supreme proof of His love for us by His death on the cross, it was on this day that His Sacred Heart was opened by the lance to be our place of refuge; it is just, therefore, that on each Friday we should show the Sacred Heart some new marks of our love. Jesus Christ has made known to us how pleasing it would be to Him that this whole day be specially consecrated to honoring His Sacred Heart. Therefore, on each Friday morning we should offer the day to the Sacred Heart of Jesus, and consecrate to Its honor all the good works of the day, forming the intention to do as many good works as possible and to do them well.

The motive of all the devotional practices of the day should be to make reparation for all the contempt and all the outrages which Jesus Christ has suffered in the Blessed Sacrament, and to give Him in this adorable Sacrament some marks of our love and gratitude. Priests should offer the Holy Sacrifice of the Mass for this end. Those who are not priests should receive Holy Communion for this intention also, if possible; they should at least assist at Mass with greater respect and devotion than usual with the intention of making reparation, as far as they are able, by their love and homage for the outrages and indignities to which His love exposes Jesus Christ in this adorable Mystery; they should unite with the priest in offering up this divine Sacrifice for this end, and if they do not receive Holy Communion they should at least make a spiritual Communion.

Those who are prevented by their duties from assisting at Mass should perform some other exercises of devotion to the Sacred Heart instead.

But the following three exercises can and ought to be performed by all who are devoted to the Sacred Heart: The first exercise consists in conceiving great regret during this day on which Jesus Christ was crucified for us at seeing Him so forgotten, so little loved, and so much outraged by men in the very Sacrament in which He gives the most striking proofs of His excessive liberality and love.

The second exercise consists in visiting the Blessed Sacrament on Fridays more frequently, and with greater respect and devotion than usual, from this motive of making reparation by our love for the ingratitude of men to Jesus Christ in the Blessed Sacrament. But if their occupations, or distance from the church, prevent some from making these frequent visits, they should, at least, in their own homes, or at their occupations, adore our Lord in spirit, and by interior acts make up for the want of external marks of devotion. All should from time to time enter in spirit into the adorable Heart of Jesus Christ, and consider the loving sentiments which this amiable Savior entertains towards us and His ardent desire to fill us with His graces and inflame us with His love.

These considerations which can be made at any time and in any place cannot fail to inspire us with tender sentiments of love in harmony with the object of this devotion. All that is required is to enter into oneself from time to time, observe a little silence, be less distracted and a little more recollected. This practice is easy and suitable to everybody; it is extremely useful and has procured innumerable graces and favors, even such as can be visibly perceived, for all those who make use of it often.

The third exercise consists in performing some good act or some little mortification, either exterior or interior, from the same motive and for the same end.

On Fridays, the Litany of the Sacred Heart as well as the Beads and Office of the Sacred Heart should be recited if possible. Some passages of this or other books on the Sacred Heart should be read on Fridays and all should endeavor to find a half-hour, or a quarter of an hour, to make the meditation indicated for the particular Friday.

III

THE PRACTICE OF THE DEVOTION TO THE SACRED HEART OF JESUS FOR EACH DAY

Besides these exercises of the devotion to the Sacred Heart of Jesus for each year, each month and each week, we should have each day certain hours set apart for thinking more particularly about Jesus Christ and honoring His Sacred Heart by giving Him some special proofs of our gratitude and love. The morning on rising, some time in the afternoon when Jesus Christ is less remembered and at night before retiring to bed are the most suitable times.

In the morning on rising, after the example of many Saints, we should prostrate ourselves in the direction of the nearest church where the Blessed Sacrament is kept, and thus prostrated make an act of faith; adore Jesus Christ in this august Sacrament, make a fervent act of love to Jesus in the tabernacle, thank Him for having instituted this Mystery of love, express our sorrow at seeing Him so abandoned, and resolve to visit Him as soon as possible and love Him unceasingly. The Litany of the Sacred Heart of Jesus and of the Blessed Virgin or some other prayer should be recited, and we should resolve not to entertain during the day any thought or sentiment not in conformity with the sentiments of the Sacred Hearts of Jesus and Mary.

Attendance at the Holy Sacrifice of the Mass is assuredly the best means of honoring and loving the adorable Heart of Jesus. We shall not give here any particular practices for this precious time; love for Jesus Christ crucified, which should take complete possession of our hearts during all this time, will not fail to suggest to each one the practices which will best suit his needs. Above all, everyone should endeavor to bring home to himself that the Sacrifice of the Mass is the same as that of Calvary, and should assist at it with the most profound respect and reverence like people who believe that the Sacrifice of Calvary is here renewed. The Beads of the Sacred Heart might be said during Mass; and the Act of Consecration to the Sacred Heart recited before the priest's Communion. Those who do not receive Holy Communion at Mass should make a spiritual Communion with great love and with a great desire to receive sacramentally. The rest of the time of the Mass should be employed in thanking Jesus Christ for having loved us to such an extreme as to institute this adorable Mystery, in asking pardon for the ingratitude of men who treat the Mass with coldness or with contempt and irreverence, and finally in making up for this indifference and irreverence by profound adoration and ardent love.

Priests who have the happiness of offering this divine Sacrifice will find their devotion increase day by day and their faith become more perfect, Jesus Christ will fill them with His greatest graces and their love for Him will increase daily, if they remember to offer this Sacrifice each day with the intention of making all possible reparation through this adorable Victim for the indignities which Jesus Christ suffers in this adorable Mystery, and if they take care to adore the Sacred Heart of Jesus when they have Him really present before them. All those who visit the Blessed Sacrament or assist at Mass should do in like manner; a person can be certain that he will feel true devotion and reverence in the presence of Jesus Christ in the Blessed Sacrament, if he comes before Him with the intention of making reparation by this act for the irreverences and indignities which He has suffered.

The afternoon is a most suitable time for visiting Jesus Christ in the Blessed Sacrament in order to honor His Sacred Heart by our love and homage. As it is the time when people think least about Jesus Christ, and when few people visit Him, those who visit Him at this time are sure of being well received. Practically all will be able to find some time after dinner, a quarter of an hour or so to visit Jesus Christ in the Blessed Sacrament. Now, as it is neither custom or routine that brings us at this time, nor the crowd that attracts us, it is evident that these visits are visits of love, and consequently sources of great graces, for Jesus Christ never allows Himself to be surpassed in generosity. Love for Jesus Christ should occupy the whole time of these visits, and it will be the more perceptibly felt as they are proofs of true, faithful, constant love.

In the evening, before retiring to bed, we should adore the Sacred Heart of Jesus which we are to regard as a sanctuary, a place of retreat in which we are going to repose. We should again thank Jesus Christ for having instituted the Blessed Eucharist, the greatest of all benefits, both on our own behalf and for those ungrateful ones, alas! very numerous, who refuse to thank Him. We should make several acts of contrition and acts of love to a God Who is so amiable and Who loves us with an infinite love. St. Aloysius of Gonzaga was accustomed before going to sleep to recite three Hail Marys, in order to put himself under the protection, and, as it were, in the heart of the Blessed Virgin; and then he made a profound bow in the direction of the church to adore the Blessed Sacrament, asking the Sacred Heart of Jesus to watch unceasingly over Holy Church, and especially over those who love Him tenderly, and begging to be preserved through His mercy from all the snares of the devil; protesting that it was in this Sacred Heart that he wished to take his rest, saying with the Psalmist: "In peace in the self same," that is, in Thee my supreme Good, "I will sleep and I will rest" (Psalm IV, 9).

The above are some practices which we suggest for the exercise of the devotion to the Sacred Heart of Jesus. As true love of Jesus Christ and special respect and veneration for the Blessed Sacrament are the characteristics of this devotion and of all its exercises, so all those who practice this devotion should be distinguished by these certain marks of the ardent love of Jesus Christ: by their assiduous attention, by their profound respect and great reverence before the Blessed Sacrament; that is to say, ardent love for Jesus Christ and special devotion to the adorable Sacrament of the Eucharist should be the distinctive marks of their character.

This love for Jesus Christ should be the source of all their desires, the end of all their thoughts, the principal object and motive of all these practices. If we are faithful in the observance of these practices, we shall certainly feel the perfect love of Jesus Christ increase perceptibly in our souls. This devotion is so pleasing to Jesus Christ that He can refuse nothing to those who practice it. He made this promise to St. Margaret Mary Alacoque, whom He used to propagate this devotion, and this has been confirmed by the experience of those who have practiced this devotion and it is finding additional confirmation every day.

In concluding this chapter, we ask all to bear the following points in mind: (1) Never to forget to adore the Sacred Heart of Jesus tenderly and affectionately each time that you present yourself before the Blessed Sacrament; (2) to visit our Lord as often as possible and with great respect and reverence; (3) to recommend this devotion to people of every walk of life, since perfect love of Jesus inspires us not only with the desire of loving Him but also of seeing Him every day better known, more respectfully adored, more frequently visited and more ardently loved.

Chapter IV

Visiting the Blessed Sacrament

I

THE MOTIVES WHICH SHOULD URGE US TO VISIT THE BLESSED SACRAMENT

If, before the coming of the Savior into the world during those centuries of rigor when the Lord was called the God of vengeance, the strong God, the God of Hosts, when He spoke only by the voice of thunder, when even princes and kings were not permitted to enter into the place that was specially consecrated to Him, when He insisted on being worshipped with such reverence that He punished severely the smallest faults committed against the respect due to Him, when kings and priests, seized with holy fear, dared not enter the Temple because they saw a mere cloud which was but an external sign of the presence of the Lord in this place, when the appearance of this cloud caused the people to prostrate themselves on the ground and, penetrated with the tenderest sentiments of gratitude to cry out in admiration: Oh! how amiable is the God Whom we adore! we will sing His mercies forever because He has deigned to choose for Himself a Temple among us; if, I say, they had caught even a glimpse of what we have seen and experienced since, if they had been told that this God, so terrible, would abase Himself so far as to become man for the love of men, and that having died to redeem and save these same men, He would work without ceasing the greatest of miracles in order to remain with them to the end of time, could they have believed it?

However, there had happened something which would have appeared to them still more incredible. Would they have ever believed, could they have even imagined, that men would have refused to love this God Who abased Himself to such an extent, that they would neither pay court to Him nor visit Him? That, however, has happened. There are Christians, and even great numbers of them, who regard it as a penance to render these duties to Jesus Christ; and the disrespectful manner in which many of these who visit Him acquit themselves of the obligation of visiting Him would suggest that what our Savior foretold about the last ages of the world might be applied to our time: "But yet the Son of Man, when He cometh, shall He find, think you, faith on earth?" (Luke XVIII, 8).

But if this faith is not extinct, is it not a still more amazing prodigy to believe in the real presence of Jesus Christ upon our altars, and to treat Him with indifference; to be no more eager to render homage to Him than those who do not believe in Him? Courtesy, friendship, gratitude and self-interest are the usual motives which induce people to pay visits. People of the world would not think of dispensing themselves from doing their duties in this respect towards men of great merit or high office or noble rank. True friends part only with regret, and they allow no opportunity of meeting again to be lost. Visits at least of courtesy are paid to people who have rendered us some service, and men pay court assiduously to those from whom they expect some benefit or dread some chastisement.

Does Jesus Christ not occupy a sufficiently high rank in the world to deserve that we pay court to Him? Has He not loved us exceedingly? Have we received no favors from Him? Have we no reason to expect that He can render us some service? And since He is to be our Judge, since on Him depends our eternal happiness or misery, have we not some advantage to gain? It is strange that so many people are agreed about what they ought to do; and that so few are willing to put themselves to a little trouble to do it. If, when Our Divine Savior was about to ascend into Heaven, we were allowed the choice of asking Him for some signal proof of His love, for some remarkable favor, would we ever have thought of asking Him to remain with us on earth until the end of the world? And if He Himself had offered to do so, with what sentiments of admiration and reverence and gratitude would we not have accepted His offer? Jesus Christ has conferred on us this signal favor; the excess of His love has induced Him to give us this extraordinary proof of His love, but it would seem that this excessive love has only served to push our ingratitude to the limit. What would be said of a man, who would visit only rarely and with extreme indifference, a person of highest rank and great merit who had come on purpose to render him some service and who had consented to make a long sojourn in a foreign country for love of him?

What motive induced Jesus Christ to remain with us after the work of our redemption was accomplished, and after His glorious Ascension into heaven? Why does He return to our earth every day in an invisible manner? Why does He remain day and night in a humble and obscure state on our altars, except that He cannot endure to be separated from men; that His delight is to be with the children of men? Grieve not, My children, He says to us, I will not leave you orphans; I ascend into heaven but at the same time I will remain with you on earth; you are weak, sick, languid, you will often be afflicted, you will fear my judgments, you will dread the anger and the justice of My Father, but you will find in Me in the Blessed Sacrament, a Father Who will console you, a Physician Who will heal you, a Guide Who will lead you safely, a Master Who will solve all your doubts, a heavenly Nourishment that will give you new strength, and finally a Redeemer and a Savior.

And does all this not suffice to touch the hearts of men who are so much alive to their own interests and naturally inclined to gratitude! They would be less ungrateful for the smallest benefits from anyone else, but one would say that when it is to Jesus Christ that we owe this gratitude, it is no longer a crime to be ungrateful.

Jesus Christ is left alone, abandoned and forgotten on our altars. People always find sufficient reason and sufficient time to pass several hours of the day in vain amusement or in idleness; if they have to find some time in the afternoon to go and adore Jesus Christ, to pay Him a visit, they say that their business will not permit them, that they cannot find time. But does it really require much trouble to acquit ourselves of this duty which all are agreed is reasonable and just? Must much time be sacrificed in order to visit our Divine Lord a little oftener? By no means, a quarter of an hour or ten minutes will suffice and very often a person has only to go a very short distance to pay Jesus Christ this homage; but our want of love for Him makes this visit difficult and inconvenient. People find at hand a hundred false reasons, a hundred obstacles which would make no impression on them if there were questions of visiting anyone else, but which prevent them from paying their respects to Jesus Christ. In Africa, Canada, India, Japan and China, new Christians are found who go very long journeys in order to adore Jesus Christ in some church; others who are not able to undertake long journeys often prostrate themselves a hundred times a day in the direction of some church, in order by these frequent adorations to satisfy their eager desire to pay homage to Jesus Christ in the Blessed Sacrament. On the day of Judgment what excuse will those mean-spirited Catholics give who hardly ever visit our Divine Lord, although they live near the Church where He makes His abode, and even pass by it several times a day? But what reply can those Religious give who, although they have our Divine Lord under their roof, are reluctant to visit Him? "My people hath forgotten Me days without number" (Jeremias II, 32). Those who profess to be completely devoted to My service and whom I regard as My chosen people — even these have forgotten Me!

"There hath stood one in the midst of you, whom you know not" (John I, 26). We do not know, and we do not wish to know Him Who is day and night in the midst of us. He is none other than our Lord and our God Who is present on our altars for the express purpose of hearing our petitions and receiving our homage. If we are sick, unhappy, or afflicted, let us have recourse to Jesus Christ, let us go to Him and tell Him, Who is our good Father, of the misfortunes which have happened to us, and of the evils which threaten us. If we have some important decision to make, if we want to restore peace in some family, if we want to bring about the conversion of some person, if we are remiss in the service of God, inconstant, imperfect, let us run to Jesus Christ and let us ask Him humbly and with respectful familiarity for the graces that we need, and above all let us ask with great confidence; this perseverance in asking, this confidence will gain the Heart of Jesus Christ, it is all-powerful. If sometimes Jesus Christ delays in answering our petitions, it is only to induce us to visit Him oftener.

What a loss it is for Catholics to neglect a means so easy and at the same time so powerful, of being happy, of becoming saints! But what will not the regret of many Religious be, who

make no account of this loss! Let such people not be astonished if they have little devotion, if all their lives they make
no progress on the road of piety, if they receive from the Father of Mercy neither consolations not interior sweetness, if
they live in uneasiness and melancholy, and in the end die in
regret and fear. Negligence in visiting Jesus Christ frequently
in the Blessed Sacrament, distraction and want of reverence
and respect during these visits, are the commonest source of
most of our misfortunes.

On the contrary, those who are faithful to visiting our Lord
in the Blessed Sacrament as often as they can, know by experience that there is no easier or surer means of obtaining all
their requests from Jesus Christ; they know that if they visit
Him frequently and with respectful confidence, especially at
those times of the day when few people visit Him, He will
grant them His choicest graces, especially true devotion and a
tender love for Himself. "Come to Me all you that labor and
are burdened: and I will refresh you" (Matt. XI, 28).

II

PRACTICE FOR THE VISITS TO THE BLESSED SACRAMENT

Our visits to the Blessed Sacrament should be frequent; they
should also be respectful. We should always enter the church
where our Divine Savior is present with great reverence, and
while we remain in the church we should be filled with sentiments of profound respect, gratitude, confidence and love. To
render any place holy, it suffices that this place be set apart for
honoring God. From the moment when it is solemnly consecrated to this use, it becomes an object of veneration to the
Angels and of terror to the demons; it is just, then, that the
Majesty of God, with which our churches are filled because
Jesus Christ makes them His dwelling-place, should render
them objects of reverence and awe to all men, especially to
Catholics.

Whatever holiness the birth of the Son of God communicated to the stable of Bethlehem, whatever sanctity His Precious Blood communicated to Calvary, and His Sacred Body to
the Sepulchre, is all found in our churches, and infinitely

more. If, then, when we enter into the Divine Presence in our churches, if when we approach the altar where Jesus Christ is present, we do not feel that holy fear which this holiest of places should inspire, if we do not feel ourselves touched by these sentiments that draw sweet tears from those who are privileged to see the manger where our Savior was laid at birth, or the place where He expired, it is because of our want of faith or absence of recollection.

To ensure proper dispositions, we should, before entering a church where Jesus Christ is present, reflect on the holiness of the place and the Majesty of Him Whom we are going to visit. If it were as easy to enter into the palaces of the Great and to approach their persons as it is to enter into our churches, how many people would esteem themselves happy; but these same people set no value on the privilege which is theirs of being able to approach the adorable Person of Jesus Christ at every hour of the day.

Profound reverence and respect in the church where Jesus Christ is present should, then, be the external signs of our faith, but tender love for Jesus Christ should be the soul of all our prayers. We should not forget to honor and adore the Sacred Heart of Jesus in a special manner every time that we visit the Blessed Sacrament. This devotion is extremely pleasing to Him and will bring down great blessings on those who practice it. During our visits to the Blessed Sacrament we should meditate much and speak little. A loving, adoring silence, which might be called the language of the heart, is much more pleasing to Jesus Christ in these visits, than a great number of vocal prayers said hurriedly and with little attention. The excessive love of Jesus Christ for us, His goodness, His meekness, His liberality and patience should excite in us the tenderest of affections. These sentiments of reverence, gratitude, confidence, and tender love for Jesus Christ should occupy us nearly all the time. We should visit Jesus in the same spirit and for the same end as the Angels, the shepherds, and the Magi visited Him at Bethlehem after His birth, namely, to adore Him; or as the Apostles, to hear Him teach; or as Mary Magdalen, prostrate at His feet, to weep for our sins or to contemplate His admirable perfections; or finally, as the sick, to ask to be healed. One of the reasons why we do not derive more fruit from these visits is because we do not approach Our

Savior with sufficient simplicity and confidence. We sometimes spend the time of the visit in exercises in which the intellect has more share than the heart, instead of very simply and humbly laying before Jesus Christ our wants, our infirmities, our weakness and, as the Prophet says, pouring out our hearts (Psalms LXI, 9); at one time saying to Him: "He whom Thou lovest is sick" (John XI, 3); he for whom Thou hast become man, for whom Thou hast shed Thy Precious Blood, to whom Thou givest Thyself every day in the adorable sacrament of the Eucharist, for the love of whom Thou dost remain day and night on the altar, he has been suffering from such and such an infirmity for a long time and needs Thy help, needs a special grace; at another time, saying with the lepers: "Lord, if Thou wilt, Thou canst make me clean" (Mark I, 40); Lord, Thou canst heal me, if Thou wilt, and why shouldst Thou not wish; after all that Thou hast done for me and all that Thou still dost, can I doubt that Thou wilt, and Thou hast the divine power to do so. At other times, let us seat ourselves at the feet of Jesus like Magdalen, and if we have not sufficient devotion to pour out tears like her, let us imitate her silence, or if we speak, let it be to express with St. Thomas the sentiments of reverence, admiration and love with which we are filled, saying to Him with a lively faith: "My Lord and my God" (John XX, 28); and repeating often with the Centurion: "I believe, O Lord, help Thou my unbelief" (Mark IX, 23). We should then ask our adorable Savior earnestly and perseveringly, like the Chanaanite woman, for all the graces we stand in need of. Fully persuaded that Jesus Christ loves us tenderly, that He is present on the altar in order to confer His benefits upon us, that He has both the power and the will to grant us all we need, say to Him with confidence: "Jesus, Son of David, have mercy on me" (Luke XVIII, 38); and even if He seems to reject our petition, even if He answers nothing and seems to refuse us everything, let us ask with still greater earnestness, and as if we did not notice the seemingly harsh way that He treats us, let us cry out the louder: "Son of David, have mercy on us" (ibid, 39); I know that "it is not just too take the bread of the children and throw it to the dogs, but the whelps eat of the crumbs that fall from their master's table"; treat me in like manner (Matt. XV, 29).

But if by our sins we have forfeited the right to have our

prayers heard, let us say to Jesus Christ with confidence: Thou hast solemnly promised to grant me all that I ask in Thy name; in Thy name, I ask Thee for the grace to correct myself of this imperfection which has so long hindered my progress in virtue, to conquer this predominant passion which is the source of so many faults, to acquire this virtue which is so necessary for my salvation and for my perfection. In Thy name, I ask for the conversion of this child, for the restoration to health of this husband, the success of this affair, and all the help I need in such and such a necessity. Thou knowest, O Lord, that I have this defect, that I have not this virtue, that I have need of courage in adversity, of moderation in joy, of strength on such an occasion, and of Thy great graces always. Thou knowest that my faith is not sufficiently strong; that my confidence sometimes fails, that I love Thee only feebly; in fact, that I have scarcely the desire to love Thee. Give me, O Lord, all these graces, all these helps, but above all, efficacious helps; it is in Thy name that I ask for these efficacious graces, and remember, O Lord, that Thou hast promised to refuse me nothing that I ask in Thy name. Perhaps what I ask is not pleasing to Thee and Thou dost refuse me because I do not know what I ask, but there is not the same danger, and Thou canst not make me the same reproach when I ask Thee for Thy perfect love. Inflame me, then, O Lord, with ardent love, with generous, faithful, constant love, with genuine love even though it be not accompanied with sweetness, with love that will make me love only Thee. "Give me Thy love and Thy grace, and I am rich enough."

It is a useful practice to think from time to time, what must be the sentiments of Jesus Christ on the altar at seeing Himself forgotten and abandoned by almost everyone, and imagine that He is saying to us as He said to His Apostles when "many of His disciples went back and walked no more with Him": "Will you also go away?" (John VI, 67, 68); and answer lovingly with St. Peter: "Lord, to whom shall we go? Thou hast the words of eternal life. And we have believed and have known that Thou art the Christ, the Son of God" (ibid, 69, 70).

In order to excite ourselves further to greater love and to bring loving compulsion to bear on Jesus Christ to inflame us with more ardent and generous love, we can imagine our amiable Savior on the altar, putting us the same question as He put to St. Peter by the sea of Tiberias: "Simon, son of John, lovest thou Me?", while we should reply with St. Peter: "Lord, Thou knowest all things, Thou knowest that I love Thee" (John XXI, 17); Thou knowest that I have an ardent desire to love Thee.

It would be very desirable that we should detach our hearts from all that is not God so that we might be able to say frequently these beautiful words of the Prophet: "For what have I in heaven; and besides Thee what do I desire upon earth? Thou art the God of my heart, and the God that is my portion forever" (Psalms LXXII, 25, 26). I know, O Lord, that Thou art the way, the truth and the life, and that "they who go far from Thee shall perish" (Psalms LXXII, 27). As for me, O my amiable Savior, I have found my repose, my joy, and my sovereign happiness in adhering to Thee, and in never being separated from Thee. "It is good for me to adhere to my God, and to put my hope in the Lord God" (Psalms LXXII, 28). In Thee, O Lord Jesus, I place all my confidence; all my consolation will be to pass the rest of my days at the foot of the Altar; and if I cannot be continually present in body, I will come to Thee every hour in spirit. My treasure is on this altar, my heart will be in the ciborium, or rather my heart shall be eternally united to Thy Sacred Heart which will henceforth be my sanctuary, my place of abode. "This is my rest forever and ever; here will I dwell, for I have chosen it" (Psalms CXXXI, 14).

Penetrated with these loving sentiments, and full of confidence, we should sometimes say to Him with great simplicity, but respectfully and familiarly: Thou art present here, O Lord, for the sole purpose of conferring Thy favors on me, what is the obstacle that prevents Thee from doing so? If it be my imperfections, deign Thou to begin to deliver me from them; heal those wounds which render me displeasing in Thy sight. Hitherto, I have not loved Thee, it is true, I am grievously sorry and now desire to love Thee sincerely, and, as proof of my sincerity, I will come often to visit Thee and ask Thee, Who seest the depths of my heart, for Thy love; and until I am all inflamed with this love, I will never cease to ask Thee for it earnestly and perseveringly. "I will love Thee, O Lord, my strength and my refuge" (Psalms XVII, 1, 2).

During the visit, each one, according to his devotion, can spend some time making acts of Faith, Hope, Adoration, Thanksgiving, Reparation and Love, and might say: I believe, O Lord, that Thou art really present on this altar; in Thy divine presence I humbly offer Thee my reverence and respect as a proof that I believe; I thank Thee for having loved me so much as to wait on the altar all these centuries for my visit; humbly prostrate at Thy feet, I make Thee an act of reparation for all the indignities and outrages which Thou hast suffered since the institution of this august Sacrament. I hope in Thee, O Lord, and I am sure that Thy Providence will never fail me in my wants, but that it will guide me happily in the accomplishment of Thy designs by the way that is most pleasing to Thee. Open to me, O Lord, Thy Sacred Heart, for It is my place of refuge; I wish to remain in It all my life and in It to give forth my last sigh at the hour of my death. Other acts can be made during the visit according to each one's devotion.

To conclude the treatment of this subject, we give here the advice of St. Francis de Sales: "Many people have made a collection of aspirations which indeed are very useful; but, in my opinion, you should not confine yourself to any set formula of words, you can express with your heart or with your lips those sentiments which love will suggest to you, for love will furnish you with all the aspirations which you desire. It is true that there are certain forms of words which have a particular efficacy to content in the heart in the Divine Presence, such as the aspirations of love, etc., found all through the Psalms of David, the various invocations of the holy Name of Jesus, and the aspirations of love found in the Canticle of Canticles. Hymns are useful also to excite devotion provided they are sung with attention." (Introduction to the Devout Life, Part II, Chapter XIII.)

III

PRACTICE FOR DAILY VISIT TO THE BLESSED SACRAMENT OF A QUARTER OF AN HOUR OR HALF AN HOUR, SUITABLE FOR ALL CLASSES OF PEOPLE

This practice of devotion is easy, since it consists chiefly in loving Jesus Christ and in making use of Jesus Christ Himself to love Him. We give the following suggestions for spending the time of the visit:

(1) Salute Jesus Christ in this mystery with all the respect which His Real Presence demands; then unite yourself to Him and to all His divine operations in the Blessed Eucharist, in which He never ceases to adore, praise and love God, His Father, in the name of all men, in the most perfect way possible, namely, in the state of victim. Then meditate on and try to form an idea of His recollection, His solitude, His hidden life, the complete privation of all things to which He is reduced, His obedience to the word of the humblest priest, His humility, and His other virtues according to the model which He gives us of them in this His Eucharistic state. Then excite yourself to imitate these virtues and resolve to do so when opportunities offer. Dwell especially on the admirable dispositions of His Sacred Heart in our favor, and on all the sublime virtues of which It is the source; the immense love of that divine Heart for the eternal Father and the ardent charity for all men with which It burns and Its eagerness for their salvation. Then endeavor to discover in this divine Heart all the abysses which It contains; abysses of humiliation, of abasement, of poverty, of suffering, of love, of consolation, of sweetness, of conformity with the will of God, of mercy, of strength, of knowledge, of abundance, of gratitude, of meekness, of holy joy, of confidence . . . Consider then what are the sentiments of His holy Soul at the sight of the ingratitude of men who have nothing but indifference for Him; excite yourself to acts of reparation; resolve by your gratitude and especially by your ardent love for Jesus Christ to make reparation for all these indignities, to the utmost of your capacity.

(2) Offer to the Eternal Father Jesus Christ His Son, as the only Victim worthy of Him, by which Victim alone we can render homage to His supreme dominion, recognize His benetits, satisfy His justice, and oblige His mercy to come to your assistance, saying with the Prophet: "Look on the Face of Thy Christ" (Psalms LXXXIII, 10). It is true, My God, that I deserve to be treated as a rebellious servant, but look, Eternal Father, on Thy Beloved Son Who is perfectly obedient and Who at this moment is Himself offering to Thee the most profound state of abasement in which He has placed Himself to obtain for me pardon for my infidelity and my disobedience: "Look on the Face of Thy Christ." From whatever direction Thy Justice may come upon me, I will immediately present to it this

Beloved Son to disarm it. If I were to see Thy anger about to burst upon me a hundred times, a hundred times would I say to Thee the same thing: "Look on the Face of Thy Christ." For myself I have no merit, but I offer Thee a Victim of infinite merit; as all the satisfaction I can make myself is of no value in Thy sight, it is just that Thou shouldst refuse me both pardon for my sins and new graces, but I offer Thee a Victim That has made complete satisfaction to Thee: Thou canst refuse me nothing that I ask in virtue on the merits of Thy Divine Son, Jesus Christ, in virtue of His sufferings and death, the recompense for which has been transferred to us by Him, and made ours. I am asking Thee for much, O Eternal Father, but I offer Thee the Body and Blood and the very life of Thy Divine Son, which is immolated on this altar, in payment for all that I ask; and what I ask, however great it may be, will be infinitely less than what I offer to Thee.

(3) Offer yourself to God by the hands of Jesus Christ; offer to Him in sacrifice your life, your employment, your inclinations, your passions; offer in particular some act of virtue which you propose to do or some practice of mortification which you have resolved to adopt in order to conquer yourself, and offer these for the same ends for which our Savior immolates Himself in the Blessed Sacrament.

(4) Offer yourself to Jesus Christ to be united more closely to Him, asking Him to fill you with His spirit and His sentiments, and above all, ask Him to be permitted to enter His Sacred Heart never to leave It. Then consider Jesus Christ as your Head, and yourself as one of His members, as one of His associates, one of His brethren to whom He has given over all His merits and bequeathed all the recompense due to Him from His Heavenly Father for His holy labors and death on the cross. It is in this capacity of associate of the Eternal Word, of one of His brethren, of His members, that we dare to appear before God with confidence, to speak to Him familiarly, and in union with the Eternal Word, in a manner, to oblige Him to give us a favorable hearing, to grant our requests and bestow on us His graces in virtue of this association, this union which we have with His Divine Son and, in particular, in virtue of the infinite value and dignity of the Victim which we offer to Him in the Blessed Sacrament. Then finish the visit by a Spiritual Communion, accompanied by a perfect consecration of all

your affections and desires to the Sacred Heart.

This kind of prayer is excellent; we should make ourselves very familiar with it, because our happiness in this life depends on our union. with Jesus Christ in the Blessed Sacrament. It would be desirable that we use this method of prayer before the Blessed Sacrament once a day but especially for certain hours of the afternoon when Jesus Christ is rarely visited.

The following is another very useful method of prayer for visits to the Blessed Sacrament: Make an act of faith in Jesus Christ present on the altar and adore Him; then excite yourself to acts of fervent love and ask our Savior to inflame you daily more and more with His love. Then endeavor to enter into yourself and see the state of your soul, its defects, its passions, its weakness, its infirmities, and represent all these miseries to Jesus Christ very simply. Submit yourself entirely to His holy Will, and bless Him equally for the chastisements of His Justice as for the favors which you receive from His Mercy. Humble yourself before his Sovereign Majesty, confess to Him sincerely your infidelities and sins; ask His pardon for them, make acts of sorrow for your sins and resolve to amend your life.

Then enter into the adorable Heart of Jesus Christ and consider Its sentiments; Its contempt for all that the world esteems, for all the vain honors, for the fleeting goods of this earth, and those pleasures that, so far from satisfying the heart, fill it with bitterness. At the same time consider the esteem of the Sacred Heart for all that the world rejects; how It regards poverty, obscurity, humiliations and contempt as precious favors. Who is deceived? Is it those who esteem and love passionately all that Jesus Christ despises, or Jesus Christ, who holds in the greatest contempt and has expressly condemned all that worldlings seek after so eagerly? Reflections like these, when seriously made, will help to disabuse us of numerous false ideas by which we are deceived, and will inspire us with the true wisdom which we admire in all the Saints.

This method of prayer is very useful and leaves us free in the choice of affections. It can be used at any time; but it is especially suitable when something unforseen happens to us; it helps us to submit ourselves to the chastisements of the Justice of God, and to put ourselves in a state of recollection after distracting occupations.

Finally, if we visit Jesus Christ frequently in the Sacrament of

His love, we shall learn from Him how to make the visit well, and we shall infallibly taste the ineffable pleasure that is found in conversing with our amiable Savior, with this most lovable Person in all creation, with this, our truest Friend Who loves us most tenderly. We shall never grow weary conversing with Him; only those who do not know the divine sweetness of His presence are embarrassed about spending the time of the visit, about making acts of faith and love and asking the graces they stand in need of. If we are unhappy in this world, it is because we do not know how fortunate we are; we do not know Him Who is in the midst of us, for if we knew Him, could we help loving Him ardently? Can we have any love for Him if we visit Him but rarely?

IV

SOME SUGGESTIONS FOR THOSE WHO VISIT THE BLESSED SACRAMENT FREQUENTLY

The following suggestions will, we trust, enable those who visit the Blessed Sacrament frequently to derive abundant fruit from these visits:

(1) Never enter a church in which the Blessed Sacrament is reserved without great reverence, as an outward sign of your faith and of your veneration for the holiness of the place. All that is needed for this is a moment's reflection on what you are doing. A humble and respectful posture, a reverential air accompanied by interior recollection are splendid dispositions, and are most necessary in order to receive the tender caresses of Jesus Christ.

(2) Vocal prayers recited during the visit should be short but tender and affectionate; the simplest and least affected are best; prayers during the visit should come from the heart.

(3) Although every time is suitable for the discharging of our duties and paying our homage to Jesus Christ in the tabernacle, there are certain hours of the day and certain days of the year when our visits are most pleasing to Him. These hours are the morning for Religious and Ecclesiastics who have the Blessed Sacrament in their own house, and the afternoon for all classes of people. For the former, who have the Blessed Sacrament in their houses, diligence in paying a visit as soon as they have

risen in the morning will infallibly bring very special blessings. This alacrity which they show in going and adoring Jesus Christ as soon as possible, and in being the first to pay homage to Him, is extremely pleasing to Him. We know that if a servant or a friend or a child showed the same alacrity and ardor and diligence towards ourselves, he would be sure to gain our hearts; judge, then, what sentiments these dispositions must excite in our favor in the loving Heart of this amiable Savior. This fervor and punctuality will draw down upon us from Jesus Christ the special graces which we stand in need of during the day for the proper discharge of the duties of our state of life. This eagerness to give the first moments of the day, to our Lord in the Blessed Sacrament, as is right and just, is certainly not the characteristic mark of ungenerous, imperfect souls who have hardly any love for Jesus Christ, but is the result of ardent love of Jesus Christ and will infallibly lead to a further increase in His love.

(4) The afternoon is also a most propitious time for visiting our Divine Lord in the Blessed Sacrament and showing Him that we love Him, and is a time when He confers great graces on those who come to Him, for during several hours of the afternoon He is rarely visited; in fact, He is almost completely forgotten. As at such times it is neither the crowds, nor custom, not human respect that brings us, but love for Jesus Christ, He will be more liberal than usual to us with His graces; this custom of visiting Our Lord when He is most abandoned has gained for some of the great Saints such special graces as have enabled them in a short time to reach the highest perfection.

(5) Besides the great Festivals which are consecrated to the service of God, there are certain other days on which our Divine Lord wishes His friends to pay special visits to Him. These are days of amusement, such as the Carnival, when the minds of most people are completely occupied with pleasure, and times when God is very much offended. Those generous and faithful friends of Jesus Christ who consecrate these days to visiting Him in His abandonment will receive His choicest graces, graces so great that they have brought many of the Saints who were faithful to this custom to the pinnacle of sanctity.

(6) You should never leave the divine presence of Jesus in the Blessed Sacrament without saying to Him with Jacob: "I

will not let Thee go except Thou bless me" (Genesis XXXII, 26).

(7) Remember always to have reverence for the church or oratory in which Jesus Christ resides; do not let yourself be outdone by worldlings, who show such obsequious respect and courtesy in the houses of the great.

(8) Never forget to pay some special homage at each visit to the Sacred Heart of Jesus; offer your heart to Jesus and beg Him to unite it altogether to His Own, so that the two hearts may henceforth form but one.

(9) A final word of advice suitable to all is: that the best way to become recollected, spiritual, and solidly virtuous is to visit Jesus Christ in the Blessed Sacrament frequently, and to make those visits with great reverence, simplicity and confidence, speaking little, listening to Him attentively and loving Him tenderly like people, who know and believe that they are really visiting Jesus Christ.

Chapter V

The Holy Mass

As there is no form of worship on earth that gives more honor to God than the holy Sacrifice of the Mass, the celebration of each Mass should be regarded as the greatest and the most important event in the whole world. In this Mystery, everything is great, everything stupendous; the power of God shown in the Mass is infinite, His love excessive, His patience extreme. Everything in connection with it should excite admiration and reverence. We know that God has the power to perform the miracles demanded by the Mass, and He has given us most convincing proofs that He has willed to do so. But in the light of this, what should appear most incredible and amazing is to see any priest at the altar without gravity, devotion and reverence, or any of the laity assisting at these dread Mysteries only to profane them by their want of reverence, the uncleanliness of their hearts, the distraction of their minds and the wandering of their senses.

We can understand that a man may carry ingratitude to the extent of despising the gifts of another man, but we cannot understand how a man, who every day has the happiness of conversing familiarly with Jesus Christ, of holding Him in his hands and distributing Him to the faithful, should set no value on such a sublime dignity, or how he can treat Jesus Christ with coldness and indifference; how, while believing in the real presence of Jesus Christ in the Mass, he can ascend the altar filled with many serious imperfections and without devotion or love, and how he is as little moved by the excellence and sublime dignity of this adorable Mystery when he has finished as when he began.

The priest at the altar is the mediator between God and man; he treats with God in the name of the whole Church, and he offers to God a victim proportioned to the benefits which we have received from Him and to those which we may ask for; a victim capable of taking away all the sins of the world, a victim, finally, infinitely pleasing to God and certain to be heard. In spite of all this, are there not some priests on whom this most holy and exalted ministry makes no impression? Are there not found some, who are not known to be priests except when they are seen at the altar, and who even at the altar dishonor the sanctity of their ministry by their want of devotion?

Is not the haste with which some offer this dread Sacrifice a visible proof of their little faith? They spend whole hours with pleasure in useless conversation, and they find difficulty in remaining half an hour in the company of Jesus Christ! Is it possible that Jesus Christ is the only one that causes them ennui?

If the severity of the account which we shall have to render at Judgment is in proportion to the sublimity of our calling and to the graces which we have received; and if, in order to be saved, our virtue must correspond to our state of life and to our ministry, has not a priest of only mediocre virtue, who has offered this adorable Sacrifice thousands of times, and who is not more devout, but, perhaps, more imperfect than before his ordination, reason to fear the formidable judgments of God? And can he, who remains unmoved even while he holds the Body and Blood of Jesus Christ in his hands, hope that there is anything in the world capable of touching his heart?

The priesthood is, indeed, one of the most sublime dignities and the most excellent favors that God has ever conferred on a mere creature; it is evident that this exalted dignity demands men of great virtue. Although the virtue of the Anchorites who lived at the time of St. John Chrysostom had reached very high perfection, and although many of them had the gift of miracles, this Saint said that their virtue was as much below what is proper and necessary to the state of the priesthood, as the condition of a private citizen is below the majesty of a king.

Great graces are required to arrive at this high state of virtue. But has not the priest all-powerful means at his disposal of acquiring this virtue? Is not the Mass an infallible means of obtaining all kinds of graces?

Blessed Claude de la Colombiere, who had an extraordinary devotion to the Mass, writes as follows:

"When I pray or fast or give alms, I do so with distrust; I say to myself: I dishonor God more, perhaps, by my bad intentions, by the circumstances of my action, than I honor Him by what I do; this penance which I perform, far from effacing my sins needs, perhaps, another penance. But when I say Mass or hear Mass, when I offer the adorable Sacrifice either as a minister of God or as a member of the Church, I can then, full of confidence and courage, O my God, challenge Heaven to do anything which can please Thee more; then, without being terrified either by the number or enormity of my crimes, I dare to ask pardon for them, doubting not that Thou wilt grant it to me in a more perfect manner than I could desire. However vast my desires may be, however great my hopes, I make no difficulty in asking all that can satisfy them. I ask for great graces, for all kinds of graces, for myself, for my friends and for my most deadly enemies; and, far from blushing at my *demands or being distrustful that I may not receive so many things at the same time, I find that I ask for little in comparison with what I offer: I even believe that I do wrong to this living Victim by asking infinitely less than It is worth.*

I fear nothing so much as not to hope firmly and perseveringly both for all that I have asked for, and something still greater, if possible, than all that I have asked for. Would to God that we might know the value of the treasure we have in our hands! Happy a thousand times are those Catholic countries that know how to take advantage of their greatest treasure! What a source of all kinds of blessings do we not find in this adorable Sacrifice! What graces, what favors, what temporal and eternal wealth for the body, for the soul, for this life, for eternity! But we must confess the truth, we do not even think of making use of our riches, we do not even deign to put our hand into the treasure which Jesus Christ has left us.

We have here at our disposal a remedy for all kinds of evils, a Tree of Life, which can give us not only health, but even immortality; and nevertheless, we are weighed down with infirmities! When you assist at Mass, if you wish to profit by it, you will obtain for yourself what you would have obtained on Calvary, if you had been present: if you had been on Calvary you would not have been refused pardon for your sins; the effect of the Holy Mass is the same.

Jesus Christ in the Mass puts Himself in our hands as a Victim of infinite value to obtain for us from God all that we can desire, however great or precious it may be. In the Sacrifice of the Mass, Jesus Christ not only makes Himself our Intercessor with His Heavenly Father to ask by His merits all that we desire, but He offers His Blood and His merits in payment for all we ask for. What can you desire, however great it is, that is of less value than that which you present in order to receive it? How comes it then that all people complain; some of their temporal misfortunes, others of their defects and imperfections? Whence comes it that our passions tyrannize over us, that our bad habits hold us chained; that one is troubled with vain desires, and that another succumbs to temptations so often; that anger and impatience carry away some, while others are overwhelmed by grief and chagrin? How comes it that this woman cannot soften her husband or maintain peace in the family, that the majority, even of those who make profession of piety, pass their lives with gross imperfections and especially with extreme tepidity in the service of God? People wish to correct their own faults and reform those of others, nevertheless they do neither the one nor the other. They are like a miser who lives in want of everything, although he is rolling in wealth.

Have you asked for your needs at the Mass as you should? How many times have you heard it for this intention? Can it be thought that God would refuse such a small thing for such a great price, that He would have set so little value on the Blood and the Life of His Divine Son, that He did not think that it was worth this grace, this virtue, this temporal or spiritual good which you desire for yourself or for someone else if it conduce to salvation? Is is possible that you have asked sincerely for a great love of Jesus Christ and that Jesus Christ has refused you? No, I will never believe it and I am sure that you do not believe it yourself. What is the reason then? It is that we neglect to assist at the holy Sacrifice of the Mass and to present our miseries to God with simplicity and confidence during this precious and acceptable time, and to ask of Him the graces which we stand in need of. Finally, the reason of our remaining in want in the midst of plenty is that we do not offer or assist at this adorable Sacrifice like people who believe in it and who reflect on what they believe."

II

PRACTICE FOR THOSE WHO OFFER UP THE HOLY SACRIFICE

If the priest is aware of the excellence of his state and the sublime holiness of his ministry, he will never approach the altar without holy fear, or leave it without infinite gratitude. God is more honored by a single Mass than He would be by all the actions of men and angels, however fervent or heroic they might be. We should then consider the offering up of the Mass as the greatest and most important function of our life, and perform it with all possible perfection. All the employments with which God honors the angels are of less excellence and dignity than this: to say a Mass is something greater than to govern the whole universe, or to raise the dead to life or to perform the greatest miracles. Judge then what preparation and thanksgiving should be made for so holy a function!

The whole life of the priest ought to be spent in preparation and thanksgiving for the holy Mass. A priest should do nothing which is not referred to the saying of Holy Mass, or to thanksgiving for it; that is to say, that all his words and actions ought to be so holy that they can serve as dispositions for the celebration of these divine Mysteries or as continuous proofs of his gratitude and love. There is no one on earth who, by his ministry, approaches so near to the Person of Christ; there is no one who ought to resemble Him more by the holiness of his life. Hence, the purity and holiness of his life should be the principal preparation; without these all other preparations are defective.

The priest's preparation for the celebration of Mass should

begin as soon as he gets up, his thanksgiving should end only with the day; the time which immediately precedes or follows the Mass should be employed in deeper recollection — renewing the intention which we should have in offering this adorable Sacrifice, and endeavoring to render ourselves less unworthy of what we are going to do or of what we have done by acts of faith, of contrition, of humility, of thanksgiving and of love.

The priest going to the altar should consider himself no longer as a man, but as Jesus Christ Who is about to speak by the priest's mouth and offer Himself by his hands: thus he should do no exterior act of the Mass of which we could not say: "Behold an act of Jesus Christ"; he should be extremely exact in observing the smallest ceremonies, if that can be called little which serves in the celebration of the greatest and most august of all sacrifices. He should perform these ceremonies with an air of grandeur and majesty, and with such modesty that his very bearing and presence will inspire all with awe and reverence; he should offer this adorable Sacrifice in a manner so grave, so devout and respectful, that Almighty God will be honored by it, that Jesus Christ will be recognized in the person of His minister, and that all who assist, will be edified.

As Jesus Christ immolates Himself and offers Himself up in sacrifice by the hands of His minister, His minister should offer himself up and immolate himself with Jesus Christ. He is chosen and deputed by the whole Church to render the homage of adoration to God, to thank Him for His benefits, to appease His anger and implore His mercy. He should acquit himself with care of his commission, especially after the Consecration; it is then that he should, like Moses, tie the hands of God's justice (if we may use the expression).

It is then, that he should recognize by means of this precious Victim the infinite greatness of this first Being, and should especially annihilate himself before Him as the Son of God does at the altar; it is then, that he ought to represent to Him all the necessities of the people, feeling sure that he will obtain all that he asks because he offers up a Victim of infinite value and a Victim eminently acceptable to God.

We are not to be surprised that the Apostles and disciples

who conversed familiarly with Jesus Christ received great graces, but we should be surprised that a priest at the altar is not all-powerful, that he should only love Jesus Christ imperfectly, and be little touched with devotion when offering the Holy Sacrifice.

The priest can be in the company of Jesus Christ whenever he wishes and for as long as he wishes; but, unfortunately, many priests do not like to be long in His company.

We sometimes complain that we have no tender love or sensible devotion at the altar; but do we lead pure lives and practice interior recollection? If priests celebrate the Holy Sacrifice hurriedly and are eager to have it over quickly, they do not allow Jesus Christ to make them feel the sweet effects of His presence and much less to let His voice be heard.

Lively faith and serious reflection on his ministry will teach the priest how to say Mass as he should. The priest takes the place of Jesus Christ and should, therefore, say Mass as Jesus Christ would say it. The realization of this great fact alone should make the priest celebrate with the greatest devotion. During the celebration of Mass he should say to himself from time to time: I represent Jesus Christ here at the altar, I speak in the name of Jesus Christ, I hold Jesus Christ in my hands. This thought will help to give the priest at the altar that grave majestic air which this holiest of functions demands and which the faithful who assist at Mass expect of him.

Devotion to the Sacred Heart of Jesus is a most effective means of making priests say Mass with great reverence, in the first place because the object of the devotion is most proper to excite sentiments of reverence during Mass and, secondly, because Jesus Christ has attached to the devotion very special graces to help priests to perform the duties of their state. It is the experience of priests who practice devotion to the Sacred Heart of Jesus that it inspires them with sentiments of love and reverence during the celebration of Mass such as they have never previously experienced; faith becomes more lively, and love for Jesus Christ increases perceptibly.

During the celebration of Mass the priest should attend carefully to the following:

(1) To say Mass with attention and avoid haste; haste to leave

the altar is a visible sign that the company of Jesus Christ is irksome to the priest; an extra ten minutes at very most would ensure that the Mass be said with due reverence: is it not a great pity that any priest should, for such a small thing, deprive himself all his life of the fruit of the grandest, holiest, and most important of all his functions?

(2) Each time he says Mass, to make an act of reparation to Jesus Christ by means of the holy Sacrifice for the outrages and indignities which He suffers in the Mass and in the Blessed Eucharist;

(3) To thank Jesus Christ for all the benefits and all the graces which He has conferred on the Blessed Virgin; this act of thanksgiving is very pleasing to Him;

(4) To ask Him with great simplicity and confidence for many things and, above all, for His perfect love; the priest should say to Him sometimes: O Lord, make me a saint, all the glory for it will be Thine; Thou wilt find everywhere more worthy subjects for Thy graces than I, but I make bold to say that Thou wilt find none more grateful; "I have found him Whom my soul loveth. I held Him and I will not let Him go" (Cant. III, 4). Permit me, O Lord, to say to Thee: however great the benefits which Thou hast conferred on me, Thou hast not given me enough, if Thou dost not give me Thy love. O my Divine Savior, give me a heart like Thine Own, give me Thy Heart.

Truly, a priest who does not feel the effects of a Sacrifice which is sufficient to blot out the sins of the whole world has great reason to fear. My God, what great graces Thou dost pour out on a soul that is well disposed! And who can express the sweetness that Thou dost make Thy devout priests experience at the Altar?

Blessed Claude de la Colombiere writes what he himself experienced at the altar, as follows:

"I have received such great graces and I have felt the effects of this Bread of Angels so perceptibly that I cannot think of it without being touched with the greatest gratitude. From the celebration of the Mass, I have conceived great confidence that I shall persevere in good and in the desire which I have to belong entirely to God, notwithstanding the terrible difficulties that present themselves to my imagination during the course of my life. I shall say Mass every day, that is my hope, that is my only resource. The power of Jesus Christ would indeed be very little, if He were not able to sustain me from day to day; He will not fail to reproach me for my slothfulness as soon as I begin to relax my efforts; every day He will give me fresh advice and new strength: He will instruct me, console me, encourage me, and grant me, or obtain for me by His Sacrifice, all the graces which I ask from Him. If I do not see that He is present, I feel Him; it seems to me that I am like one of the blind men who threw themselves at His feet and who doubted not that they touched Him, although they did not see Him."

Such is the way in which priests should celebrate Mass, and such are the sentiments which ought to animate them in the presence of Jesus Christ.

III

PRACTICE FOR THE FAITHFUL WHO ASSIST AT MASS

The faithful who assist at Mass should be convinced that there is no action which they should perform with such respect, attention, and devotion as this act of assisting at Mass. As the Mass is really and truly the representation of the Sacrifice of the Cross, and at the same time the real Sacrifice of the same Victim that was immolated on Calvary; that is to say, of Jesus Christ Who offers Himself still to His Eternal Father as a holocaust in expiation for our crimes, and as He applies to us the price of His Blood poured out on Calvary for us on the Cross, we should assist at the Mass with the same sentiments we would have had if we had been present at the death of our Savior on Calvary; or rather, we should try to enter into the sentiments which our Blessed Lady and the Beloved Disciple then had.

Modesty, recollection, silence, a humble posture, and profound respect are necessary dispositions; but they must be animated by a lively faith. We must recollect that we are in a place sanctified by the presence of Jesus Christ and filled with the majesty of God Whom we ask for the graces of which we stand in need. We are assisting at a sacrifice of which Jesus Christ is the Victim and it is for us that this Sacrifice is offered. How great then ought to be our respect and confidence!

We should carefully avoid everything capable of distracting our attention from what is taking place at the altar, for of all the ways for hearing Mass, the holiest way, and the one most in conformity with the spirit of the Church is to follow the actions of the priest. Vocal prayers are very useful when they are said with devotion, but they should not occupy the whole time of the Mass; we should not make ourselves troublesome by speaking all the time, we should stop and listen from time to time to hear what the Lord speaks to us. We should imitate the poor; they tell about their miseries, hold out their hands and then remain in silence waiting for alms. This silence during the time of the Holy Sacrifice is not lost time; it is a mark of alertness and attention in the presence of God and of humble confidence in His mercy. Some serious reflections on what is taking place on the altar, and acts of faith in the truth of this Mystery will not fail to excite in us great devotion.

But it may be said that of all the ways of hearing Mass the way which the devotion to the Sacred Heart suggests is one of the most useful. It consists chiefly in interior acts. Immediately after the Consecration, animated with a lively faith, adore Jesus Christ with the sentiments of a person who has come to Mass to offer Him his homage and to make atonement for all the indignities, contempt and outrages to which His love has exposed Him in the august Sacrament. Then adore His Sacred Heart, and thank the Divine Savior for all the love with which His Sacred Heart burns and the admirable dispositions of this Heart towards us; then enter into this Divine Heart to admire all the treasures of virtues and graces which It contains. Admire in It the most profound humility imaginable, the most heroic patience that is proof against the most vexatious treatment, excessive meekness towards all, infinite sorrow for our sins with which He consented to be laden; contemplate there the infinite zeal for the glory of His Father and love for all men, the solicitude, zeal and extreme eagerness for men's salvation and for yourself in particular; think of what must be the sentiments of Jesus Christ on this altar at the sight of so much contempt and so many outrages; and penetrated with sentiments of love and gratitude, from the depths of a heart moved to generosity, tell Him of your sorrow and your love. If you do not receive Holy Communion, dispose yourself for a spiritual Communion, which consists in an ardent desire to receive Jesus Christ sacramentally in order to make reparation by your sentiments of reverence and love for the coldness, insensibility and want of proper dispositions with which many receive Him.

It is strange that Catholics are found who feel wearied and who do not know how to occupy the time of Mass; they are like a sick person who gets annoyed at seeing someone working efficaciously to cure his malady, or like a man burdened with heavy debt who does not know what to do in presence of a powerful Monarch who offers him all His treasures. Blessed Claude de la Colombiere expresses this thought very forcibly in his sermon on the Mass. He says: "What! Have you never received any favor from the good God? We all are actually surrounded with, laden down and overwhelmed with God's benefits, and we have never thanked Him as we ought; so many dangers averted, so many crimes overlooked, such an amiable and constant exercise of Providence over us, such sweet and continual eagerness to draw us to Himself, to gain our hearts, and make us saints. The list of the graces which you receive in a single day would suffice to occupy you during the whole time of Mass. Do not all these favors deserve to be thought over again and again? Having then recalled to your mind all these benefits, say boldly to the Eternal Father: Behold the immense benefits which I have received from Thee; but look upon this Victim, this Divine Body, this Precious Blood, this adorable Sacrifice. Behold what I render to Thee for all Thy benefits; I can have no doubt that they are well repaid by such a magnificent Offering. But what can I give Thee, O my adorable Master for having given me the means by which I can requite Thy Heavenly Father liberally for all His benefits, and expiate all my sins? I have but one heart to offer Thee, wilt Thou deign to accept it, this heart disturbed by so many passions and sullied by so many sins? At least it is broken with sorrow; in this state I offer it to Thee. Thou dost open Thy Divine Heart to me, Thou dost give It to me, could I dare, O my amiable Savior, to refuse Thee mine? O God of majesty, who am I that Thou shouldst deign to accept the sacrifice of my heart? It will henceforth belong to Thee, creatures will have no more share in it. Be, then, my amiable Jesus, my Father, my Friend, my All: since Thou deignest to be content with my heart could it be otherwise than content with Thine? Henceforth, I wish only to live for Thee; receive, then, my most amiable Savior, the sacrifice which the most ungrateful of men offers to Thee, to repair the wrong which up to the present moment I have never ceased to do Thee by offending

Thee?"

"You say that you do not know what to do during the Mass! Have you never offended God? Do you not offend Him every day and every hour of the day? Go over in your mind during the Mass all the faults of which you have been guilty since the previous Mass. Ask pardon of Jesus. But have you no favor to ask for? You are complaining every day of your relatives, your friends, your children; ask God to make this enemy of yours more reasonable, this daughter more modest, this husband less passionate, ask Him to change the heart of this son; ask for yourself greater meekness, more patience, more courage and zeal for your salvation, but ask especially for the perfect love of God; and in order to obtain all these things, offer to Him Jesus Christ on the altar; it cannot be that He will refuse you, for what you offer is worth infinitely more than all that you can ask for.

It is strange that the Lord cannot fill His house, except by using threats,* except by compelling† (in a certain sense) people to enter; but it is still more strange that we enter so often into the House of the Lord, that we assist every day at the most august of all sacrifices, and that we derive no fruit from it, that we do not even know of the ineffable fruits which we might have derived. This want of knowledge is one of the things most to be deplored in the Catholic Church. What a misfortune to live in want, while we have an immense and inexhaustible treasure at our disposal, but do not know about it! But is it not a still greater misfortune if we know about this treasure and derive no advantage from it?"

*John VI, 64.   †Luke XIV, 23.

Chapter VI

Holy Communion

As the Blessed Eucharist is the greatest and most sacred of all the Sacraments, the use which we make of It is the most important concern of our lives as Christians; consequently, this Sacrament demands more care and application for its worthy reception than anything else in the temporal or spiritual order. If we were only to receive Holy Communion once in our whole lives, even if we lived to the age of those before the Deluge, our whole life would not be too much to spend in preparation for the worthy participation in so holy and so awe-inspiring a Mystery. That consideration should not, however, keep us away from the holy Table, but should urge us to have the proper dispositions for approaching. We should not, therefore, say: I do not wish to receive Holy Communion because I feel that I am unworthy; we should rather say: I wish to endeavor by every means in my power, by the holiness of my life and by my upright conduct, to render myself worthy of receiving Communion. We will approach in a worthy manner, if we believe that we are unworthy and at the same time do all in our power to make ourselves worthy. One good Holy Communion would suffice to make a saint, and all that is required to make it good is a good will and serious consideration on the greatness of this Sacrament.

Those who receive Holy Communion without becoming more devout, more mortified, more recollected, without making any increase in the love of Jesus Christ are in a more dangerous state than they think. What would we think of people who conversed frequently with Jesus Christ, ate at the same table with Him daily, and who did not become daily more virtuous? Would any hope remain for the cure of sick people whom Jesus Christ did not heal when they were presented to Him?

Death and famine are not the most terrible chastisements by which God sometimes punishes His people; the most dreadful, says the Prophet Isaias, is when He threatens to make them die of hunger in the midst of an abundant harvest; they will press many grapes without getting a drop of wine: "For behold, the Lord of hosts shall take away from Jerusalem and from Juda the whole strength of bread and the whole strength of water" (Isaias III, 1). Behold the most terrible of all chastisements; the bread which you eat will have no more strength for you, you will eat much and nevertheless you will die of languor and weakness, you will die of hunger.

However dangerous the malady may be, there is always some hope as long as the person can have recourse to the last remedies; but when the most powerful remedies have been applied several times without effect, what would be our sentiments about the malady? If we were sick, and if we had taken the most excellent of all remedies without any effect, we would tremble with fear, we would believe that we should surely die! But we have received the Adorable Body and the Precious Blood hundreds of times, perhaps, and if there is no fruit, have we reason to be satisfied with ourselves? This want of fruit from Holy Communion may come from several sources; each one should examine himself on this point.

The general dispositions which we should bring to Holy Communion are profound humility, sincere acknowledgment of our nothingness, spiritual hunger, which is at the same time a sign that we need this heavenly nourishment and a proof that we wish to profit by it, great purity of heart, ardent love for Jesus Christ, or at least an ardent desire to love Him and to carry out the designs He had in giving Himself to us in the Blessed Eucharist, which are to unite us more intimately to Him by perfect conformity of heart and mind with Him. Those who at Communion have no feeling of devotion, no fervor, no tender love, assuredly lack some of these dispositions.

It is a common defect of people who receive Holy Communion often that they do not make sufficient preparation. Prayer books give a great choice of excellent methods for preparing well for Holy Communion; each can choose the one that suits him best. The means suggested by the devotion to the Sacred Heart of Jesus will suit everyone; experience shows that there is, perhaps, no other practice so helpful to communicate well as this devotion. But all these practices should be accompanied by serious reflection on the admirable qualities of this Divine Nourishment which we are going to receive. Great purity of life, generous mortification, the gifts of the Holy Ghost which are the recompense of perfect mortification, imitation of the virtues which we admire and love in Jesus Christ are dispositions which will ensure great fruit from Holy Communion. We should imagine that the Communion for which we are preparing is to be the last of our life, and we should bring to each Holy Communion the same preparation as if, on leaving the Holy Table, we were to pass from this life to eternity.

If we wish that the Sacrament of the Blessed Eucharist produce in us sentiments of love for God, let us reflect on the immense love which God had for us when He instituted this Mystery, and His design to draw us on through it to His perfect love. This excessive eagerness about external things which

Jesus Christ reproved in Martha should teach those uneasy people who are completely occupied in reciting many vocal prayers that tranquillity of heart, interior recollection, and listening attentively from time to time to Jesus Christ after the example of Mary Magdalen, are the better part. Accordingly, we should employ the greater part of this precious time which precedes, accompanies, and follows immediately after Holy Communion in making many interior acts, principally acts of the love of God; these acts will have the effect of increasing the love of God in our hearts. We can recite vocal prayers before Holy Communion, but let us spend at least a quarter of an hour in reflecting seriously on the great act which we are about to perform. If a man is persuaded that he is going to receive Jesus Christ, if he desires eagerly to do so and seriously reflects on it, he cannot fail to be profoundly moved.

The fact that a prince comes in disguise diminishes in no way the reverence due to him in those who really believe him to be a prince; a remarkable favor which he confers, or a special proof of love which he gives while he is in disguise, will make us love him all the more, especially if it is in order to render us some important service that he has adopted the disguise. Apply this to Jesus Christ: "Jerusalem, if thou didst know Who it is that comes to visit thee, and the blessings which thou couldst have reaped from this visit!" Consider above all that you are about to receive the adorable Body of Jesus Christ with His Sacred Wounds which He allowed His disciples to touch, and with this Body, you are about to receive His Sacred Heart.

It is into this Sacred Heart Which is opened to us that we are about to enter; in this Sacred Heart we are to learn how to pray, to thank our God, to praise Him, to annihilate ourselves in His presence, but above all to love Him. How many miracles will not Jesus Christ operate during these precious moments in a pure soul, in a soul that truly loves Him! The very thought of this Sacred Heart will make us feel extraordinary devotion at Holy Communion.

If Jesus Christ on entering into our souls gives us perceptible marks of His presence, as happens ordinarily to those who have a tender devotion to His Sacred Heart, let us profit by these precious moments, let us observe great interior recollection, let us listen to Our Divine Lord and lovingly receive His graces.

Jesus Christ will work miracles in our souls if we do not prevent Him from acting in us, by our voluntary distractions and dissipation, by which the devil seeks to deprive us of the fruit of Holy Communion.

The occupation of a fervent soul during this precious time should be principally to abandon itself completely to the love of this Divine Savior and to enjoy the sweet effects of His presence. A sincere and tender love is, at the same time, the best disposition for receiving Holy Communion, and the principal fruit that we should derive from it. Usually we keep silence in the presence of Jesus Christ when we love Him much, and we show our love for Him by fervent interior acts. St. Mary Magdalen, seated at the feet of Jesus in silent admiration, is the model for a soul which has just received Holy Communion; if it speaks at all, its words should be the expression of its love, admiration, and joy.

After receiving Holy Communion, say from time to time: "I found Him Whom my soul loveth, I held Him and I will not let Him go" (Cant. III, 4); or "my God and my All"; or "my Beloved to me and I to Him" (Cant. II, 16); or "Put me as a seal on Thy Heart" (Cant. VIII, 6); or "For what have I in heaven? And besides Thee, what do I desire upon earth?" (Psalms LXXII, 25).

We should then endeavor to enter into the sentiments of Jesus Christ and consider what He finds in us that displeases Him, what are His designs over us, what He wishes us to do, and what prevents us from carrying out His designs for us. Let us keep ourselves prostrated at His feet in spirit, and renewing our faith in His Divine Presence from time to time, let us adore Him continuously with profound respect mingled with astonishment at seeing the God of Majesty, before Whom the Seraphim tremble, abasing Himself to such an extent as to come and lodge in the heart of a man, of a sinner, and reversing the laws of nature and working an astounding miracle to accomplish this. Then passing from sentiments of admiration to those of gratitude, and recognizing our own inability to thank Him adequately, let us invite all creatures to unite with us in blessing Him; let us offer to Him the love of all the Saints and the fervor with which so many holy people receive Communion; let us offer to Him His own Divine Heart with all the immense love with which It is inflamed.

Then, with great confidence and sincerity, let us lay before Him our weakness, our misery, and our wants; we can say with Martha and Mary Magdalen: "Lord, behold, he whom Thou lovest is sick" (John XI, 3). Can I doubt of Thy love after what Thou hast just done for me? If Thou lovest me, canst Thou see my infirmities and not cure them? But, above all, canst Thou see that I love Thee so little and not inflame my heart with the sacred fire of Thy love? Even if Thou wert to refuse me all the rest, canst Thou refuse to grant me Thy perfect love? I know that I have put great obstacles to Thy merciful designs in my regard, but do Thou in Thy great mercy remove these obstacles.

Each time that we receive Holy Communion, let us not fail to make some sacrifice to Jesus Christ which will be pleasing to Him; let us promise Him that we will begin at once to correct some fault which we know displeases Him most; and let us remember that we will never experience the sensible effects of Holy Communion unless we take care to pass the rest of the day in interior recollection. In the case of those who receive Holy Communion frequently, coldness, want of generosity, distractions immediately after Holy Communion, are nearly always the signs of the unhappy state of a soul that is insensible to the greatest of all benefits, of a soul that has all the more reason to fear because it is not alive to the danger of the state of tepidity in which it is living, and is not on its guard against the false security in which it sleeps.

St. Bonaventure distinguishes eight kinds of motives which should urge the faithful to receive Holy Communion: (1) Some should receive Holy Communion because, being aware of their spiritual infirmities, they wish to be visited by the heavenly Physician Who alone is capable of curing them; (2) others, because having sinned much, they have nothing to offer to Divine Justice but this holy Victim, this Lamb without stain that taketh away the sins of the world; (3) others, because they are either overwhelmed with sorrows, or buffeted by violent temptations and have no recourse except to the God of Omnipotence Who is always ready to assist them and defend them; (4) others, who have some favor to ask of the Eternal Father and hope to obtain it by the merits of His Son, our only Mediator; (5) others, with the intention of offering this Holy Communion in gratitude for favors received; (6) others, in order to honor God and His

Saints by making this offering of their Holy Communion to God in honor of the Saints; (7) others, urged by charity for their brethren whether living or dead, employ the Blood of Jesus Christ to obtain for the living pardon for their sins, and for the dead alleviation in their sufferings; (8) finally, generous souls inflamed by a true desire of loving our Divine Savior, receive Him in the adorable Sacrament of the Blessed Eucharist in order to be still more inflamed with His love. This last motive is the most perfect and most in conformity with the designs of Jesus Christ in giving Himself to us" (St. Bonaventure, Process VII, Relig Cap. 12).

This Divine Savior comes to us in order to unite us more closely to Him; He opens to us His Heart, He gives It to us, will we dare refuse Him ours? Let us enter into this amiable Heart, and since It comes to us, let It henceforth take the place of our heart so that we will have no longer any sentiments but Its. But let us enter well into these sentiments; let us consider what Jesus Christ loves, what He esteems, what He despises; we can have no doubt that His judgment is infallible and that if we judge differently from Him, we are sure to be wrong. What does He think of these honors, these pleasures which I seek after so passionately? On the contrary, are not these humiliations, these crosses which I abhor, the object of His complacence, of His special predilection?

By these reflections we can easily discover whether the Sacred Heart of Jesus is united to ours and whether we have truly the spirit of Jesus Christ.

Chapter VII

What are the marks of perfect love of Jesus Christ and of true devotion to His Sacred Heart?

The marks of the true love of Jesus Christ are the qualities opposed to the faults which we have enumerated in Part II, Chap. II of this book. Jesus Christ is not only the object and source of all solid virtue, but He is also the most perfect model of all the virtues, and nothing except what is in conformity with this divine Model merits the name of virtue. The imperfections of people reputed to be pious do great injury to the cause of piety. Those people who pass for pious are often filled with self-love and esteem for themselves and are sensitive to the least contempt; many of them are melancholy, obstinate, moody; they are sometimes carried away by fits of anger and are unduly solicitous about their own ease and comfort. Excessive fear of injuring their health often renders them slothful, negligent, useless, extremely indulgent to themselves and always severe towards others. People of the world insensibly get accustomed to judge virtue by the imperfections of those people who pass for pious. They come to the opinion that a person cannot be pious without being melancholic, odd, obstinate, disobliging, filled with self-love and very repellent. Thus the high esteem that genuine piety should enjoy is lost through being mistaken for what is seen in the lives of the imperfect. Under this false idea, worldlings think it no great misfortune not to have the virtue accompanied by numerous defects which they see in very many who pass for pious people.

Although the inperfections of the one do not excuse the vices of the other, nevertheless it is true that they give occasion for dislike for virtue to many people who, repelled by conduct so much out of harmony with the true idea of this devotion (to the Sacred Heart), have then imagined either that the virtue of true lovers of Jesus Christ is not genuine, or that it is impossible to have true virtue. We shall endeavor here to refute this false reasoning. All the Saints refute it by the holiness of their lives. We shall confine ourselves to pointing out who are the really virtuous people by giving the unmistakable marks of true devotion and by tracing the character of a man who loves Jesus Christ perfectly.

I

THE CHARACTER OF A MAN WHO LOVES JESUS CHRIST PERFECTLY

The Character of the truly charitable man, which St. Paul sketches so beautifully in the thirteenth Chapter of his first Epistle to the Corinthians, is also the character of the man who loves Jesus Christ perfectly. St. Paul says: "If I speak with the tongues of men and angels . . . If I should have prophecy and know all mysteries and all knowledge, and if I should have all faith that could remove mountains. . . . If I should distribute all my goods to feed the poor and if I should deliver my body to be burned, and not have charity, it profiteth me nothing" (1 Cor. XIII, 1-3). True charity, he says, is "patient, is kind: charity envieth not, dealeth not perversely, is not puffed up, is not ambitious, seeketh not her own, is not provoked to anger, thinketh no evil; rejoiceth not in iniquity, but rejoiceth with the truth: beareth all things, hopeth all things, endureth all things" (ibid. 4-7). That is the character of a man of solid devotion and true virtue; if one of these traits is wanting, his devotion is defective and his love for Jesus Christ is imperfect.

A person, then, who is solidly virtuous and who loves Jesus Christ perfectly is a man without self-love, without guile, without ambition; he is a man who is at all times severe on himself, granting himself no indulgence, but kind towards others and interpreting all that they do in a good sense. He is honest without being affected, polite without being cowardly, obliging without seeking his own interest, he is extremely exact without being scrupulous, he keeps himself continually united to God without contention, he is never idle, yet never allows excessive eagerness to appear, he is never too much preoccupied or distracted with his occupations because he keeps his heart always free and is constantly concerned with the great affair of his life; his eternal salvation; like the great Saints, he will have a low idea of himself and a great respect for others, because he looks only at their virtues and does not pass judgment on their faults. Guided solely by spiritual maxims, he does not think that those who despise him do him wrong, because he does not think that the honor which men refuse him is due to him. Finally, he is a man who is never in bad humor, because he has always what he wants, and provided it is pleasing to God he never wishes for anything different; he is always content, always at peace, always even-tempered; he is neither puffed up by success nor disheartened by failure, because he knows that the blessings and the crosses of life come from the same Divine Hand, and as the will of God is his sole rule of conduct, he always does what God wishes and accepts what God sends him.

Guided by these principles, he does not seek to do what may

bring him most fame; and because he knows that what we do has no merit except insofar as it is in conformity with the wishes of God, he does not strive to accomplish much, but he endeavors to do perfectly what his Divine Master wishes him to do. Accordingly, he is constantly on his guard against his natural inclinations and his self-love, and prefers the unpretentious duties of his state of life to great actions of his own choice that suit his own tastes. Animated by this pure love for Jesus Christ, he is completely resigned to the privation of talents which it has not pleased God to give him, of virtues which God has not called him to practice, and of good that He has not wished him to do; he is equally faithful in corresponding with the graces which God gives him, and in practicing the virtues and doing the good that God puts in his way and gives him the desire to do.

Finally, he is a man who is distinguished among the multitude of the faithful by his meekness, his humility, and especially his ardent love for Jesus Christ and tender devotion to the Blessed Virgin, and by the air of sanctity about him, all of which are in themselves an excellent form of apostolate. His reverent use of the Sacraments will make him increase daily in virtue, and give him that hunger and thirst for justice of which Our Savior speaks, and being a man of faith, he never assists at the adorable Sacrifice of the Mass without sentiments of profoundest gratitude and respect. He seeks honestly to know the will of God in all circumstances which arise and is always generous with God Who has given us all things without reserve, even Himself, to induce us to refuse Him nothing. He is extremely mortified at all times, at every age of his life and in all circumstances, because he knows that our crucified Savior, Jesus Christ, is our Model in all things. Being filled with the spirit of Christ, on every occasion, both in prayer and when occupied with his duties, he endeavors to make all his opinions and all his thoughts agree with the simple will of God, which is his guide in everything, and to fix on God as on his center all the movements of his heart by a simple, loving acquiescence in His holy will.

This is the character of a truly virtuous man traced by Jesus Christ Himself, which all the Saints have so well expressed by their lives and which is the foundation of the holiness and the merit of all the Saints; it is also the truest portrait of a man who really loves Jesus Christ. By the traits of this character we can easily see how false it is to say that real virtue is ugly and repulsive, and that the accusation against truly pious people that they are disobliging, melancholic, impatient, irascible, full of self-love, jealousy and ambition, is devoid of all foundation. It can be seen even more clearly how people with a reputation for piety, but who foster in themselves the above-mentioned gross defects, injure the cause of true piety and prejudice the faithful against it; by their manifest defects they bring the virtue which people attribute to them into disrepute, and their example serves as a rampart of defense for the position of the licentious.

And let it not be said that this perfect love for Jesus Christ and this true piety, such as is here depicted, exist only in the imagination; or that if they are really found in the world, a life regulated according to such principles would be very strange, and a man who lives according to them, very unhappy. The life and conduct of all the Saints is the model from which this portrait has been drawn; and there is not a single one of them who, while living in conformity with these principles, has not enjoyed a peace and joy which surpass all understanding. If many people who pass for being very pious do not recognize themselves in this portrait, it is because they have not the courage to do all that is necessary to arrive at this degree of perfection. These people in the beginning make serious efforts, they even make some progress on the road to virtue, but they often stop in the middle of the way, and many who had but a few steps more to go deprive themselves of all the advantages of the perfect life because they have not the courage to make this last effort.

But, says St. Francis de Sales,* the greater number of this class of peope are those who form a false idea of piety. Most

---

*The following is the passage from the Devout Life of St. Francis de Sales referred to by Father Croiset: "You aspire to devotion, my dearest Philothea, because, being a Christian you know it to be a virtue extremely pleasing to the Divine Majesty. But since small faults committed in the beginning of any business in the course of time grow infinitely greater, and become in the end almost irreparable, you must know in what true devotion consists; for since there is but one true devotion, and many vain and counterfeit, if you cannot distinguish which is the true one, you may easily deceive yourself in following some fantastic and superstitious devotion.

"As Aurelius painted all the faces in his pictures after the likeness of the woman he loved, so everyone paints devotion according to his own fancy and passion. He that practices fasting thinks himself very devout if he fasts, though his heart be at the same time full of rancour; and while being so temperate as to scruple about moistening his tongue with wine or even with water, he makes no difficulty about drinking deep of his neighbor's blood by detraction and calumny. Another accounts himself devout for reciting daily a multiplicity of prayers, though he immediately afterwards utters the most disagreeable, arrogant and injurious words amongst his domestics and neighbors. Another cheerfully draws an alms out of his purse to relieve the poor, but he cannot draw meekness out of his heart to forgive his enemies. Another readily forgives his enemies but never satisfies his creditors except under compulsion. These, by some, are esteemed devout, while in reality they are by no means so.

"When Saul's servants sought David in his house, Michol by laying a statue in his bed, and covering it with David's clothes, made them believe that it was David himself, in like manner, many people, by performing certain external actions of devotion, cover themselves with a cloak of piety and thus lead the world to believe them to be truly devout; whereas they are nothing but statues and phantoms of devotion." (Introduction to the Devout Life, First Part, Chap. 1.).

of them represent it according to their humor, their natural bent, or their passions. A naturally melancholic person makes solid virtue consist in being gloomy, and he cannot imagine that a person could be joyful and pious at the same time. Some others, who look only at the exterior of the spiritual life, make it consist in the use of instruments of penance, fasting, vigils and similar bodily austerities. Many others imagine that they have arrived at the height of virtue when they have acquired the habit of reciting long vocal prayers, hearing many Masses, remaining long in the church, assisting at the whole divine office and receiving Holy Communion frequently.

Some people, even some Religious, believe that for perfection it is sufficient to be attentive in Choir, to love retreat and silence and to observe carefully the rules of their Order. Thus they make perfection consist in one or other of these exercises, but that is not the fact. Exterior works are either means of arriving at perfection or are the fruits of perfect holiness, but perfection or the perfect love of Jesus Christ cannot be said to consist in these works. These exterior works may be the excellent fruits of consummate virtue in people who are really holy, but in the case of those who neglect to watch over the movements of their hearts, who have no true interior mortification, or who refuse to conform their will to the will of God, they may be harmful.

True love of Jesus Christ and true devotion such as consti-
tute the spiritual life, as we have seen by the character of the
perfect man, consist solely in loving God and hating ourselves,
in submitting ourselves not only to Him, but to every creature
for the sake of Him; in renouncing our own will entirely to
follow His, in mortifying our pride and self-love, and above all
in doing these things for the glory of His name, without any
other motive but that of pleasing Him, and for the sole reason
that He wishes and deserves that creatures love and serve Him.
These are the dictates of the law of love which the Holy Spirit
has engraved on the hearts of the just. By observing them, we
shall put into practice that self-denial so much recommended
by Our Savior in the Gospel; they will make His yoke sweet,
and His burden light.

We read in the Sermon on the Mount: "Not everyone that
saith to Me, Lord, Lord, shall enter into the kingdom of heaven:
but he that doth the will of My Father Who is in heaven, he
shall enter into the kingdom of heaven. Many will say to Me
in that day: Lord, Lord, have not we prophesied in Thy name,
and cast out devils in Thy name, and done many miracles in
Thy name? And then will I profess unto them: I never knew
you. Depart from Me, you that work iniquity" (Matt. VII, 21-23).

This is a striking but terrible lesson for those who labor even
with success for the salvation of souls and who, having pointed
out to others the road to perfection, make no effort themselves
to attain it and die in the great imperfections in which they
have lived.

We should therefore be fully convinced that the love of
Jesus Christ, true devotion, Christian virtue and solid piety,
consist solely in sincere humility, universal and continual mortification and perfect conformity of will with the will of God.
If one of these three virtues is wanting, there can be no true
devotion, no solid virtue.

These are the sentiments of St. Paul and of all the masters of
the spiritual life: or rather they are the sentiments of all who
are worthy of the name of Christian, since they are sentiments
of Jesus Christ, and consequently of all those who have the
true spirit of Jesus Christ. In all our designs and enterprises,
says a great Servant of God, we should rather purpose to do
the will of God, than to procure the glory of God, for by doing

the will of God, we will infallibly procure His glory, but if we propose as the motive of our actions to work for the glory of God, we may sometimes allow ourselves to be deceived and do our own will under the pretext of working for the glory of God.

Oh! how common is this kind of illusion in those who are employed in good works and in ministrations of zeal for souls! Real perfection about which there can be no mistake, consists in accomplishing the will of God; but how few are those who are sufficiently enlightened to know the excellence of this perfection, or sufficiently pure to taste its sweetness!

God has loved us too much, says a faithful friend of Jesus Christ, for us to give Him only grudging service; the very thought of being wanting in generosity to Him should cause us horror. What! Shall we refuse to belong entirely to Him after the great mercy which He shows us daily? Shall we keep back something from Him after all we have received from Him? My heart shall never consent to adopt this course. When I think of the little that we can do for the glory of God even when we employ ourselves entirely in His service, I blush at the very thought of reserving anything. There is no safety in taking a middle course, since it is so easy to go to the wrong extreme. Only those who give themselves to God without reserve need expect consolations from Him at the moment of death, and it is only those who lead a sweet and tranquil life.

It is easy to see from this how perfectly the sentiments and the lives of God's true servants accord with the character-sketch which we have given of the man who loves Jesus Christ perfectly, and what great consolations those true servants of God enjoy. How miserably those people are deceived who themselves having never tasted these heavenly consolations because they have never had true devotion, imagine that it is the same with the truly devout who love Jesus Christ perfectly!

By these same principles we can judge how far removed from the true love of Jesus Christ are those people who adopt some external practices of devotion, and who never cease talking about them; those people who are devout only when it suits their whim or their natural inclination, who are recollected for a few days during their Retreat but retain all their imperfections; those people who deny their senses nothing, who perform the holiest exercises of devotion in a perfunctory manner, who spend their days in company without any guard on their hearts, always exposed to surprise attacks of the enemy, always agitated by various passions, always in trouble and guided by no rule; those people who are so excessively touchy that the least word offends them, the least want of respect wounds them; these people finally, full of guile and deceit, always seeking their own interests and not scrupling to attain their ends by underhand means, changing every hour of the day because they are following the various promptings of their passions.

It is easy to see that these various classes of people have not the spirit of Jesus Christ, that their virtue is not genuine, and that as long as they persevere in this unhappy state, their devotion to the Sacred Heart of Jesus will be too imperfect to gain for them an entry into that Divine Heart, or at least to make a long sojourn in It.

II

THE ORDINARY EFFECTS OF THE PERFECT LOVE OF JESUS CHRIST

From the foregoing we can easily see that the ordinary effects of the perfect love of Jesus Christ may be summed up by saying that, by making us imitate His adorable virtues perfectly, this love renders us as comfortable to our Divine Model as it is possible to be in this life, by the perfect imitation of His admirable virtues. Our exterior and interior life will thus become a living expression of His; and as He is the living image of God, His Father, so we shall become living images of Him, expressing in ourselves all the traits of His various roles, of His mysteries and of His virtues. We find it easy to imitate those whom we love much; now this perfect imitation of Jesus Christ will be rendered visible by unalterable meekness, perfect control over our minds, entire dependence on Jesus Christ in all our actions, and a great love of the Cross.

These virtues are the ordinary effects of the true love of our Divine Savior; they will be possessed in greater or less perfection according to the measure of our love for Him.

Meekness is to such an extent the distinguishing mark of the character of Jesus Christ that the Prophets make use of it almost exclusively to describe Him. Among the Saints of the Old Testament, those who have been figures of Jesus Christ, such as Moses and David, excelled in this virtue. It was said of the former that "he was a man exceedingly meek above all men that dwelt on the earth" (Numbers XII, 3), and of the latter it was said: "O Lord, remember David and all his meekness" (Psalms CXXXI, 1). Jesus Christ Himself teaches us both by word and example that meekness is the dominant note of His character, and that it is impossible to be like Him without being meek. Perfect love always demands some resemblance: now it is particularly this unalterable meekness that imprints on us the exterior and visible marks of resemblance to Jesus Christ; it is also the ordinary effect of His love.

This amiable virtue contains in itself many others; it is impossible to be always in good humor, always to receive people with a smiling countenance, to show unalterable meekness on all occasions, without having sincere humility, continual mortification, perfect charity and unalterable peace of soul that is proof against all accidents. If we are wanting in meekness it will be found that we are lacking in some of these virtues. Difficulty of approach, an austere and repelling exterior with an air of severity often found in people who pass for pious, are usually the effects of unmortified natural inclinations, and are never found in a true disciple of Jesus Christ Who wishes that meekness and humility of heart be the distinguishing marks of His disciples. Thus it is an everyday experience that the people who display most meekness towards their neighbor are those who have the tenderest love for Jesus Christ. It was by meekness that the Apostles converted the most hardened sinners, and apostolic men must acquire this amiable virtue if they wish their labors to be fruitful.

A heart free from the tyranny of the passions renders our interior conformable to that of Jesus Christ by our complete unselfishness and our perfect acquiescence in His commands, and makes us consider in all things the will of God which we are always disposed to accomplish without anxiety or uneasiness. It is a certain sign that a person has little love for Jesus Christ, if he finds no attraction for the perfect acquiescence in His will. Seeing that people experience very great pleasure when what they do is pleasing to those whom they love, how can they be said to have true love for Jesus Christ, if they find no inclination to do what He desires? If we love Him we will do what is pleasing to Him, and nothing will give us pleasure but what He desires.

Once we have given our hearts to the love of Jesus Christ, this love will suffer no sentiment of self-love there. It strips us of all attachments and gives us that holy indifference which makes everything equally pleasing to us; it wishes for nothing for self and wishes for everything that is the will of God; we do not trouble about how God wishes to employ us, whether it be at something of great importance, or something trifling, something disagreeable, or something according to our taste; success and failure will be equally welcome, because wishing only what God wishes to happen, we will be content with whatever does happen. Those who are attached to their employments, to their place of residence, to their own ease, or to anything else, cannot serve God with this liberty of spirit, because they are slaves of their own will. This causes them to live with little merit, to be troubled in mind, to refuse to be guided by the Holy Spirit and the inspirations of grace; it makes the yoke of Jesus Christ feel rough and heavy, and exposes them to all sorts of illusions and dangers. Fervent souls should therefore leave aside all preoccupations for the love of Jesus Christ when he demands it, and nothing should be judged worthy of consideration, nothing should be capable of touching them but the love of Jesus Christ, everything else being indifferent to them. Care should be taken, however, that this indifference does not degenerate into carelessness and cowardice.

All our endeavors and all our pleasure should be to do what God wishes, when and how He wishes it; without this there is no virtue, only illusion and self-love. This perfect conformity to the will of God, this perfect submission to the orders of Divine Providence — esteeming nothing but what God wishes us to do, whether it be something brilliant that attracts attention, or something hidden and obscure — is not only the surest and shortest road, but properly speaking, it is the only road to acquire perfect purity of heart, great love for Jesus Christ and, within a short space of time, great stores of merit. A man who leans on God is immovable, he cannot be shaken; if his enterprises do not succeed, he is content because he has no other will but the will of God. O happy state of peace and calm! It is well worth striving to attain.

The third effect of this love is entire dependence on Jesus Christ in all our actions. It consists in a continual remembrance of Jesus Christ by which we keep this Divine Savior before us as our Model in everything which we do. We try to make ourselves conformable to this Model in all things; we not only try to do what He wishes, but to do it in the manner in which He Himself was accustomed to do it when He was on earth, so that it is the example of Jesus Christ that regulates our whole conduct. This will give to our manner a stamp of modesty and piety which will charm and edify all, and will inspire both veneration for our person and love for virtue.

Very great advantages are derived from this exercise of the love of Jesus Christ, which consists in making Him the Model of all our actions. By this means, the heart insensibly becomes detached from creatures, self-love is diminished and finally killed, our defects are corrected, and we advance with great strides towards perfection.

Esteem and love for the Cross are also among the ordinary effects of the perfect love of Jesus Christ. When we love our amiable Savior tenderly, we shall have no difficulty in entering into His sentiments, we shall find it easy to conform to His inclinations and desires, we shall have respect for all that He esteems and find an attraction for all that He loves; we shall have nothing but disgust for all that displeases or offends Him; in fine, we may say that this conformity of desires and sentiments with those of our Divine Savior is a necessary effect of true love. It is also from this source that such extraordinary love of the Cross has sprung up in the hearts of all ardent lovers of Jesus Christ. For the tepid and sinful, the exercises of piety are irksome and disagreeable, the yoke of Christ feels heavy, the very name of humiliation and of the Cross frightens them, but there is an almost infinite number of persons of every age and sex and of every walk of life who find such an attraction in the Cross that they would be inconsolable if they were a moment without suffering.

Whence comes such a great difference of sentiments? The privation of sufferings in this life appeared to St. Teresa harder to bear than death. St. Magdalen de Pazzi found death hard only because it deprived her of the pleasure which she experienced from the sufferings of this life; the ardent love of both these holy souls explains their love for suffering. The sight of Jesus Christ, says a great Servant of God, renders the cross so lovable to me, that I think I could not be happy without it; I find myself disposed to spend my whole life without any consolation, even spiritual; for me the love of Jesus Christ takes the place of everything; the Cross has its charms, if anyone loves Jesus Christ perfectly, he will find ineffable delights in the Cross. If we have not the same sentiments, it is because we have not the same love for Jesus Christ.

Many people, says the Author of the Interior Christian, flee from the Cross under the delusion that they can bring more glory to God by brilliant achievements, and be more useful to their neighbor; they do not see that this is the result of self-love and not of the love of Jesus Christ. We must serve God according to His will, not our own; His love should inspire us with sentiments in conformity with His own. Jesus Christ had an extreme love for the Cross, we cannot help loving the Cross, if we really love Jesus Christ. In our own times we find that in those who love Him, love for Jesus Christ is still accompanied by a great desire to share His Cross, and the more perfect this love is, the greater is the desire for His Cross.

The last effect of this love is a high esteem and a great veneration for everything that has reference to Jesus Christ. This love for Him gives us an insatiable hunger for Holy Communion; the very image of Jesus Christ inspires us with new devotion to Him; and under the influence of this love, we will always pronounce with profound respect the words which He spoke; the very name of Jesus will excite sentiments of love for Him in our hearts.

In the world, people honor even the valets of noblemen, they show respect to their coat of arms, to their livery, or to anything that bears their name. Among Christ's followers, the poor stand in a special relation to Jesus Christ and they wear His livery, so when we assist them, it is Jesus Christ Himself that we assist in their person: it is, then, evident that charity towards the poor should be an ordinary effect of true love for Jesus Christ. This love for Jesus Christ should inspire us not only with compassion for the poor, it should inspire us also with love and respect for them; such love for Jesus Christ has induced even great Kings to serve His poor with their own hands. People who love Jesus Christ truly experience an indescribable pleasure in giving alms, they cannot bring themselves to run a poor man away, for they feel that they would be turning away Jesus Christ in his person, and they find that this charity for the poor increases in them in the measure that their love for Jesus Christ increases.

By these marks we can recognize whether we love Jesus Christ perfectly. The more ardent our love for Him is, the more visible will be its effects, and the best proofs we can have that we love Jesus Christ are the effects which that love produces.

As we do not undertake to give here all the effects which the love of Jesus Christ produces in pure souls, we pass over those marvels which are uncommon because perfectly pure souls are rare. The following, however, are some of the more ordinary effects: a soul that is inflamed with this divine love loses its affection for creatures, its desires no longer tend towards the things of this earth, and its inclinations are to go to Jesus Christ as the center of all its interests and its place of repose; signs of love appear from time to time; a mysterious languor consumes the body slowly; the impressions of this divine love increase to the point that the soul can do nothing but seek its God incessantly; this is its occupation at all times and in every place; whether at work or repose, whether awake or asleep, whether at prayer or recreation, the soul thinks continually on the object of its love, and its only care is to love God and please Him, all other cares being happily lost in this one care. But to arrive at this perfection of love, a person must purify himself more and more; he must renounce all other love and efface from his mind all ideas which have no relation to Jesus Christ.

Devotion to the Sacred Heart of Jesus according to the manner proposed in this book, is a sure and easy means of arriving at this sublime state of perfection, and of acquiring the exalted virtue described in this chapter, since all the practices of this devotion tend to make us love Jesus Christ perfectly and tenderly, and the sublime virtue here described consists in the perfect love of Jesus Christ.

PRAYER

Adorable Heart of my Divine Savior, seat of all the virtues, treasury of all graces, retreat of holy souls; O Sacred Heart of

Jesus Which is the object of the complacence of the Eternal
Father; O Heart worthy to reign over all hearts, to possess all
the hearts of men and angels; O adorable Heart of my amiable
Jesus Which loves us with such prodigious tenderness but
Which, alas! is so little loved even by those It loves so tenderly;
would that I could, O my amiable Jesus, travel over the whole
world, and make everyone experience the ineffable sweetness
and the extraordinary graces which Thou dost pour out in such
abundance on all those who honor Thee and love Thee with
their whole heart. Deign to accept at least the sacrifice which
I make Thee of my heart and my ardent desire that Thou be
blessed and praised by all men and angels, and eternally loved
and eternally honored and glorified. Amen.

Chapter VIII

The Exercises of this Devotion

We understand by these exercises the various vocal prayers
such as the Acts of Reparation and Consecration to the Sacred
Heart, the Litany of the Sacred Heart, etc., which are said on
certain days of the year more particularly consecrated to honoring the Sacred Heart of Jesus, and the Meditations assigned
for these days.

It is well to remark here that these exercises assigned to certain days of the year are not so closely connected with these
days that they cannot be said with fruit at all times, provided
they are said with devotion.

MEDITATIONS FOR CERTAIN DAYS OF THE YEAR MORE PARTICULARLY CONSECRATED TO HONORING THE SACRED HEART OF OUR LORD JESUS CHRIST

The two following meditations are given at great length in
order to make the use of them easy for all classes of people,
even those who have not learned how to make a meditation.
We ask those latter to read over these meditations attentively,
to stop and reflect on what they have read, and we trust that
they will derive fruit from this reading; and as this reading will

be accompanied with sentiments of love for Jesus Christ, which the grace of God is sure to inspire, it will be a true prayer.

Those to whom the use of meditation is familiar may confine themselves to going over the subject of each point.

MEDITATION FOR THE FIRST FRIDAY AFTER THE OCTAVE OF CORPUS CHRISTI, I.E., FOR THE FEAST OF THE SACRED HEART. THE INCOMPREHENSIBLE LOVE WHICH JESUS CHRIST SHOWS US IN THE BLESSED SACRAMENT OF THE ALTAR

The subject of this meditation is the incomprehensible love which Jesus Christ shows us in the Blessed Sacrament where He is so little known by men and still less loved even by those who know Him. The end we should propose to ourselves in this meditation, and which should be its fruit, is to be sensibly touched by the extreme ingratitude of men, most of whom are insensible to the signal proofs of His love found therein, so that we may make reparation as far as it is in our power, by a return of love, by our acts of adoration and by every kind of homage, for all the indignities which the Sacred Heart of Jesus has received until now in the Blessed Sacrament.

The subject matter for the three points of this meditation will be taken from the three motives, or the three desires of the Heart of Jesus Christ in the institution of this mystery.

1. The ardent desire which Jesus Christ has had to be continually with us.

2. The desire which He has to share all His possessions with us.

3. The desire which He has to unite Himself intimately with us, although men are insensible to such remarkable proofs of His love.

First Prelude — We represent to ourselves the Supper-room where the Son of God, seated in the midst of His apostles, instituted this adorable mystery. He did not allow the contempt to which He was to expose Himself to prevent Him from doing so, nor did the presence of the traitor Judas, who was to make the first sacrilegious Communion at His divine hands, make Him delay even for a moment the institution of this mystery of His love.

Second Prelude — Having made an act of faith in the truth of this adorable Mystery, and disposed ourselves by an act of contrition to receive the lights and graces which God is ready to give us on this occasion, we ask the Holy Spirit in the name of Jesus Christ Himself, and through the intercession of the Blessed Virgin and of our Angel Guardian, for the grace to conceive a great regret for such contempt and ingratitude, while penetrating deeply into the loving sentiments of the Sacred Heart of Jesus Christ in the Blessed Sacrament.

First Point — *The ardent desire of Jesus Christ to be with us.*

Consider that the Sacred Heart of Jesus Christ was no sooner formed in the womb of the Blessed Virgin than It was inflamed with an immense love for all men: but, as it is the property of love to wish to be always with those loved, a life of thirty-three years appeared to Him too short to satisfy the ardent desire which He had to be always with us; in order to satisfy this greatest of all His desires, He must needs perform the greatest of all His miracles; the Sacred Heart could not suffer any reserve in the excess of Its love. Be not afflicted, My apostles, said our amiable Savior, if I am obliged to leave you to ascend into heaven; *My Heart desires more ardently to be with you than you desire to be with Me:* and as long as there will be men on this earth, I will be with them all days even to the consummation of the world.

All the motives which had induced the Son of God to clothe Himself with our human nature had ceased; the work of the Redemption had been accomplished. It was the ardent desire alone of being always with us which induced Him to perform this continual miracle, this abridgment of all miracles by which His immense love put Him in a state of being no longer able to be separated from us. Jesus has ascended to His Father: why does He return every day to this *earth invisibly, if it is not because He cannot separate Himself from men,* and because His delights are to be with them? Could we have ever imagined that Jesus Christ would love us to this excess? It is from the highest pinnacle of His glory that He thinks of coming to lodge in our hearts, as if something were wanting to His happiness so long as He remained away from us. This desire must be very extreme when it can continue to exist in heaven where all desires are satisfied. Jesus Christ must indeed love men passionately, since, without being held back by the immense glory which He enjoys since His Ascension, He puts Himself daily in a humble and obscure state on our altars in order to satisfy the excess of this tender love, thus fulfilling what was spoken by the Prophet: "My delights are to be with the children of men" (Proverbs VIII, 31).

REFLECTIONS

(1) These are the tender sentiments with which the burning love of the Sacred Heart inspires Jesus Christ: but what must be His sentiments at the sight of the neglect and indifference of those whom He loves to such excess, but who love Him so little.

(2) Jesus Christ has no need of men, nevertheless, He loves them so much that He reckons it as nothing to be enclosed in a consecrated host to the end of time, so much does He esteem the pleasure of being with then. Men, on the contrary, cannot do without Jesus Christ; nevertheless, they love Him so little that they set no value on this marvel of His love, or on the happiness of conversing with Him.

(3) What were the sentiments of Jesus Christ when He saw Himself abandoned by all the people on whom He had lavished His benefits, and even by His most zealous disciples? What must be the sentiments of this same Savior in the Blessed Sacrament of the Altar where almost everyone abandons Him for the greater part of the day, and where even some Religious who have Him in their own house only rarely visit Him!

(4) Is it not exceedingly strange that Jesus Christ dwells corporally among us, and that there are no eager crowds of worshippers in the places where He dwells? All places of business and amusement are filled with people, there are always crowds in the palaces of the great, and people always find sufficient time to pay them court, although these great people are often in such bad humor that they do not even acknowledge the services paid to them. However, they leave Jesus Christ all alone in our churches, although He never rejects anyone and receives with extreme joy and sweetness all those who visit Him. He complains of this treatment by the mouth of His Prophet, saying: "I have watched, and am become as a sparrow all alone

on the housetop" (Psalms CI, 8). I am left all alone in My churches; My people will not spend even a few minutes in honoring Me in the Sacrament of My love.

(5) Visits among men are customary; it is only our amiable Jesus Who is visited only rarely.

(6) If sweetness of conversation or self-interest attracts us, what conversation could be sweeter or more useful than that which we can have with the most accomplished and the most powerful Person in the world, and the One Who loves us most? His conversation hath neither sadness nor tediousness, as witness those chosen souls who are filled with consolation in His Presence, and who would be willing to pass entire days and nights at the foot of the altar (Vide Sap. VIII, 16).

(7) Amiable Jesus, what must be the sentiments of Thy Heart at the sight of the insensibility and ingratitude of men? Thou dost offer Thyself daily on our altars in sacrifice for them; and yet a half an hour spent at this august sacrifice appears too long to them, while they are willing to sit up all night for useless and harmful amusements.

(8) Ungrateful men! You do not know Him Who unceasingly dwells among you (John I, 26). Eternal life consists in knowing Jesus Christ; without this knowledge we are lost. But it is not sufficient to know Him, we must also love Him.

(9) Can we honestly say that we love Jesus Christ? Would we be satisfied if He loved us no more than we love Him? Or that men should love us as we love Jesus Christ? Or that our friends should show no more friendship to us than we show to Jesus Christ? How would we like it if people to whom we had rendered great services showed us no more gratitude than we show to Jesus Christ? Would we allow servants or children to show as little reverence in our presence as we sometimes show in the presence of Jesus Christ in the Blessed Sacrament?

The angels crowd around the altar to adore and love Jesus Christ, although it is not for them that He is present in the Blessed Sacrament; men for whom alone He has performed this miracle are the only people who will not condescend to visit Him. "I am forgotten as one dead from the heart" (Psalms XXX, 13).

O Lord, Who to satisfy Thy ardent desire to be always with me, hast invented this miracle of love, what dost Thou think of the ingratitude which I have hitherto shown Thee? Is this how I respond to Thy love? There is no man who would have shown me even a little kindness that I would not have visited more frequently and more willingly; there is no creature that I would not have loved more. I have forgotten Thee, O Lord, and hitherto I have not loved Thee. How can I, miserable and ungrateful that I am, expect that Thou shouldst think of me? But when hast Thou ceased to think of me? Shall I wait until my abandonment of Thee, my hard-heartedness, my neglect, and my ingratitude oblige Thee to think of me no more? O my amiable Savior, do not take an account of these things; in the past, on innumerable occasions I have given Thee reason to forget me, to despise me, to think of me only to precipitate me into hell; that Thou hast not done so, I thank Thee, O God of mercy, I resolve for the future to visit Thee more frequently. I most humbly ask Thy pardon for my ingratitude towards Thee. With the help of Thy grace, I hope by my assiduous attention in visiting Thee in this adorable Sacrament to make reparation for the injury which I have done Thee by my indifference, and if it is not possible for me to make Thy Temple my ordinary dwelling place, I hope at least to have an assured place of refuge in Thy adorable Heart Which, from this moment, I choose as my dwelling place and from Which I wish never to depart. "Here will I dwell, for I have chosen it" (Psalms CXXXI, 14).

Second Point — In the Blessed Eucharist, Jesus Christ eagerly desires to share all His blessings with us.

Consider that Jesus Christ, Who is the Source of all Blessings, has condescended to remain always among us because He wishes to be present at all times in order to share His treasures with us. And not only has our amiable Savior graciously consented to share with us in this august Sacrament all the blessings of which He is the Source, but by giving Himself to us, He has willed to give us the very source of these blessings: "I will show you every kind of blessing; but in what other place except in the Blessed Eucharist, can you find every kind of blessing!" (St. Bernard).

The princes of this world bestow their gifts only at certain times, and on certain persons; Jesus Christ in the Blessed Sacrament bestows His blessings at all times and on everyone who approaches Him. "Come to Me all you that labor and are burdened, and I will refresh you" (Matt. XI, 28). One might say that it suffices to be poor or afflicted to have the right to approach this source of all blessings and graces, and that it suffices to be unfortunate to be well received. "Come to Me all you that labor..." This bountiful God, foreseeing our infirmities and our weakness, gives Himself to us as our nourishment in order to restore our strength and be a sovereign remedy for all our evils: "And I will refresh you..." "Why weepest thou? And why dost thou not eat? And why dost thou afflict thy heart? Am I not better to thee than ten children?" (1 Kings I, 8). Why do you weep?, says our Divine Savior in the Blessed Sacrament, and why are you afflicted at the loss of your health, of your children, or of your goods? Will you not find in Me all these things and more? Our Divine Savior did not rest content with opening His Sacred Heart to us in token of His love, and pouring out on us all His blessings and graces; He wishes to be Himself our strength and our defense against all the efforts of our mortal enemies. Finally, what could Jesus Christ have done for us, what gift could He have given us, that He has not given us when He gave us Himself? "He that spared not even His own Son, but delivered Him up for us, how hath He not also, with Him, given us all things" (Romans VIII, 32).

REFLECTIONS

(1) This Divine Savior comes to us full of goodness and full of the most ardent love; and yet we go to Him daily with coldness and indifference. He comes to us laden with graces and treasures to enrich us; how long will we continue to go to Him with our hands empty of good works, and our hearts so full of creatures that they cannot share in the bounty of this Divine Savior?

(2) There is no kind of blessing which Jesus Christ does not give us when He gives us Himself in the Blessed Eucharist; and yet there is no kind of irreverence or outrage, which men do not commit against Jesus Christ in this august Sacrament.

(3) He has given us His Sacred Body as our food, and His Precious Blood as our drink; and yet He has become the opprobrium of men... He is despised for being too good and for loving us too much.

(4) The houses and the persons of the vilest and most criminal of men have not been so badly treated as the churches of Jesus Christ and even His Sacred Body.

(5) Love has induced Jesus Christ to disguise Himself in order to come on our altars; but to what treatment did He not expose Himself by this disguise? What contempt, what outrages has He not received from infidels and even from Christians? How many godless men, how many heretics, treat Him on our altars as a mock divinity and renew all the outrages which He suffered in His passion because he called Himself the Son of God.

(6) The Jews exercised less cruelty to the sacred Person of Jesus Christ than the impious have shown towards His sacred Body in the Blessed Sacrament. They have trampled the consecrated Hosts under foot, they have pierced them with knives a thousand times, they have broken them, burned them, not to speak of abominable uses to which they have put them, the very thought of which makes us shudder.

(7) The free choice which Jesus Christ made of the insults and outrages which He received at Jerusalem took some of the bitterness out of them; but dare we think that the Sacred Heart of Jesus, Which puts Itself in this state in order to be the better known and honored by men, endures with complacence the strange contempt shown It?

(8) Persons have compassion for a man who is despised and maltreated; it is only to the outrages committed against Jesus Christ that they are insensible; wicked men seem to take pleasure in ill-treating Him.

(9) Children are made to keep silent and to behave well when brought to visit people, but are given liberty to do as they like in churches; to run about, to play and talk even during the adorable Sacrifice of the Mass. Some people show more reverence at an assembly for amusement and give more attention to a profane entertainment than to the Sacrifice of the Mass. Some young people show insolence at the foot of the altar and sometimes even boast of it; yet Turks do not dare to lift up their eyes in their Mosques, and it would be a crime punishable with death to laugh or speak there.

(10) How many houses are more richly furnished than some of our churches, while the altar linens on which the adorable Body of Jesus Christ reposes are sometimes such that many

people would disdain to wear them on their bodies!

(11) What answer could Catholics give to heretics if these latter reproach them with the want of reverence of many Catholics in church and if they claim that there is more respect shown in their own? If, they say, you, Catholics, believe that Jesus Christ is really present on the altar in this Host, you who understand so well what duty and courtesy demand, and are so well-conducted not merely in the palaces of the great, but even in the houses of your friends, if you believe in the Divine Presence in your churches, how comes it that you do not show more respect there? We have contempt for your Sacraments, a heretic might say, but do you yourselves not teach us to despise them?

(12) It cannot be denied that very many pagans treat their pagan ceremonies with great respect; Catholics have in reality the holiest of all Mysteries, nevertheless, many of them treat them with great disrespect. Which deserve the more severe judgment; the pagans who practice their superstition with respect, or those Catholics who treat the most real and most holy of Mysteries with disrespect and sometimes even with sacrilege? Have not many Catholics reason to fear that the very pagans will rise in judgment against them and condemn them?

(13) Jesus Christ has always the greatest compassion for our miseries but He Himself endures contempt, outrages, and profanations daily at the hands of all classes of people; yet how few people grieve at this treatment which He receives and endeavor to make fitting reparation.

O incredible hardness and insensibility of the hearts of men! O most adorable and amiable Heart of my loving Jesus! O Heart worthy of the respect and adoration of men and angels! O Heart worthy to possess all hearts and to reign over all hearts, what must be Thy sentiments at seeing Thyself treated with such ingratitude! But what should be the sentiments of my heart at seeing Thee so badly treated? Thou seest, O Lord, that I am deeply grieved at such ingratitude. Humbly prostrate before Thee, I wish to make reparation and I most humbly ask Thy pardon. Would that I might be able to make fitting reparation for so many outrages that Thou has received, or at least to prevent them from being again committed against Thee! But, alas! my amiable Savior, my desires are futile; for even if I were to shed all my blood, I could neither make adequate reparation for the past nor prevent the recurrence of these outrages. But, at least, I have a heart capable of loving Thee, capable of rendering Thee homage, and this thought consoles me. I have a heart, and this heart will love Thee; henceforth it will love none other than Thee. With this heart I offer Thee all the desires and all the activities of which it is capable. I offer Thee, O my Savior, all that I can do which, by the help of Thy holy grace, is capable of pleasing Thee; all that is capable of honoring Thee. I invite and humbly ask all Thy Angels, all Thy Saints, and Thy Blessed Mother to render Thee the honor which I desire, but of which I am incapable. I pray them to honor, praise, adore and love Thee for me and for all men. As fitting honor and homage to Thee, grant me to offer Thee Thyself. Thus I will be able to say that Thou belongest to me, and that henceforth all Thy desires are mine. I will praise Thee, O my amiable Savior, and I will publish everywhere that Thou alone art worthy to be loved, served, praised and honored eternally.

Third Point — The ardent desire of Jesus Christ to unite Himself to us.

Consider that union of hearts is the ultimate effect towards which love tends. This union of hearts was the object which Jesus Christ had in mind when He instituted the Blessed Eucharist, in which adorable Mystery He acts like one passionately inflamed with love for men, since in it, love makes Him, in a manner, go out of Himself in order to live only in the object of His love. "At this holy Table," says St. Augustine, "Christ has consecrated the Mystery of union with us." This Sacrament is a Mystery of union. It is true that by the Incarnation God has united Himself perfectly to our human nature, but the hypostatic union was not the end of the Incarnation as sacramental union was the end of the institution of the Blessed Sacrament. He united Himself to our human nature in order to have a body capable of enduring the pains which He wished to suffer for us; but He gives Himself to us in the Blessed Eucharist for the purpose of uniting Himself intimately to us. He invites us to this heavenly banquet by His promises: "Come to Me all you that labor and are burdened, and I will refresh you" (Matt. XI, 28). He uses threats to induce us to come:

"Except you eat the flesh of the Son of Man and drink His blood, you shall not have life in you" (John VI, 54). He recommends that compulsion be used to make men come to this banquet: "Go out into the highways . . . and compel them to come in" (Luke XIV, 23). Finally, He uses every means to enkindle in us a great desire to go to Him, in order that nothing may prevent Him from coming to us and uniting Himself closely with us. Has there ever been a greater proof of most ardent love? But, my amiable Savior, didst Thou not foresee to what outrages this excess of love would expose Thee? It is true that for Thee the heart of a chaste and fervent Catholic is an agreeable dwelling place, but how many of these dost Thou find? How canst Thou endure the coldness, contempt and lack of faith of the great mass of tepid Catholics and above all the terrible corruption of the hearts of many? These indeed are obstacles, especially for a Heart that cannot endure anything sullied, but the greatness of Thy love surmounts all these obstacles. Imagine, if possible, the hatred of God for sin; this hatred is infinite. It is less, however, in a certain sense, than His desire to come to us, since He prefers to abandon Himself to the sacrilegious embraces of infamous sinners rather than forego the delights experienced in close union of those who love Thee. Behold to what an excess our Savior loves us in this adorable Mystery: Almighty God wishes to be Himself our recompense. "I am thy reward exceedingly great" (Genesis XII, 1). But that Jesus Christ Himself should be our food: "For My flesh is meat indeed; and My blood is drink indeed" (John VI, 56), is a miracle of love that passes our understanding; it is an act of liberality in which Jesus Christ, in a manner, exhausts Himself. Those are all the effects of the immense and tender love of our Savior.

REFLECTIONS

(1) Catholics believe in this marvel and yet for the most part are insensible to this excess of love.

(2) It is astonishing that our Savior should have loved men to this excess, but it is more astonishing that they will not love Him in return, and that no motive, no benefit, no excess of love can inspire them with gratitude.

(3) Ungrateful man! Unfeeling man! What is it that you find in this amiable Savior that repels you? Perhaps He has not done enough to merit our love? But He has done more than we could have dared to hope for, more than we can comprehend; more than, to our feeble human judgment, befits His infinite Majesty; and yet we coldly deliberate whether we will respond to these marvelous advances, or whether we will continue to despise them!

(4) A mere show of friendship, a service rendered, gains the hearts of men; must it be that it is only our loving Savior Who fails to evoke any gratitude, although He has given His Blood for our redemption on Calvary and His Sacred Body as the food of our souls in Holy Communion?

(5) All the faithful are agreed that Jesus Christ has loved us infinitely, that He is infinitely amiable, and that in order to gain our love, He has gone to extremes that pass our understanding and yet how few there are who love Him perfectly.

(6) What is the explanation of the fact that Jesus desires so eagerly to come to us and that we have to be compelled to go to Him? It is because He loves us ardently and we do not love Him at all.

(7) How is it that we remain so cold after receiving Holy Communion, although we have been nourished with the Sacred Heart of Jesus, Which is a furnace of love capable of consuming the world? The reason is that we go to Holy Communion with hearts filled with the love of creatures and impenetrably closed against the darts of His love; that although we receive this Sacred Heart into our souls, our hearts, not being sufficiently purified, cannot enter into this adorable Heart to be there inflamed with His love.

(8) Many people prefer to deprive themselves of Holy Communion rather than give up their vices. They would be obliged to be more reserved, to love Jesus Christ more, to live a more regular life, if they approached oftener to the Holy Table. The love of Jesus appears inconvenient to them; they prefer to abstain for long intervals from this Bread of Life; they even condemn frequent Holy Communion, because they have a great aversion for the Body and even for the Sacred Heart of Jesus Christ.

(9) I desire ardently, eagerly to unite Myself closely to you: "With desire have I desired to eat this pasch with you" (Luke

XXII, 15).

(10) Jesus desires to come to us often in Holy Communion because He knows that this is the only way to render us daily less unworthy; there are, however, Catholics who, under pretext that they are unworthy to receive Holy Communion, render themselves every day more unworthy by keeping away from Jesus Christ.

(11) If it were really humility that keeps these people away, they would have the virtue which renders us most worthy to receive, but it is aversion for the Sacred Body of Jesus Christ that makes them both stay away, and even condemn those who approach frequently!

(12) The pretended humility of St. Peter when he refused to allow our Savior to wash his feet was so severely condemned by our Savior that it would have been his ruin if he had not changed his mind: "If I wash thee not, thou shalt have no part with Me" (John XIII, 8). How many people, through pretended respect and false reverence, keep away from the source of life, which Holy Communion is, and thus ruin themselves?

(13) Pagans and uncivilized tribes of the East cried out when they heard of this Mystery: Oh! how good the God of the Christians is! How kind! How amiable! But what would they have thought if they were told that this God, so amiable, is hardly loved by Christians; that not only does this exquisite food not excite their appetite, but that they have an aversion to it, and that they even take advantage of this humble and obscure state, to which the excess of His love has reduced Him, to commit the greatest sacrileges and the most abominable profanations?

(14) What must be the sentiments of the Sacred Heart of Jesus, the Source of all purity, when It is buried in a heart full of uncleanliness, in a heart which breathes only hatred and vengeance and even imprecations against the Savior it receives! But what should be our sentiments when we know with what malice people treat this innocent Lamb, Who utters not a word amidst such contempt and outrages, and Who allows Himself to be led to the altar and slaughtered for our sake!

(15) Does this excessive goodness and meekness make no impression on you? It touched the heart of Pilate, it changed the insolence and rage of His executioners into respect and love and made the Centurion cry out: "Indeed, this was the

Son of God" (Matt. XXVII, 54); it changed the hearts of the most barbarous peoples; is it only our hearts that are insensible to its appeal?

(16) All are horrified at the mention of the treason of Judas and the rage of the Jews; we are everyday witnesses and perhaps accomplices of the sacrileges and outrages committed against our amiable Savior in this adorable Mystery, and we remain unmoved.

(17) "In Thy sight are all that afflict Me" (Psalms LXVIII, 21). You have before your eyes those who treat Me so badly in this Sacrament of love, says Our Savior to us by His Prophet, You are witness of their irreverence. "My heart hath expected reproach and misery" (ibid). My Heart, exposed to so many indignities, endures their outrages with patience. "And I looked for one that would grieve together with me" (ibid); I have waited day and night, and no one comes; "And for one that would comfort Me" (ibid); I have waited for someone who would endeavor to make reparation by his love, adoration and homage for the indignities which evil men make Me suffer in My Heart, and for the contempt which they show for My love; "And I have found none" (ibid).

No, no, my Savior, it shall not be said that Thou are thus abandoned, I will put an end to Thy just complaints. Is it thus, my amiable Savior, that people respond to Thy love? Why hast Thou loved us so much? Rather why do we love Thee so little? Why is it that we do not love Thee? I have not been content to remain insensible to the love and the tender sentiments of Thy Sacred Heart; to the outrages which men have committed against Thee; I have myself been of the number of those who have offended Thee. My amiable Savior, Whose Heart is always burning with love for me, always open to receive me, always ready to show me mercy, to pardon me for my past neglect, for my tepidity, for my want of faith, for my irreverences, receive the act of reparation which I make to Thee prostrate here before Thee. Thou thinkest of me unceasingly in this august Sacrament, Thou lovest me unceasingly, Thou has always the tenderest sentiments for me: how, then, could I forget Thee, or show Thee indifference, or refuse to love Thee? Ah! my God, may I cease to live, if I continue to love Thee so little! May my heart be annihilated if it should henceforth be insensible to the greatest of Thy benefits which is Thyself, O Lord; for in giving Thyself to us Thou hast given us the most precious gift, Thou hast conferred on us the most signal favor that is in Thy divine power to give.

"And now, Israel, what doth the Lord, thy God, require of thee: but that thou fear the Lord, thy God, and walk in His ways, and love Him, and serve the Lord thy God, with all thy heart, and with all thy soul" (Deut. X, 12). Listen, Christian, to what the Lord demands of thee: He demands that thou love Him, He demands thy heart. What! Shall it be necessary that the Lord demand my heart after all He has already done for me? Is it possible that I should refuse it, although I lavish it every day on creatures? Ah! my amiable Savior, I now offer it to Thee; deign to accept it: "A contrite and humble heart, O God, Thou wilt not despise" (Psalms L, 19). My heart is contrite and humble, it cannot fail to be pleasing to Thee. Receive then this heart which I offer to Thee with all the emotions of love and gratitude of which it is capable, to honor and love Thee for the rest of my life. The greater number of my years that are passed have been lost, because I have not loved Thee, but my happiest years remain, because I will use them to love Thee. I will love Thee, O most Sacred Heart of Jesus That was wounded for me, wounded on the Cross for my sins, wounded in the Blessed Eucharist with love for me. I will honor Thee for the rest of my life, I will consecrate to Thee the days that remain; Thou shalt be my place of repose, my dwelling place and my place of refuge. "This is my place of rest, here will I dwell." For the future let those that seek me, seek me in the adorable Heart of my amiable Jesus, and they will find me there. This Sacred Heart shall be my dwelling place, It shall be my nourishment, in It I will repose after all my toils, and burning with the same fire of love with which It burns, I shall love in It and with It, and the Object of my love shall be this Sacred Heart of Jesus.

The meditation may be concluded with the following prayers:

Soul of Christ, be my sanctification.
Body of Christ, be my salvation.
Blood of Christ, fill all my veins.
Water of Christ's side, wash out my stains.
Passion of Christ, my comfort be.
O good Jesu, listen to me.
In Thy Wounds I fain would hide.

Ne'er to be parted from Thy Side.
Guard me should the foe assail me.
Call me when my life should fail me.
Bid me to come to Thee above,
With Thy Saints to sing Thy love
World without end. Amen.

(Indulgences: (i) 300 days every time; (ii) seven years, if said after Communion; (iii) Plenary once a month, when this prayer has been said devoutly every day).

LET US PRAY

O Lord Jesus Christ, Who by an ineffable miracle of love, in order to gain for Thyself the hearts of all men, hast deigned to give them Thy Sacred Heart for their nourishment, hear the prayers of Thy suppliants, and pardon the sins of those who confess Thy name; turn Thine eyes, all beaming with goodness and mercy, on those towards whom Thou dost direct the affections of Thy most amiable Heart, in order that we who abhor and grieve for the impious insults, contempt, derision and sacrileges committed by Thy ungrateful creatures all over the world, may by offering worthy homage to Thee in this Sacred Mystery, be inflamed with the affections of Thy most Sacred Heart and may accompany Its loving sentiments towards us with worthy praises for all eternity. Who livest and reignest with the Father and the Holy Ghost, world without end. Amen.

MEDITATION FOR THE FIRST FRIDAY OF EACH MONTH

On the sentiments of the Sacred Heart of Jesus at the sight of the ingratitude of men, and the outrages to which His ardent love for them has exposed Him.

Let us represent to ourselves the pitiable state to which the Son of God was reduced when He permitted His imagination to picture to Him most vividly, with all their most afflicting circumstances, the dreadful torments and humiliating insults which He was to suffer from three classes of people until the end of the world: from the Jews who were to reject Him; from heretics who were to recognize Him, but who were to refuse to believe in His benefits; and from Catholics who, while believing in His benefits, would repay them with the greatest ingratitude. It was at this sight that He began to fear, as the Gospel tells us, to be wearied and to be sad; and that, finally, He fell into a kind of death-agony, receiving no consolation from anyone, not even from His most faithful disciples to whom He complained, saying: "My soul is sorrowful unto death!" Let us imagine that it is to ourselves that Jesus Christ makes this complaint: you abandon Me, seeing Me reduced to such a pitiful state.

First Point: The sentiments of the Heart of Jesus Christ at the sight of the torments which He was to suffer through the cruelty of the Jews.

Consider what were the sentiments of Jesus Christ when He represented to Himself distinctly, on the one hand, the singular benefits which He had lavished on His chosen people, and on the other, the cruelties and outrages which He was about to receive from this same people, notwithstanding so many benefits. All the graces which had preceded His coming had been given to them only in view of the merits of Jesus Christ. It was particularly for this people that He had become Man, it was among them, in preference to all other people, that He had chosen His parents and His friends, that He had performed His miracles and preached His doctrine, and for all these benefits He received nothing but harshness, persecution and opprobrium. He was refused a lodging at birth; He was no sooner born than He was compelled to seek shelter in a foreign country. With what indignity was He not treated during His public life! But what has He not suffered at His death! He was seized like a robber, He was dragged like a criminal along the same streets through which He had been led in triumph a few days before as the Messiah. He was buffeted as an insolent person in the house of Caiphas, He was covered with spittle as a blasphemer; He was treated as a mock king and an impostor, being delivered up to the terrible cruelty of the demon-possessed rabble during the whole night in the dungeon of Caiphas where He suffered innumerable outrages. He was treated by Herod as a fool; He was condemned to be scourged like a wretched slave, and the criminal, Barrabas, was preferred to Him as being less wicked than He: finally, He was condemned to the most ignominious death and was nailed to the Cross on which He expired in the sight of a huge multitude of people, most of them witnesses of His miracles, and even some in whose favor He had wrought miracles, without finding a single one among that crowd to take His part, or to offer Him consolation. From insensibility to His sufferings, they even passed to contempt, and from contempt to execration. But perhaps these people were deceived? No; they knew that His life had been holy, exemplary; that it was spent doing good, working miracles for the afflicted; and it is even for that that they persecuted Him — for being too good.

All this presented itself clearly and vividly to Jesus Christ. He was perfectly conscious of the dignity of His Person, the greatness of His favors, the disinterestedness of His love, and the unworthiness, meanness, rage, and malice of those who treat Him with such cruelty.

A great soul, especially when it is possessed of great love and when it hopes by suffering to make that love known, is capable of giving itself willingly up to suffering; but the more generous and tender a person is, the more difficult he finds it to support injustice and ingratitude, especially when he sees himself sacrificed to the envy of his enemies, and betrayed by those from whom he had a right to expect help in his affliction, and when he sees that his terrible sufferings and afflictions are not capable of inspiring these men with the least sentiment of compassion.

Never has any person more clearly and vividly represented to himself things in all their circumstances than Jesus Christ. Never had anyone a more generous heart, and consequently, no one was ever more sensible to ingratitude. With what torrents of bitterness was not that Sacred Heart of Jesus inundated, when It represented to Itself what He had done for this people and what that people was going to do to Him. Let us, who are so sensible to contempt, especially contempt from people whom we have most obliged, let us judge what must have been the sentiments of Jesus Christ at the sight of this spectacle.

The sorrow which crushed His Sacred Heart must have been especially bitter, because it is the only torment of His Passion of which He complained. "Attend and see if there is any sorrow like to My sorrow" (Lamen. I, 12). O what ingratitude and cruelty! And in this mortal sadness, no consolation!

"Is this the return which you make to the Lord, O foolish and senseless people?" (Deut. XXXII, 6). Ungrateful men, unfeeling Christians, is this the gratitude which you have for your Savior and your God?

No, my Savior; it shall not be said that Thou art so universally abandoned; it shall not be said that Thou wilt find no one to share in Thy sorrow. I ask Thee for at least a drop from that ocean of bitterness with which Thy Sacred Heart was inundated at the sight of such ingratitude and contempt, in order that, if I am not happy enough to blot out my sins by shedding all my blood, I may at least so grieve for them, that I may wash them away by my tears.

Second Point — The sentiments of the Sacred Heart of Jesus at the sight of the outrages that He was to suffer from heretics.

Consider that the second cause of this fear and mortal sadness with which the Sacred Heart of Jesus was fillled, was the number of insults and outrages which He was to endure from the malice of heretics until the end of time, and which His imagination represented to Him without hiding a single one. There is nothing more painful to a generous heart than ingratitude, especially when it is accompanied with contempt; but of all kinds of ingratitude, the blackest is when people not only return no thanks for favors received, but even deny that they have ever received favors so that they may have full liberty to maltreat their benefactor without passing for ungrateful people. Jesus Christ knew distinctly that, in the future, Christians would be found in great numbers who would renew on His Sacred Body in the Blessed Eucharist all the outrages that the malice of demons could be capable of, and who would deny His real presence in the Blessed Eucharist in order to give themselves full liberty to vent their rage and hatred against Him.

Could we have imagined that men would be capable of such malice and contempt, that they would use His greatest mark of love to outrage Him to excess? Our Divine Savior in the Garden of Olives saw clearly and distinctly all the outrages that would be inflicted on Him in the Sacrament of His love down through the ages to the end of time; He saw His temples profaned, His altars demolished, His priests slaughtered, His Sacred Body dragged on the ground and trampled underfoot, and become the object of the mockery and derision of the greatest criminals, and the horror and execration of the impious.

What must have been the sentiments of this tender and generous Heart in the Garden of Olives! Must Thou, O, my Savior, work such a miracle to furnish impious men with a means to treat Thee so unworthily? Must Thou, by an excess of love, remain among men to the end of time to be the object of their contempt and rage? Is not such a vision sufficient to make the heart dry up with sadness and sorrow? Is it not Thou, O King of glory, Whom I see covered with opprobrium and ignominy in so many places? Is it not Thou, O God of Majesty, before Whom the Seraphim annihilate themselves with respect, Whom I see so insolently treated by the wretches of this earth? Is it not Thou, in fine, the object of complacence of Thy Eternal Father, Who art become an object of horror and execration for Thy creatures, for Thy slaves, for Thy own children? And all this because Thou hast loved them too much!

Could we have ever imagined, O Lord, that to the excess of Thy goodness, men would reply by an excess of malice? To Thy excess of love, by an excess of ingratitude?

But, O my amiable Savior, is not my excess of ingratitude still greater, if I show no sympathy to Thee at the sight of such treatment?

It is, indeed, in this point, O my Savior, that I discover the meaning of the words of Thy Prophet: "The last of men, the Man of Sorrows" (Isaias LIII, 3). Heretics have treated Thee as the last and the most despised of all men, and they have fulfilled the prophecy which said that Thou wouldst be "filled with opprobrium" (Lam. III, 30). But, my Savior, will these heretics, these unnatural children, these impious ones, be never satisfied with treating Thee so insolently?

And shall I be ever touched at seeing Thee so ill treated?

This terrible vision of sin and ingratitude caused Thy death-agony and the bloody sweat in the Garden. I ask of Thee that it may touch me unto tears, and that if I cannot feel the same sorrow that weighed down on Thy Sacred Heart, at least my shame at being so insensible to Thy sorrow may in some manner supply for my insensibility.

Third Point — The sentiments of the Heart of Jesus Christ at the sight of the ingratitude of the majority of Catholics.

Consider that it was no less afflicting and sad for Jesus Christ to see the ingratitude of the majority of the faithful, who would have only coldness and indifference for Him in the Sacrament of His love. He saw the little esteem, nay, even the contempt with which they would treat this greatest proof of His love; He saw that no matter what He might do to be loved by the faithful, even dwelling always amongst them in the Blessed Eucharist, neither this excess of His love, nor His benefits, nor His very presence, would be capable of making the greater part of them love Him or would prevent them from forgetting Him: He saw that those churches in which He was to be sacramentally present would be left for most of the time without adorers: He saw what little reverence, nay, what disrespect would be shown in His presence: He saw clearly how the greater part of His followers, who spend long hours in vain amusements and useless visits and complete idleness, would rarely find a quarter of an hour to spend before Him in the Blessed Sacrament; He knew how many others would visit Him only under compulsion and without either devotion or reverence, and finally, the very small number who would eagerly visit Him and devoutly adore Him. He saw clearly that the greater number would take no more notice of Him than if He were not really present in the Blessed Sacrament or if present as if He were a person of no consequence.

The harsh treatment which He received from the Jews, Gentiles and heretics was indeed very painful to Him; but they were His open enemies, and such treatment might be expected from enemies. But could we ever have thought it possible that those who recognize His benefits, that those who make profession of being faithful to Him, that His own children, should not only be insensible to His benefits and in no way touched with compassion at the sight of the grief caused by such contempt, but that they should themselves treat Him with contempt by their irreverences and sacrileges? Our Savior might well say: "If pagans and Turks and infidels had treated me so, I might have endured it." "For if my enemy had reviled me, I would verily have borne it" (Psalms LIV, 13), but that Christians, Catholics whom I have not only redeemed, but have fed and nourished with My Body and Blood, should have nothing but contempt for Me, that they should treat Me with ingratitude, is too much. "But Thou, a man of one mind, My guide, My familiar: who didst take sweet meats together with Me!" (Psalms LIV, 14-15).

What must be the sentiments of this most generous and tender Heart of Jesus Which has so loved men, and Which finds in the hearts of those men only coldness and contempt? "I am become a reproach among my enemies" (Psalms XXX, 12). If after exposing Myself to the contempt and hatred of my enemies, in the midst of the outrages which I suffer, I could at least find a large number of faithful friends who would console Me! but it is quite the contrary. "They that saw Me without fled from Me" (Psalms XXX, 12). The greater number seeing that I have disguised Myself under the feeble appearance of bread in order to have the pleasure of dwelling among men, abandon Me and forget Me as a person who has no place in their hearts. "I am forgotten as one dead from the heart" (Psalms XXX, 13).

Can we say that there is any exaggeration in this terrible picture of torments, contempt, outrages, and coldness that was presented to Our Savior's mind in the Garden of Olives? Is it really true that people, even Christians, have treated Jesus Christ with this contempt, with this coldness? What has my own conduct been towards Him in the Sacrament of His love? Have I remained indifferent at seeing Him treated with such contempt?

Alas! I have only to consider my present sentiments; and since this pitiable state to which our sins has reduced our loving Savior has touched the hearts of the most hardened sinners, am I not a prodigy of insensibility if I remain unmoved?

Ah! how can I think of all this, and, at the same time, realize that it is God made man Who endures this sadness "even unto death," with which His Sacred Heart is inundated at the sight of such monstrous insults and such terrible torments; when I reflect that this is God Who most freely accepts to suffer these insults and torments, how can I not die of grief and love?

If a man, if a slave, had endured the hundredth part of what Jesus has endured and still endures daily on our altars for love of us, we could not help loving him, being grateful to him, offering him our sympathy and saying sometimes: After all, this poor unfortunate man loved me, and would not have met with misfortune if he had not loved me. Is it, then, only to the proofs of love which Jesus Christ has given us that we make no response? He showed His love for us by dying on the Cross for us, and still shows it by remaining in the Blessed Sacrament for our sake in spite of the insults and outrages which He receives from wicked men; and is coldness and ingratitude our only recompense to Him? What hardness of heart! What insensibility! Is it possible that the heart of man is capable of such ingratitude?

Alas! O my Savior, it is only too capable of it, and it would show only too clearly that it is, if this same love which induced Thee to endure such outrages and indignities for us, did not also induce Thee to soften the hardness, and warm the coldness of this unfeeling heart, and render it capable of loving Thee. For what would all the prodigies which Thou has performed and all the torments which Thou hast endured, avail, but to harden this heart still more and to make it more criminal, if it is not touched by these proofs of love, if it is not more grateful for them, if it does not love Thee more for them.

As I hope, O Lord, that Thou wilt not refuse me Thy grace, I now make a firm resolution to give Thee henceforth unmistakable proofs of my love and of my just gratitude. I have been hitherto insensible to Thy favors, insensible to Thy sufferings, indifferent towards Thee, although I know that Thou art always with us in the Sacrament of Thy love. I have good reason, O my amiable Savior, to distrust my promises, having been in the past so insensible to Thy sufferings and to Thy benefits, and so faithless in Thy service; but Thy great mercy now inspires me with confidence that I will henceforth be more constant and faithful. I promise to show Thee the sincere devotion which I have to Thy Sacred Heart, by my respect in Thy presence and by my frequent visits to Thee in the Sacrament of Thy love, and by my ardent desire to spend the rest of my life in making reparation to Thee, as far as is in my power, by my love and homage, for the outrages Thou dost suffer from wicked men, and the coldness and indifference which Thou dost experience in the Blessed Sacrament even from people consecrated to Thee. "I will love Thee, O Lord, my strength: the Lord is my firmament, my refuge and my deliverer" (Psalms XVII, 1).

DIFFERENT SUBJECTS FOR MEDITATION FOR ALL THE FRIDAYS FOR EACH MONTH

Besides the meditation that has been indicated for the First Friday of each month, a day particularly consecrated to honoring the Sacred Heart of Jesus, we think it advisable to give here subjects of meditation for all the Fridays of the year, as they also are days destined for honoring in a special way the Sacred Heart.

The subjects for these meditations are taken from those parts of the Gospel which describe the sadness which Jesus Christ experienced during His life on earth, and which give His own most touching account of the extreme affliction which His Sacred Heart experienced. We shall endeavor to refer the sentiments of this afflicted Heart as described in the Gospels, to the sentiments which must be evoked in that Heart at the sight of the coldness, contempt and outrages which It receives daily in the adorable Sacrament of the Eucharist, where wicked Christians unceasingly renew the treatment which He endured from the Jews. We shall try, as far as possible, to adapt these subjects to the Gospels of the Sundays of the various months.

We give the two points of the first of these meditations at a little greater length; but in order not to unduly increase the size of this book, we shall merely propose the subject of the others, and make on each some reflections suitable for the end proposed in the meditation.

JANUARY

Meditation for the Second Friday in January

"If I had not done among them the works which no other man hath done, they would not have sin; but now they have both seen and hated both Me and My Father" (John XV, 24).

First Point:
Consider that even if the Jews had not been convinced by the testimony of the Prophets, as they should have been, that Jesus Christ was the Messias, the miracles which He wrought, His admirable virtues, His indefatigable zeal for their salvation,

His great meekness and especially the prodigious benefits which He lavished on this people in favor of whom He performed so many miracles, should have been more than sufficient to gain the hearts of all who knew Him.

But, alas! all this had quite the contrary effect; Jesus Christ was persecuted, hated, treated with greater indignity than if He had been the greatest criminal. Perhaps they had forgotten His benefits and His miracles? By no means: they remembered them, they spoke of them; they made His very benefits and miracles a crime, and He was treated with indignity by the Jews precisely because He loved them too much and was too liberal in their favor. Imagine then, if possible, what must have been the sentiments of Jesus Christ, what the affliction of His Sacred Heart at the sight of such black ingratitude!

Second Point:

But consider what must be now His thoughts at seeing Himself treated every day with such indignity in the Blessed Eucharist even by Catholics, although He instituted the Blessed Eucharist to satisfy His ardent love for these same Catholics. Even if Jesus Christ had not wrought this miracle, even if He had not loved us to this excess, would Catholics have any reason for not loving Him? Ungrateful Catholics, has this amiable Savior not done enough to merit your love? And if His extreme love has induced Him to do what seems to us too much, must this excess of love make us not love Him, nay, even despise Him? And has not this happened since the institution of this adorable Mystery? Are not the words of the Prophets, who said: "He shall be filled with reproaches," "despised and most abject of men," fulfilled in our day in the treatment which He receives in the Blessed Sacrament? The ingratitude and impiety of the Jews excite in us just indignation against this unhappy people. We see, however, this impiety and ingratitude incessantly renewed in the indignities to which His love exposes Jesus Christ daily in the Blessed Sacrament, and are we never touched by it?

Hitherto, O my Savior, I have been ungrateful to Thee. I have replied to Thy bountiful favors by coldness and neglect; but do Thou continue to show Thy mercy in spite of my infidelity; grant me either to die of sorrow or to live in continual regret for having so little loved God Who has loved me to excess, and Who gives me continually in the Eucharist the most extraordinary proof of the greatest love that ever existed.

I will henceforth love Thee, O my Savior, and will eagerly render Thee love and homage in the Blessed Sacrament. I will begin to give proof of my love by my modesty and respect in Thy divine presence, by my ardent devotion to Thy Sacred Heart, and by my eager desire to repair, as far as is in my power, the outrages that have been offered to Thee, and which, alas! are still offered to Thee daily in the Sacrament of Thy love; grant that these dispositions may continue until my death.

Meditation for the Third Friday of January

"And they were all scandalized in His regard. But Jesus said to them: A Prophet is not without honor, save in His own country and in His own house. And He wrought not many miracles there, because of their unbelief" (Matt. XIII, 57, 58).

In what way could Jesus Christ have been a source of scandal to them, unless it were by disguising Himself too much among them and being too liberal with them? The love which He bears us is excessive, it knows no moderation; but His love which should have gained for Him the hearts of all men, brings Him into contempt with many. Those among whom He has lived longest are those who know Him least and who render themselves most unworthy of His graces; and as it is only among strangers that He finds faithful servants, it is only among them also that He works His greatest miracles and pours out His favors most liberally.

It is strange that a prophet is not without honor except in his own country, in his own house; but it is much more strange that Jesus Christ receives so many outrages in His own house, that He is so little known by those among whom He dwells unceasingly, and so little loved even by those to whom He is known. It is strange that when He opens to us all His treasures in the Blessed Sacrament, that when He gives Himself to us, we feel so little the marvelous effects of His presence; that those who approach oftenest and nearest to Him are not always the holiest nor those who love Him the most. It is strange that Jesus Christ, Who is continually amongst us, works so few miracles, that He is to some an object of scandal. But will it be not still more strange if I myself, in spite of making all these reflections today, do not love Jesus Christ more, if I am insensible to the outrages which He receives in the Blessed Sacrament, and if I do not use all possible means to make reparation for them?

Meditation for the Fourth Friday of January

"Then the Lord of the vineyard said: What shall I do? I will send My beloved Son. It may be, when they see Him, they will reverence Him; Whom when the husbandmen saw . . . casting Him out of the vineyard they killed Him" (Luke XX, 13, 14, 15).

The sense of this sad parable was only to literally accomplished in the person of Jesus Christ Whom the Jews treated in that manner; but is not the accomplishment of this same parable renewed every day among Christians in the unworthy manner in which they treat Jesus Christ in the Blessed Sacrament?

Could the Eternal Father employ a means more proper to acquire for Himself faithful servants among men than by sending them His own Divine Son? And could Jesus Christ find a means more proper to make Himself honored and loved than by instituting the Blessed Eucharist? However, do people love Jesus Christ more for it? Is He not on the contrary worse treated on account of this? The ingratitude of the Jews makes us indignant, but why are we not touched by our own ingratitude? It is indeed surprising that the presence of Jesus Christ, His meekness, His generosity, His miracles had no effect on the hearts of the Jews, but is it not more strange that the real presence of Jesus Christ in the Blessed Sacrament, His abasement, His silence, His liberality, and all the favors which He is ready to confer on us, should have so little effect on the hearts of Christians?

FEBRUARY

Meditation for the Second Friday of February

"And Simeon said to Mary His Mother: Behold, this Child is set up for the ruin and for the resurrection of many in Israel, and for a sign which shall be contradicted" (Luke II, 34).

This prediction pierced the heart of Mary like a sword; but

what an impression did it not make on the Heart of her Divine Son! Jesus Christ then offered Himself to His Eternal Father for the salvation of all men, and the price which He offered was infinitely beyond the debt which He paid. Nevertheless, this Victim immolated for all, will be useless for a very great number, and this infinite price offered for all men will be for the ruin and the resurrection of many. This same Victim is still offered and immolated daily on our altars for our salvation by the hands of the priest, and may we not say that this same Victim is for the ruin and resurrection of many? And how could it be otherwise, since He is still an object of contradiction for men? Some refuse to recognize Jesus Christ, others while recognizing Him, despise Him, the majority forget Him, and even those who think of Him are not always grateful. Was it not enough, O my Divine Savior, that this prophecy should have been accomplished during Thy mortal life; must it be still renewed daily by the contempt with which Thy Sacred Person is treated in the Blessed Sacrament? It has pierced the heart of Thy Mother with sorrow; will it never touch my heart?

Meditation for the Third Friday of February

"Then Jesus took unto Him the twelve and said to them: Behold we go up to Jerusalem; and all things shall be accomplished which were written by the prophets concerning the Son of man. For He shall be delivered to the Gentiles and scourged and spat upon" (Luke XVIII, 31, 32).

What must have been the sentiments of Jesus Christ! Do you see, said He to His Apostles, this people on whom I have lavished My benefits and in whose favor I have wrought so many miracles? This people is going to repay these benefits by the blackest ingratitude; I am going to give myself into their hands, and they will deliver Me to the Gentiles; I am going to become the object of hatred of this people, the mockery of the soldiers, the laughing-stock of the people of the court and a Victim sacrificed to the malice and impiety of the priests. There will be no contempt which I will not suffer, no outrage which I will be spared, no torment which I will not be made to suffer. But what would this amiable Savior have replied if He had been then asked, why foreseeing all this did He put Himself in their hands? Would He not have replied that His love was still greater than all those outrages, and that He exposed Himself willingly to them to testify the excess of His love? His love is daily renewed in the adorable Eucharist, Jesus Christ has still the same sentiments in our favor; but, O my God, what are my sentiments with regard to Jesus Christ so little loved and treated with such contempt?

Meditation for the Fourth Friday of February

"And all were astonished at the mighty power of God. But while all wondered at all the things He did, He said to His disciples: Lay you up in your hearts these words, for it shall come to pass that the Son of man shall be delivered into the hands of men" (Luke IX, 44).

It required an authority as great as that of Jesus Christ to persuade His disciples, who were witnesses of these miracles, that those miracle which were then attracting the admiration of all, would not prevent men from treating Him with indignity. The Jews had refused to love Jesus Christ, and in order to be at liberty to maltreat Him, they closed their eyes in order not to know Him. Heretics follow the example of the Jews in this; but could we ever have believed that there would be found men who would treat Jesus Christ with the last indignity and contempt in the Blessed Eucharist, while making profession of believing in this Jesus Christ Whom they treat thus unworthily?

O Lord, Thou dost command Thy disciples to fix these sad truths well in their hearts; grant that they may be fixed in ours also.

MARCH

Meditation for the Second Friday of March

"My soul is sorrowful even unto death. Stay you here and watch with Me . . . And He cometh to His disciples and findeth them asleep. And he saith to Peter: What? Could you not watch one hour with Me? (Matt. XXVI, 38-40).

A person must be of a very harsh and unfeeling nature, if he remains calm and unconcerned when he sees his friend afflicted with great calamity and plunged into sadness; but how painful is not this indifference to the friend thus afflicted?

Jesus had taken only three of His Apostles into the Garden of the Agony; the pitiable state to which He was reduced could not make them watch even one hour with Him.

Jesus Christ is treated in the Blessed Eucharist with coldness and contempt by the majority of men; how few of those who make profession of being His followers and of loving Him are touched by these outrages! Jesus Christ is incessantly being delivered into the hands of His greatest enemies, but how few even of those who claim to be faithful to Him come to the foot of the Altar to keep Him company, and to how many people could Jesus Christ still make the reproach: "Could you not watch one hour with Me?" What could I answer, O Lord, I who lose so many hours in vain assemblies and in vain amusements?

Meditation for the Third Friday of March

"And Judas, coming to Jesus, said: Hail, Rabbi. And he kissed Him. And Jesus said to him: Friend, whereto art thou come?" (Matt. XXVI, 48, 49). Judas, dost thou betray the Son of man with a kiss?" (Luke XXII, 48).

It is very hard to bear, when an ungrateful person adds hypocrisy to malice, when he tries to deceive us by an exterior show of friendship, when in public he makes use of familiarity and marks of friendship to destroy us. My Divine Savior, what must be Thy sentiments at seeing this great number of Christians whom Thou dost invite so cordially to Thy banquet, whom Thou dost admit with so much love to Thy table! Thou dost thereby give them a testimony of Thy extreme love; on their part, they perform an act which is in itself a visible mark of the tender love which they have for Thee; but to how many of them couldst Thou not say: "Friend, whereto art thou come? Dost thou betray Me with a kiss?" To how many impure souls hast Thou delivered Thyself? To how many hearts sullied by a thousand vices? How many sacrileges have been committed under this false appearance of piety? And shall I be always insensible to all this?

Meditation for the Fourth Friday of March

"And the soldiers led Him away into the court of the palace: and they called together the whole band: and platting a crown of thorns, they put it upon Him . . . and they began to salute Him: Hail, King of the Jews. And they did spit on Him. And bowing their knees, they adored Him" (Mark XV, 16, 18, 19).

Would the most infamous and most criminal of men have been treated with such indignity? But these mockeries, these outrages, these unheard-of cruelties which the soldiers perpetrated on the Sacred Person of Jesus Christ, causing the Precious Blood to flow, only lasted at most a few hours, and they have been accompanied by the tears which compassion and love have drawn from so many faithful servants of Jesus Christ down the ages. But is not this terrible tragedy renewed daily in the outrages which are offered to Jesus Christ in the Blessed Sacrament? And have not the most terrible of these acts of contempt mentioned in the Gospel been renewed hundreds of times by wicked Christians and infidels? How many people seem to enter a church only to insult our Savior? How many people throw discredit on the most dread of all mysteries by their want of reverence? Would that there might be found, O my Savior, at least a number of faithful servants who, sensibly touched at seeing Thee daily so little honored and loved, and treated with such indignities, would make Thee fitting reparation!

APRIL

Meditation for the Second Friday of April

"And Pilate, answering, said to them: What will you, then, that I do to the King of the Jews? But they again cried out: Crucify Him" (Mark XII, 12, 13).

Pilate did not know what to do with Jesus as if He were a useless person; the Jews were in haste to have Him crucified. A stranger at the trial would have thought from the conduct of Pilate and the Jews, that Jesus Christ was fit for nothing but to be despised, outraged and crucified. Wretched people! You do not know what to do with this Savior Who has been sent especially to you; this Savior will be taken away from you and given to the Gentiles, to barbarians who will know how to profit by this mysterious stone which you have rejected. Jesus Christ is now really present among us in the Blessed Sacrament. But is Jesus Christ in this august Sacrament more useful to us than He was to the Jews? Do we know the treasure which we possess? Do we know the infinite value of this precious Victim, and do we profit by the treasure which we have? Unhappy are the kingdoms and provinces where heresy reigns with such tyranny! The abuse and contempt with which your people treat this august Sacrament have reached the extreme limit. You have not known what to do with this Divine Savior, and He has been taken from you and brought to the Indians, the Chinese, the Iroquois. But, O my God, have I known how to profit by the presence of this Divine Savior Who dwells amongst us?

Meditation for the Third Friday of April

"Now when Pilate had heard these words, he brought Jesus forth ... and he said to the Jews: Behold your King. But they cried out: Away with Him, away with Him, crucify Him, therefore, he delivered Him to them to be crucified" (John XIX, 13, 14, 15, 16).

Jesus Christ was no longer recognizable; the rage of the Jews and the cruelty of the executioners had left Him in such a terrible state, that the judge himself had to tell the Jews that He Whom he presented before them was Jesus Christ. This spectacle would have touched the hearts of the most savage barbarians; even the Jews would have had compassion, even their hearts would have been moved, if it had been anyone else but Jesus Christ. Behold our Divine Savior abandoned to the rage of these demons! O my adorable Savior, Thou art overwhelmed with torments and opprobrium! It was Thy love for us that brought matters to this excess. Was not this sufficient without exposing Thyself daily to similar treatment in the Blessed Sacrament? Was it not already too much? Yes, answers our Savior, it was more than enough to appease my heavenly Father, more than enough to extinguish the hatred of My enemies, more than sufficient to blot out the sins of the whole world, more than sufficient to quench the fires of hell; but it was not enough to show Christians the excess of My love. It was enough to move My judge, Pilate, and My executioners, enough to split the rocks, and, nevertheless, neither the remembrance of My past sufferings nor the sight of the outrages which I suffer unceasingly in the Blessed Eucharist are enough to touch the hearts of Christians. Oh! the hardness and insensibility of our hearts! All these excesses of suffering and love are not enough to conquer our indifference. We see Jesus Christ daily treated with indignity in the Blessed Sacrament, and we look on with unconcern!

Meditation for the Fourth Friday of April

"Jesus cometh, the doors being shut, and stood in the midst, and said: Peace be to you. Then He said to Thomas: Put in thy finger hither, and see My hands, and bring hither thy hand and put it into My side; and be not faithless but believing" (John XX, 26, 27).

Is not this a loving condescension? How our Savior must have loved this incredulous Apostle to use such strong and loving means to convince him! The sole sight of this opened Side inflames the heart of this Apostle with love. Jesus Christ comes to us daily in the Blessed Sacrament; He gives us this same Body, and on this same Body, we find these same wounds; in fine, He gives us His Heart, He makes us touch It, and this Heart and all the fire with which It is inflamed, has not been able to inflame our hearts! With what coldness people retire after receiving Holy Communion! Their hearts are frozen in the presence of this burning love! The faith and new fervor of St. Thomas rejoiced the Heart of Jesus Christ extremely; but what must be His sentiments, at our insensibility and little faith! What should I myself think of it?

MAY

Meditation for the Second Friday of May

"So long a time I have been with you; and have you not known Me" (John XIV, 9).

It is not possible to know Jesus Christ well and not to love Him tenderly; a person who loves Him only coldly cannot be said to know Him. This complaint which He makes to His Apostles reveals to us the sentiments of His Heart. Although they had left all to follow Him, they did not love Him yet with sufficient fervor, because they still knew Him only imperfectly.

But has not this Divine Savior more reason to make a similar reproach to us and to say to us: I have been so long in the midst of you; I have been with you night and day; I have been in your midst solely for the love of you, and yet you do not know Me! For if you knew Me, would you leave Me alone almost always? Would you show so little eagerness in visiting Me? Would you be so little recollected in My presence? Would you have so little confidence in Me in all your wants? Would you not have recourse to Me before all others in all the happenings of life, and could you without pain separate yourself from Me during all your life? What reply could I make to Him?

Meditation for the Third Friday of May

"Sleep now and take your rest: Behold the Son of Man shall be betrayed into the hands of sinners" (Mark XIV, 41).

It is very painful for a person who loves much to see himself abandoned by his best friends when misfortune comes; but is it not almost as painful to see that the few friends that make profession of not abandoning him are in no way touched by his downfall and take no share in his affliction? Jesus Christ in the Blessed Sacrament is outraged by the greater part of men; He is every day delivered into the hands of sinners. The greater part of those who make profession of loving Him are in no way touched by these outrages to Him: They do not even think of showing regret at seeing Him treated in such an unworthy manner. You sleep, devout souls, religious persons, and you take your repose, while Jesus Christ is despised and outraged on every side in the adorable Sacrament of the Eucharist. In this place, heretics profane the sacred vessels and trample the consecrated hosts underfoot; in that other place, sinners daily commit the most horrible sacrileges: Our Divine Lord is everywhere forgotten, everywhere despised, and you are not affected by this contempt; and you do nothing to show Him that you feel it. We have it in our power to make reparation in some manner for these outrages; and we do not give ourselves the trouble to do so; we do not even think of it.

Meditation for the Fourth Friday of May

"And Jesus began to fear and to be heavy, and He said to them: My soul is sorrowful even unto death" (Mark XIV, 33, 34).

A person of really great soul and generous heart is, as a rule, not extremely afflicted at the sight of insults, torments and even death which he himself has chosen, and to which he has delivered himself willingly: but this same heart, which is proof against torments, cannot be insensible to the ingratitude of those for whom it suffers, and this is the torment which made Jesus complain; He Himself said so expressly to St. Margaret Mary. Let us, then, imagine Him saying to us: I do not complain that I am to be dragged through the streets of Jerusalem, torn with scourges, crowned with thorns, nailed to an infamous gibbet to suffer until death the most excruciating torments; My love for men makes Me accept all that; but I cannot resign Myself to be treated with such indignity in the Blessed Eucharist which I regard as the masterpiece of My love, the most efficacious means of gaining for Me their love and thus of making Me love them still more, and the most suitable place to receive their homage and love in reparation for the monstrous treatment which I have received at the hands of the Jews; it grieves Me that the Blessed Eucharist should be the place where I am to receive most outrages, where I am to be abandoned, despised and treated with indignity even by those who make profession of piety.

JUNE

Meditation for the Second Friday of June

"And Jesus said to them: I am the bread of life; he that cometh to Me, shall not hunger, and he that believeth in Me shall never thirst. But I said unto you, that you also have seen Me and you do not believe" (John VI, 35, 36).

How sharp a reproach after such a great benefit! It is as if Jesus Christ had said: My children, I am not satisfied with giving My Body to redeem you, I give you My Body to serve as the food of your souls. To die for a person is the greatest mark of love; but I would not consider it the greatest mark, if I did not renew the sacrifice of My death every day and hundreds of times a day; if, being no longer able to die, I did not put Myself constantly in the state of death in the Blessed Eucharist: and, nevertheless, I have already said to you: You have seen Me, but you love Me but little, because you believe only feebly.

Ungrateful Christians! You have seen what this amiable Savior has done for you, and you see daily what He still does for you, but do you love Him the more for it? If you are so little moved by what He has done for you, could you not at least be touched by what you have done against your amiable Savior?

Meditation for the Third Friday of June

"And He sent messengers before His face; and going, they entered into a city of the Samaritans to prepare for Him. And they received Him not" (Luke IX, 52, 53).

What are our sentiments about these unhappy Samaritans? What happiness for them, if they had known Who it was Who presented Himself before their gate, and to Whom they refused entrance into their city! But what were the sentiments of the Heart of Jesus Christ, when His disciples reported to Him in what manner they had been treated and the contempt which they had shown to His Person! But these wretched people have not been alone; there have been at all times people who have refused the disciples of Jesus Christ entry into their towns and who have even driven out Jesus Christ Himself. Indeed, this has happened at various times down the ages in most countries that were once Christian. Would that He were then less badly received by the rest of Christians, a little more loved, and treated with less indignity by those who receive Him!

Meditation for the Fourth Friday of June

"And the Pharisees came forth, and began to question with Him, asking Him a sign from heaven, tempting Him. And sighing deeply in spirit, He saith: Why doth this generation ask a sign?" (Mark VIII, 11, 12).

What reproaches this sigh conveys, and how well founded these reproaches were! The Sacred Heart feels keenly the callousness and malice of the Pharisees. There had not been a town or village through which Jesus Christ had passed that had not witnessed His miracles. But when people do not love those who perform wonders in their favor, they are little touched by what they see and hear. It must be that we love Jesus Christ little since the greatest and most loving of all His miracles, which is the Blessed Eucharist, touches us so little. But, O my amiable Savior, should not this amazing hardness of heart on our part be capable of making us grieve for it, as it would still be capable of drawing sighs from Thy Sacred Heart, if It were still subject to sorrow and sadness? My heart, O merciful Savior, is capable of sorrow and sadness, deign Thou to soften it by Thy grace that it may grieve over my own ingratitude and the ingratitude of men towards Thee.

JULY

Meditation for the Second Friday of July

"Then, they all cried again, saying: Not this Man, but Barabbas" (John XVIII, 40).

Where could this intense hatred come from, and what could have rendered Jesus Christ so odious? What sick person was ever presented to Him that He refused to heal, or what person in misfortune ever appealed to Him and was refused consolation? This rage and fury of the Jews certainly astonishes us, and certainly it grieved the Heart of Jesus Christ. But, my Savior, are there not people today who have a like hatred against the most august and most lovable of all the Sacraments? How many heretics are there not who, refusing to recognize Thee in this Sacrament of Thy love, cry out against Thee even in our day: "Not this Man!" How many bad Catholics who, either refusing to receive Thee in Holy Communion, or receiving Thee unworthily cry out: "Not this Man!" Finally, how many people who pass for pious, who, by their forgetfulness and indifference, and by their negligence in visiting Thee in this adorable Sacrament, show only too clearly that they do not want Thee! Have I ever been among this number?

Meditation for the Third Friday of July

"I am come in the name of My Father, and you receive Me not: if another shall come in his own name, him you will receive" (John V, 43).

How reasonable is not this reproach! But what intense pain and sorrow it shows in the Heart of Him Who utters it! What would be the sentiments of a prince, if he saw that people received with great honor the least of his father's servants, but that they treated himself, the son and heir, with the greatest contempt? People have respect for a man whom they know to have been sent by God. The relics of those who have given their blood for Jesus Christ inspire us with the veneration which these generous martyrs deserve. People even undertake long journeys at great inconvenience to do them the honor due to them, and this act of piety is solid and praiseworthy. But is our conduct reasonable, when Jesus Christ, who is ever present in the Blessed Sacrament, cannot induce us to visit Him and pay homage to Him? How many people are there not who have no devotion to the Blessed Sacrament, an actual aversion to receive Holy Communion, little or no respect in the presence of the Blessed Sacrament, and who say that they can find no time to visit It?

Meditation for the Fourth Friday of July

"He that eateth bread with Me shall lift up his heel against Me . . . When Jesus had said these things, He was troubled in spirit and said: "Amen, amen, I say to you, one of you shall betray Me" (John XIII, 18, 21).

It required a great cause of sorrow to trouble a Heart so intrepid as that of Jesus Christ. But the contempt which He receives from men in the Blessed Sacrament is for Him a cause of the keenest sorrow, and a sorrow which He cannot hide. The Divine Savior is going to institute the Blessed Sacrament; His love urges Him to do so, but His mind represents to Him distinctly the outrages to which this Mystery is going to expose Him. This sad consideration throws His Sacred Heart into an abyss of affliction; He sees those heretics who, refusing to believe that He has loved us to this excess, will take advantage of this very excess of love to offer Him cruel outrages, and these impious people who, while making professions of belief in Him, will commit horrid sacrileges against Him. If this Divine Savior had done for the demons the hundredth part of what He has done for men, would they treat Him with such indignity? O, my Divine Savior, these indignities and outrages have cut Thee to the quick, and shall I remain unmoved by them?

AUGUST

Meditation for the Second Friday of August

"After this, many of His disciples went back: and walked no more with Him. Then Jesus said to the twelve: Will you also go away?" (John VI, 67, 68).

This question came from a Heart all inflamed with love, and it was a visible proof of extreme tenderness; it had the effect of inducing the Apostles, to whom it was addressed, to love Jesus Christ more ardently. It had the effect which the Divine Savior expected, and this new fervor of the Apostles consoled Him a little in His affliction at the departure of so many followers. Jesus Christ often makes the same demand of us, and for the same reason. How happy we shall be, if it has the same effect! Every day this amiable Savior sees Himself abandoned by cowardly followers who, tired of His benefits, withdraw from Him and leave Him alone. Faithful Catholics, listen to the question which Jesus Christ puts to you: "Do you also wish to leave Me?" Are you too tired of this Divine banquet and weary of My service? Do not you act like those, who go away and if they come sometimes to render homage to Me, only do so with the crowd from custom and routine?

Meditation for the Third Friday of August

"Jesus said to him: The foxes have holes and the birds of the air, nests, but the Son of man hath not where to lay His head" (Luke IX, 58).

Is there any exaggeration in this complaint which Jesus Christ makes? Is it true that He has been everywhere persecuted and treated with contempt? Alas! persecution was waiting at Bethlehem for Him at birth; He was no sooner born than He had to take refuge among an idolatrous people; He Himself complained of the treatment He received at Nazareth; He was driven out of Jerusalem; He was refused admittance into the villages of Samaria; He was several times obliged to hide Himself from the fury of the persecution of those who wished to kill Him before the time He had chosen had arrived. But did this contempt and persecution end with His mortal life? It would have ceased, if He had not instituted the Blessed Eucharist. But He has instituted It and since Its institution, wicked men have never ceased to insult Him and persecute Him. If this had not actually happened, who could have ever imagined that Jesus Christ in the Blessed Sacrament would not have been safe from insults and outrages? Alas! it is only too true that Jesus Christ has been the object of every kind of outrage all through the ages in the Sacrament of His love, and that a very large number of Christians have in no way been moved by this treatment.

Meditation for the Fourth Friday of August

"But He answered him nothing . . . And Herod with his army set Him at nought; and mocked Him, putting on Him a white garment, and sent Him back to Pilate" (Luke XXIII, 9, 11).

How heroic is this patience, how amiable this meekness, how admirable this silence! How eloquent it is, and what good lessons it has for us! But, my God, these great virtues which alone are proofs of His Divinity, and which should have gained Him the veneration and love of all, have brought Him nothing but contempt! Have not Thy prodigious patience in the Blessed Sacrament, O my Jesus, and Thy admirable silence at the sight of the outrages Thou dost there suffer, a similar effect? If the least act of irreverence, if unworthy Communions were immediately punished, people would not be so wanting in modesty and reverence. But, this Divine Savior Who has punished so rigorously, even in this life, the least insults done to His servants, suffers without a word the contempt offered to His adorable Person in this Mystery; and He prefers to expose Himself to the outrages of sinners, rather than drive the just away from the altar rails by inspiring them with fear. O my God, what beautiful lessons this silence of Jesus Christ in the Blessed Eucharist teaches us!

SEPTEMBER

Meditation for the Second Friday of September

"And Jesus answering, said: Were not ten made clean? And where are the nine? There is no one found to return and give glory to God but this stranger" (Luke XVII, 17, 18).

People in the world cannot endure ingratitude; it is only with regard to God that people are unconcerned about being ungrateful. This miraculous cure was wrought for ten persons; of those ten, only one was found to thank his Benefactor. Of all the benefits which we have received from God, without doubt, the greatest is the Blessed Sacrament; It is even the source of most of the other benefits which we daily receive. And who thinks of thanking Jesus Christ often for this great benefit? Who thanks our admirable Redeemer for having abolished all other sacrifices and leaving us a Victim which God must accept: a Victim in proportion to the other benefits which we have received from Him, and to those which we may further demand; a Victim capable of blotting out the sins of all men; a Victim Which is a sovereign remedy for all our evils; a Tree of Life which can communicate to us not only health, but even immortality? As of old, our Savior complained of the ingratitude of the nine lepers cleansed who did not return to give thanks; so, in our days, He complains through His servant, St. Margaret Mary, of the ingratitude of men for the benefits of the Blessed Eucharist: "If men would but make some return of love to Me, I would consider as nothing all that I have done."

Meditation for the Third Friday of September

"And when He drew near, seeing the city He wept over it, saying: If thou hadst known, and that in this thy day, the things that are to thy peace: but now they are hidden from thy eyes" (Luke XIX, 41, 42).

How well those tears of Jesus express the sentiments of His Heart! Unhappy Jerusalem! unfortunate people! Into how many evils does not your blindness precipitate you! What will you say when you see that you had your happiness in our own hands and that it rested with you alone to be the happiest of all peoples, if you had only been willing to recognize on this day the best of all masters, the meekest of all kings? If Jesus Christ were still capable of feeling sorrow and shedding tears, loving us as He does, could He look on us without weeping? Could He consider the indifference which we have for Him in the Blessed Eucharist, the contempt with which we treat Him and the evils which this contempt and indifference bring down

on us, without saying to us as He said to this unfortunate people: Ah! ungrateful and cowardly Christians; if you did know
in this day which is given to you, Him Who is in the midst of
you, Who alone can bring you peace and render you eternally
happy! But now all this is hidden from your eyes. You do not
wish to know Me, for how could you be so unhappy, if, knowing Me, you did love Me?

Meditation for the Fourth Friday of September

"Behold the hour cometh, and it is now come, that you shall
be scattered every man to his own, and you shall leave Me
alone" (John XVI, 32).

What were the sentiments of the Heart of Jesus Christ when
predicting to His Apostles their cowardice and ingratitude, their
flight and their abandonment of Him? But could these same
Apostles believe that they were capable of abandoning so good
a Master? However, that happened. But, O my Savior, has
that time passed? Jesus Christ is on our altars night and day,
and how many of us are eager and assiduous in paying Him
court? When was the palace of a prince without a crowd of
courtiers, although only a few get the privilege of speaking to
him? Jesus Christ is the only one that the world treats with
indifference; He is always ready and extremely desirous to do
good to all and yet He is left almost always alone.

OCTOBER

Meditation for the Second Friday of October

"Amen I say to you, one of you that eateth with Me shall
betray Me . . . But woe to that man by whom the Son of Man
shall be betrayed" (Mark XIII, 18, 21).

That the Scribes and Pharisees, that the impious and criminals should have conspired against Jesus Christ might be expected, as they were His mortal enemies. But that Jesus Christ
should see Himself betrayed by a favorite, by an Apostle, by
a man whom this Divine Savior had chosen in preference to
so many others, and to whom He had given such striking marks
of ardent love! But, my Savior, since it is Thou who choosest

Thy servants and favorites, how long wilt Thou continue to find ungrateful ones and even traitors among those whom Thou choosest, among the many Christians whom Thou hast chosen by a pure effect of Thy love in preference to so many infidels, with whom Thou dost deign to make Thy abode, on whom Thou dost pour out so liberally Thy favors and to whom Thou dost give even Thyself? How many people abuse Thy favors! How many ungrateful people refuse to receive Holy Communion, and how many traitors there are among those who do receive Holy Communion! And, O my Savior, shall I be insensible to all this?

Meditation for the Third Friday of October

"This people honoreth Me with their lips, but their heart is far from Me: in vain do they worship Me..." (Mark VII, 6, 8).

The honors which were given to Jesus Christ must have been very insincere; the heart must have had little share in those praises which were given to Him from time to time, since all these acts of homage ended in making Him suffer the greatest outrages, and in seeing Him expire on the Cross. To how many tepid Christians can Jesus Christ make this mournful reproach? This want of modesty in the church, this lack of reverence before the Blessed Sacrament, this repugnance to this heavenly nourishment — does not all that show that our homage does not come from the bottom of our hearts? We have the exterior trappings of devotion but where is our sincerity? Ah! my Savior, how can my heart be so near Thine and not be inflamed by Thy love?

Meditation for the Fourth Friday of October

"Jerusalem, Jerusalem ... how often would I have gathered together thy children, as the hen doth gather her chickens under her wings, and thou wouldst not?" (Matt. XXIII, 37).

What shall this unhappy people reply to this reproach? But what shall we ourselves reply when it shall be made to us? This very figure which Jesus Christ uses shows forth our ingratitude more clearly, because it expresses the great love of Jesus Christ in our regard. This amiable Savior has left us Himself in the Blessed Sacrament in order that we may find at every moment a powerful Protector, a Physician, a Father: He is inceasingly in the midst of us, because He wishes to have us always near Him. But does not this coldness, this neglect on the part of the greater number of Christians, oblige Him to say to us: My poor children, how many times have I wished to gather you, as a hen doth gather her chickens, and you have gone away! You would not! Are you astonished if you are so long afflicted, so often conquered and so dangerously wounded? It is for this reason that there are so many among you who are sick and languid, and that several sleep the sleep of death. Shall I be insensible henceforth, O my amiable Savior, both to the loving reproach which Thou dost make to me, and to the contempt with which I have hitherto treated it?

NOVEMBER

Meditation for the Second Friday of November

"He fell upon His face praying and saying: My Father, if it be possible, let this chalice pass from Me: nevertheless, not as I will but as Thou wilt" (Matt. XXVI, 39).

Jesus Christ had passionately desired to give His Blood for the salvation of men, and He has testified His desire a hundred times: "I have a baptism wherewith I am to be baptized," said He, "and how am I straitened until it be accomplished" (Luke XII, 50). It is not then death which terrifies Him and renders this chalice so bitter, but the ingratitude of those men who refuse to profit by His death.

"I have desired, Eternal Father, and I desire more than ever to deliver these slaves, but I have never desired to make people ungrateful: the outrages which I am going to receive from My enemies do not terrify Me, but the contempt which I foresee that My own children will have for Me, afflicts Me: the blindness of the former touches Me, but the black ingratitude of those latter pierces My Heart with sorrow." Jesus Christ passionately desired the coming of the time for the institution of the Blessed Sacrament of the Altar, but the abuse and contempt with which people were to treat this august Sacrament were for Him a great cause of sadness, and the principal reason that caused Him to cry out: "My Father, if it be possible, let this

Chalice pass from Me" (Matt. XXVI, 39).

Truly, this chalice must have been very bitter, but do we know that it depends on us to remove this bitter chalice from Him? As it is we ourselves who, by our contempt and our indignities, have caused Him all this bitterness, it is we who present Him with this chalice. It depends on me, O my Savior, to sweeten this chalice by my homage, and shall it be said that I will refuse to do so?

Meditation for the Third Friday of November

"But Jesus, turning to them, said: Daughters of Jerusalem, weep not over Me, but weep for yourselves and for your children" (Luke XXIII, 28).

Has ever such love been known as that which Jesus Christ shows us on this occasion? His Sacred Body has been torn by the scourges; He has lost a great quantity of blood; He has become an object of mockery and derision to the whole people, and in this pitiable state, He is not concerned about His own sufferings, He feels only those which He foresees that we shall bring on ourselves by our want of gratitude. If there is any feeling in our hearts, what can touch them, if this will not? Jesus Christ forgotten, despised and outraged in the Blessed Sacrament feels more keenly the evils which we shall bring on ourselves by these acts of contempt, than the contempt itself. Weep, my children, He says to us, weep for your neglect of your Redeemer, your Father. Weep for your black ingratitude which you have pushed to extremes, weep for these acts of irreverence which you have committed so boldly in My presence; weep for so many sacrilegious Communions; weep for your loss in refusing to know Me, or while knowing Me, in refusing to love Me. For what, then, shall I shed tears, O my Savior, if I can think of ingratitude without weeping?

Meditation for the Fourth Friday of November

"The Queen of the South shall rise in judgment with this generation, and shall condemn it, because she came from the ends of the earth to hear the wisdom of Solomon, and behold a greater than Solomon here" (Matt. XII, 42).

New Christians are found in Africa, India, China, and Japan

who travel more than thirty miles several times a year to have the consolation of adoring Jesus Christ in the Blessed Sacrament, and of hearing holy Mass. They count the fatigues of their journey as nothing when they have the happiness of assisting at Mass and of passing half an hour with Jesus Christ in the Blessed Sacrament. How many people will rise on the day of Judgment against us and condemn us? We have Jesus Christ in our own town, Religious have Jesus Christ in their own houses, and they reckon this privilege as nothing. Some make so little of this privilege that they visit Jesus Christ only with indifference; many visit Him against their will and with hardly any devotion. Shall not the Queen of the South rise in judgment against these people? And shall she not condemn them, because she came from the ends of the earth, to hear the wisdom of Solomon. He Who is here on our Altars is greater than Solomon.

DECEMBER

Meditation for the Second Friday of December

"And this is the judgment: because the light is come into the world, and men loved darkness rather than the light" (John III, 19).

How deplorable was the blindness of the Jews! And what can they answer, when they will be reproached with the evils which they have brought on themselves by their blindness? You had the Light in your midst, it will be said against them, and you closed your eyes because you preferred the darkness. The Sun of Justice so long expected, had risen among you. You refused to make use of this daylight which was to make you happy. This same light is still in our midst in the Blessed Sacrament, and are all Christians wiser than the Jews? Do all Christians make use of this light? Is there not reason to fear that the presence of Jesus Christ in the Blessed Eucharist, with His Sacred Heart ever ready to pour out on us the treasures of grace which It contains and of which It is the source, will be the cause of our condemnation? Have we recourse to Jesus Christ in the Blessed Sacrament, and do we address ourselves to Him with confidence? Do we seek from Him the helps and graces necessary for us in the various happenings of life? Alas!

This light is despised because people love the darkness, and this contempt will be the cause of their condemnation.

Meditation for the Third Friday of December

"John answered them saying . . . there has stood One in the midst of you whom you know not . . . the latchet of Whose shoe I am not worthy to loose" (John I, 26, 27).

What a misfortune for the Jews that they had not known Him Who was in the midst of them! But do we know Him Who is in our midst? Great ones of this world, do you know Him — you who punish so rigorously the smallest faults against the respect due to yourselves, but who are so little touched by the outrages done to this Sovereign Whom you profess to know? You common people, do you know Him Who is in the midst of you — you who pay court so assiduously to those from whom you expect some favor and who are so reserved in the presence of those whom you fear, while you have so little respect in the church, and hardly ever find a moment of leisure to come and pay your homage to Jesus Christ in the Blessed Sacrament? Finally, ministers of the Lord, religious, do you know Him Who is constantly in your midst? And if you do know Him, whence comes it that you are so rarely in His presence? No, O Lord, we do not know Thee; I confess that hitherto I have not known Thee; but for the future my conduct towards Thee will show that I am beginning to know Thee really, since I will begin to love Thee truly.

Meditation for the Fourth Friday of December

"And it came to pass that when they were there, her days were accomplished that she should be delivered. And she brought forth her first-born Son, and wrapped Him up in swaddling clothes, and laid Him in a manger, because there was no room for them in the inn" (Luke II, 6, 7).

There is place for everyone, there is no place for Jesus Christ! The world begins to reject and despise this Divine Savior even before His birth. The Man-God is reduced to be born in a stable, while mere men are born in palaces. What were, then, the sentiments of Jesus Christ at seeing Himself so badly lodged, and what must still be His sentiments in our days at seeing

Himself so badly received, while many Christians are lodged in magnificent houses? Do the sacred vessels which continually contain Jesus Christ, do the holy places where He resides, correspond to the sumptuous magnificence which appears in the houses and in the furniture of people of the world? But at least, would that Jesus Christ did not find Himself so often in impure souls, and in hearts sullied by a thousand sins! I know, O my Savior, that Thy delights are to be in a pure heart; purify my heart then in order that Thou mayest find Thy delights there, that I may have henceforth the pleasure of receiving Thee less unworthily. Inflame this heart of mine with Thy pure love; may Thy Sacred Heart come and take the place of mine, and let mine henceforth be so intimately united to Thine that our two hearts may have henceforth always the same sentiments. Amen.